Fortress Fighters

An autobiography of a B-17 aerial gunner
by William F. Somers

...along with an extraordinary collection of stories of the brave men who fought with the 99th Bombardment Group, 15th Air Force, from March 31, 1943 until the group's 395th mission on April 26, 1945. The 99th's first mission was flown from its base in Navarin, North Africa to Villacidro aerodrome in Sardinia... its last from Foggia, Italy to an ammunition storage area in Bolzano, Italy. Old Folks, was the last plane lost to enemy action by the 99th--that being out of the 346th squadron, April 25th, on the same raid our crew flew its 30th mission to Linz, Austria.

FORTRESS FIGHTERS

An autobiography of a B-17 engineer/gunner with a collection of stories of men of the 15th Air Force who flew the heavies from North Africa and Italy to smash the formidable German underbelly during World War II.

Library of Congress Control Number: 00-092670
ISBN No. 0-9705799-1-8

PRINTED IN THE UNITED STATES OF AMERICA

Somers Printing, Inc.
304 South Rockford Drive, Tempe, AZ. 85281
Cover design by Michael W. Somers

First printing, December, 2000

> *"The B-17, I think, was the best combat plane ever built. It combined in perfect balance, the right engine, the right wing and the right control services. You wouldn't believe they could stay in the air."*
>
> *-- Lt. Gen. Ira C. Eaker,*
> *Chief of Mediterranean Air Forces*

> *"The Air Force kind of grew up with the B-17. It was as tough an airplane as was ever built. It was a good honest plane to fly-- a pilot's airplane. It did everything we asked it to do, and did it well"*
>
> *--Gen. Curtis E. Lemay,*
> *Chief of Staff, USAF*

Dedication

To my grandsons Paul, Peter and Adam that they grow to know the liberties they now enjoy have come with a price we, who preceded them, paid dearly for.

-- Papa Bill

Acknowledgements

This is to thank profusely those who contributed to this book and gave me their permission, in writing, to use their material.

Les Hansen, navigator, 347th Sqdn., Ch. II, "Take No Prisoners"

Robert A. Duffy, Commander 99th B.G. Ordnance Company, Ch. V, "Brutta Foggia"

George W. Guderley, gunner, 463rd Bomb Group, Ch. VII, "Last Mile From Hell"

Joseph P. O'Donnell, gunner, 483rd Bomb Group, Ch. VII, "Last Mile From Hell"

Delbert Laudner, gunner, 348th Sqdn., Ch. VII, "Last Mile From Hell"

Genevieve S. McGee, gunner's widow, 348th Sqdn., Ch. VIII, "Voice of Tears"

John Plummer, pilot, 347th Sqdn., Ch. X, "Tailspin"

James Bruno, pilot, 347th Sqdn., Ch. XII, "The Last Gun"

Julius Horowitz, pilot, 348th Sqdn., Ch. XIV, "Enemy Salute"

Joseph R. Kenney, son of the late Joseph C. Kenney, gunner, 346th Sqdn., Ch. XV, "Retired At Fifty"

Homer (Mac) McClanahan, pilot, 346th Sqdn., Ch. XVI, "The Evader"

Table of Contents

DEDICATED TO THOSE WHO SERVED WITH THE
99TH BOMBARDMENT GROUP (H) DURING WWII.
THEY FLEW 395 COMBAT MISSIONS IN B-17's
FROM 31 MARCH, 1943, TO 26 APRIL, 1945.
THEY WERE AWARDED TWO DISTINGUISHED
UNIT CITATIONS WHILE STATIONED IN
AFRICA AND ITALY.

"PRESENTED BY THE
99TH BOMBARDMENT GROUP
HISTORICAL SOCIETY,
28 JUNE, 1986."

99TH Bombardment
Group (H)

MEMORIAL PLAQUE

AIR FORCE MUSEUM, DAYTON OHIO

The above plaque honoring those of us who served with the 99th Bomb Group
can be seen on the memorial grounds near Air Force Museum.

MEMORIAL WALL OF PLAQUES

Air Force Academy, Colorado Springs, Colorado
Dedicated Oct. 16, 1987 to the men who died in the
Army Air Force during World War II

Bill Somers, in 1988 visit, points to 99th B.G. plaque.

CHAPTER 1

They Got Me!

The Gunner's Creed

    This is my ship. I have faith in the pilot who flies it. I know the navigator will direct a true course. I trust the bombardier to destroy our objective. I believe in the abilities of the crew. Yet the safety of my ship and the success of our mission depends on me and my guns. I vow solemnly to perform my duty. I am the ship's gunner. --George E. Mathison, 1st Lt., Air Corps.

    Patriotic fervor was sweeping the nation when I entered the service. Gold star mothers across America were beginning to adorn the windows of their homes. Poland, Belgium, Holland and France had fallen to Hitler's legions. His blitzkriegs scored heavily in those occupied countries. In May of 1940 a trapped army of 340,000 men were miraculously saved at Dunkirk and delivered to England by almost every English boat that could float. A few months later the crucial Battle of Britain began and the R.A.F. would prevail--clearly a major turning point of the war, at least for the British. The Battle of the Atlantic hadn't reached its climax, but the German U-boat was taking an extremely heavy toll of allied shipping. Though not committed to war at the time, the United States in March of 1941 signed a lend-lease agreement with England and subsequently dispatched 50 World War I destroyers and a handful of Flying Fortresses to the beleaguered island nation. All this had preceded my call to duty.

    It was my oldest sister Janet who was on that station platform in Tarrytown, New York on an overcast day in May, 1943. It felt good that somebody dear to me was there to see me off--even if it had to be a sister, not a sweetheart. She was terribly excited. Imagine, her oldest brother going off to war. A first in the family--at least for this war. My father was gassed in France in World War I.

Ready to explode with envy Janet couldn't contain herself. She wished at that moment more than anything she were me. And at that moment, she was my crutch, my inspiration. She gladdened my heart which was pounding with excitement and apprehension. I'd been on reserve status for three months and had anxiously been awaiting the order to active duty. The prospect of maybe going into combat was exhilarating. I think the feeling was contagious because Janet's eyes were a liquid pool of pride at my imminent deliverance into khaki. And the anxieties of the unknown had my whole being in turmoil.

At that very moment as we stood awaiting the train that would take me on the first step of my journey into war, the United States marines were storming the beaches of Guadalcanal. Elsewhere the American defeat at Kasserine Pass in North Africa was recent history. And over Europe, American airmen had launched their bombing offensive in a strategic effort to carry the fighting into the German heartland. Little did I know I would join that daylight bombing effort as a combat crewman.

Camp Upton on Long Island, New York received me. Much has been made of raw recruits in story and movies. Intimidation best describes my feelings at the time. We were stripped of civilian dignity and relegated into obscurity and sameness by association with massive numbers and bland dress. It was the most humbling experience of my life.

I only spent ten days at Camp Upton. But they shaped my army career--my life in that relatively short space of time. Infantry, artillery, air corps, airborne, transportation, supply, chemical warfare--all and more were the options available to us. I'm not so sure they were options. So many of us fledgling recruits lacked any job experience at all having just left high school. In my case, I had attended and graduated from a federally funded short term airplane mechanics school at Newburgh, New York. It was an NYA program, not unlike the CCC programs extant at the time. Those who evaluated me had no difficulty pointing me in the direction of the Army Air Corps branch of service.

Now a chartered path had enveloped me and my next assignment was basic training at Keesler Field, Mississippi. Thirteen weeks of intense physical and mental indoctrination lay ahead. It was a period that would transform me from civilian to GI. Spartan living in spacious 2-floor barracks, regimented physical training exercises and marching drills, K.P., instruction in military courtesy and manual of arms became a part of our daily life.

Seems like we took infantry basic. Should men destined for the Air Corp be subject to long hikes with heavy packs and rifles? Hey, this was the Army Air Corps. But that training in the deep South in summer was designed to make or break us, Air Corps or no Air Corps. We had to be fit and by god there would be no exceptions to the drill. Running hurdles with a 9-pound rifle, advancing under barbed wire and swinging from 15-foot ropes over deep 4-foot pools of water were all part of our basic training.

Private's pay was $50 a month. But you could buy a bar of candy or a coke for a nickel and a pack of cigarettes cost about 15 cents. It was the day of the Zippo lighter and the fountain pen. And the post exchange (PX) on base provided essentials and non-essentials at very reasonable prices. The service club on base afforded an excellent opportunity to pass the time away from stress. Sundays afforded a break from the rigid training schedule. Lay around on your sack and read, maybe attend church in the base chapel or go to a movie at a GI theater.

Tomorrow meant the rifle range, guard duty, kitchen police, drilling and more drilling. Always your constant companion--the unwieldy gas mask. It went everywhere you did including the special chambers rigged for tear gas drills. The 13 weeks of basic training couldn't end soon enough and on Aug. 21st we shipped out to Sheppard Field, Texas for my next stage of training. Three weeks earlier 178 bombers of the 9th Air Force in North Africa smacked the oil refineries of Ploesti, Rumania in an attempt to shorten the war by six months. The attacking B-24 Liberators suffered very heavy losses. But the daring low level raid severely impacted German war production for maybe six months.

I'll always remember our arrival at Sheppard Field. Strung out in formation with barracks bags and other gear in a squadron area, we faced a first sergeant who was determined to lecture us. The heat was stifling and our formation of mechanics-to-be was a sad one indeed. The train ride from Mississippi was suffocating enough without having to endure this protracted formation. I was so thirsty. When we were finally dismissed and I found a water fountain, much to my dismay it served up water with a strong sulphur taste. Awful. And the taste was to be found in the soft drinks we bought too. But this was Texas where winds blew in the Oklahoma dust to make marching and drilling a nightmare when not in class.

Wichita Falls was the nearest big town to the base. In it were the USO clubs. They were a kind of shelter and afforded a time of relaxation away from the base. Manned by pretty lady volunteers who served coffee and donuts, listened to your problems and generally provided nice conversation, the USO was the friendly alternative to the military.

Sheppard Field's AM (aircraft mechanics) school operated 24 hours a day, rotating 7-hour shifts every 15 days. School didn't begin for us in Flight 5 until Sept. 9, 1943. And in Italy on this day, Allied troops landed at Salerno and encountered strong resistance. Class lectures were rare. For the most part students learned by using mockups or watching demonstrations. Many of these demonstrations were conducted in giant hangars. They justified our rifle training and drills by citing the shocking Bataan experience. Because they couldn't or didn't know how to adapt to infantry attitudes and tactics, ground crews were easy prey for the advancing Japanese. We were even taught how to retreat over a simulated gorge using hand ropes. Army brass wasn't about to take any more chances with men whose primary duty was maintaining aircraft. They wanted us prepared for any eventuality. We were soldiers first. We were trained to use 2-man pup tents on bivouac while attending aircraft in the field away from the hangars under simulated combat conditions. Always--our gas masks were with us.

Our study was intense and concentrated on essentials that included engines, carburetion, structure, instruments, hydraulics, electrical, propellers to name a few. The twin engine North American B-25 and also the Martin B-26 with 4-bladed props were assigned to us. The irony here being I would one day be crewing a B-17. But much of what I was taught at Sheppard Field was easily adapted later on to the 4-engine B-17. Our class of 54 men graduated in eight weeks.

My next assignment would be factory school where we specialized in engines. We didn't ship out for this next duty until Jan. 31, 1944. The seemingly long delay between schools and the swift prosecution of the war concerned me. I surely wanted to get into combat in the worst way. At this point in time the Yanks had made a surprise landing at Anzio and the Russians, in their ongoing sweeping counter attack, had pushed German forces back into Poland.

An American Guadalcanal victory, the crucial Battle of Stalingrad, allied landings in Sicily and Italy were all significant wartime advances as my stateside studies continued. My only hope of seeing combat was to achieve flying status via gunnery school and eventually gain a combat crew assignment to medium or heavy bombers. Gunnery school was a must if I were to accomplish this so I put in for it.

Inglewood, California--Mines Field to be exact, was our factory school destination. Four weeks of engine study ended with our class of 11 graduating on March 7th. On the home front it was reported on this day that women comprised 42% of the work force in west coast aircraft plants.

I was ecstatic to learn my next assignment would be gunnery school. Strange, with gunnery schools in nearby Arizona at Kingman and Yuma, they should ship me way across country to Florida. I shipped out on March 8th and arrived March 13th at Buckingham Army Air Field, near Ft. Myers. My class would be the 8th Student Rec. Squadron. In two months, if I passed everything, I would be an aerial gunner with wings to prove it.

Gunnery school was everything I expected and more. From the waist of a bomber we learned to shoot air-to-air target sleeves. We shot skeet from the back of a moving flatbed truck encircled in a rim of welded pipe for stability and safety. Our turn around the oval track with a score of skeet houses slinging birds at us left little time but to fire our shotguns. But our slow speed and ignorance of skeet patterns aloft kept us vigilant. It was a test of our ability to lead the target and score. The intricacies of the power turret were ours to command. It was the acquisition of knowledge, of course, that made the turret a friend indeed despite the learning difficulties.

But most of all I fell in love with the Browning air cooled .50 caliber machine gun. It became our sole reason for being. It would be the instrument of our salvation in alien skies. The anxieties and stress that accompanied the learning process of this lethal weapon taxed our ability to the utmost. This phase of our training could make or break a young candidate like me desperately eager to fight his country's battles up in that wild blue yonder. Fail and I'd find myself on a flight line somewhere finishing out the war. And this, to be sure, was an unhappy option.

To earn our wings we would have to learn to detail strip the .50's more than 150 parts (give or take a few) and reassemble them in a given time frame. Further, field stripping the seven major groups of the gun blindfolded and with gloves on in the ever so short span of half an hour became the ultimate prerequisite of our successful ability to master the weapon. Our instructors zeroed in on a gunner's stamina and knowledge, the better to survive in battle, we were told. They vowed no gunner would become maimed or killed for want of skill in connection with the .50 caliber machine gun. I would go on to successfully master not only this gun, but the very complex power turret that would house the twin fifties.

Gunners wings were ceremoniously awarded our graduating class in a bit of pageantry. We turned out on the tarmac in proper Class A uniforms and we marched in review before a significant audience of civilians and army brass. I've been in the army a year now. In Europe the Allies gained three miles in their drive to capture Rome. On the home front, Bing Crosby excels in one of his few dramatic roles as a Catholic priest in *Going My Way*. I was promoted to corporal the same day I received those silver gunners wings making me a very proud soldier boy. The door was now open for me to repay a debt I felt I owed to my country. Until now I had taken the blessings offered me as a citizen of the United States of America almost for granted. And frankly, hadn't thought much about it. But the war changed all that. Now I could say to Uncle Sam: "I owe you and this is my chance to pay up."

Wearing these wings was earned recognition for having successfully completed a technical training schedule. Not just gunner, but what went into making me a competent flight engineer. I had been given the tools for the job. Now let's do it. Shoot 'em out of the sky (which I didn't do) and bomb the hell out of them (which I did do 30 times). I knew now I'd finally get to see action. It was only a matter of time and it proved out that in six months I'd be on the flight deck of a Flying Fortress winging my way into battle. I couldn't help but think back to the skinny kid I was in high school who never earned a letter in sports and what my peers would think of me now.

I was now a fully trained flight engineer waiting for assignment. To be honest the best training came on-the-job. AM school provided the foundations, but it was on the flight line and from working mechanics and crew chiefs and other tested flight engineers that we really became knowledgeable. I would also need to work with my pilot, whoever he might be. We would learn to interact, work closely briefing each other, filling in gaps that we may have missed in our education to this point. As a qualified engineer I had to know my engines and armament equipment thoroughly. The copilot and I would, of necessity, work together checking engine operation, fuel consumption and other aspects of the internal operation of the aircraft. I would be the primary source of information concerning the airplane. I must depend on the pilots to pass on whatever information about flying they consider absolute and worth sharing with me. It would be a mutual effort, teamwork from the word go.

I shipped out of Sheppard Field May 8th--destination, Plant Park, Tampa, Florida. We gathered inside a large baseball park or sports arena to meet our crew for the first time. Henry (Hank) Soriano, an Hispanic, was our ball turret operator. He was short, maybe 5-feet, six inches.

Perfect for the turret underneath the B-17. Hank was loose and easy, always ready to show his perfect white teeth in a ready smile. He was from San Diego. Another Californian was Elmer Nelson, age 21. A handsome kid, he smoked a pipe and was from Albany, in the Oakland suburbs. Kind of a showoff, but fun to be with. He was our armorer and waist gunner. Don Power, 24, from Cochranton, Pennsylvania, was our other waist gunner. He was a big fellow who took things quite seriously. John (Red) Patterson, 18, the youngest man on the crew, was from Butler, Pennsylvania. He would be our tail gunner. He was quite a character; gregarious and friendly. Tall and thin with a close crop of red hair, he provided lots of laughs when we need them most. Good man to have aboard. And then there was Alex Leitman, age 33, the oldest man on the crew. He was our radio operator and a very conservative gentleman he was. Out of Birmingham, Alabama, Alex was a Jew and born in Hungary. We understood his apprehension. Both Alex and Don's wives were with them as long as we trained stateside.

Our officers included pilot, Bob Neely, from Larchmont, N.Y. The tall, lanky individual with fine facial features and an easy manner about him wore leather gloves at the controls of his ship. Invariably the sweat soaked back of his hands stained his tan gloves on every mission. Bob was all business in flight as our aircraft commander. Jim Wyatt flew copilot. He was a Georgia boy, rather severe and private. I never could develop a warm relationship with him. John Thomas, our bombardier, from Arkansas, was a lot of fun. Accept-me-for-what-I-am kind of a guy. And Steve Kaptain, our navigator, was from Stamford, Connecticut. He too had a very little to do with enlisted men of the crew, but proved to be quite proficient at his job.

Officers and enlisted men did not socialize. We always lived in separate quarters in the states as well as overseas. Off duty was one thing, but flying we acted responsively. Be they practice missions or the real thing, we were committed to each other and the work before us.

We languished for two months in that Plant City ballpark waiting for our assignment to OTU. Yes, we next would be assigned to an overseas training unit where new crews were trained for combat. The last step before going overseas. At least now I knew the type of bomber I would fly in. It was to be the B-17 Flying Fortress. My medium bomber training would need some help. I'd be crewing a 4-engine, not a 2-engine aircraft, but there were enough similarities to ease the conversion for me. I'd be flying in America's foremost strategic offensive weapon.

During our long wait in that ballpark, D-Day, the Allied invasion of Normandy, had taken place. But two months to the day out of gunnery school, July 8, 1944, we received our orders to proceed to Gulfport, Mississippi and OTU. Two days later the Allies invaded Sicily.

We learned to interact with each other on practice missions. For the next two and one half months we worked as a team not only getting to know our people, but the airplane itself. Battle-tested engineer gunners instructed me at my job on the ground and in the air. Their assist proved invaluable overseas. After all, I was now involved with a 65,000 pound behemoth and being successfully responsible for it meant I would be likewise responsible for the safety of our crew.

Every inch of the 73-ft. 9-in. length of the Flying Fortress was a challenge. And let's face it. In the crash courses I was subjected to in Texas and California, much learning was left to my initiative, meaning interaction with experienced line personnel. The bomber's numerous systems were complex. The electrical system provided power to operate the landing gear, wing flaps, turrets, instruments, bomb doors and others. The hydraulic system controlled the cowl flaps and the wheel and emergency brakes. Heat throughout the plane was provided by using glycol fluid stored in the No. 2 engine nacelle. Heat was administered by the exhaust.

Once high altitude was attained, we plugged in our heated suits. Without the invention of the supercharger, heavy bombers of the day would have found high altitude flying impossible. Ground pressure at sea level was forced into engine carburetors. And in the B-17, each engine had a supercharger. Lack of ground pressure to feed the engines wasn't the only threat to life and limb. Oxygen too was essential to survival. It was supplied by 18 bottles through four independent systems and 16 outlets at strategic locations through the plane. Each of those 18 bottles contained a four hour supply of oxygen for one man. Walk-around bottles, with a 3-minute supply, provided crew mobility in emergencies.

The bomb load of the Flying Fortress was diverse. Its bomb racks were fitted anywhere from 100-pound fragmentation bombs to 2000 pounders. We were to carry the full range of sizes in actual combat, but the bomb used most frequently were 500-pounders. The heavier the bomb load, usually the shorter the mission, but not always.

We were assigned to fly the B-17G. It was the bomber's latest and last major design change. Overseas delivery of the Model G began in September, 1943, but peak delivery wasn't attained until April of 1944. The changes did not affect engine characteristics. In the air or on the ground with its 1200 h.p. engines in sync, there was a certain thundering rendition of sound pleasant to the ear and unique to the aircraft. Even at 160 mph cruising speed, there was nothing serene about the cry of the engines. They labored in concert with each other and when they didn't it didn't take a pilot or flight engineer to know trouble loomed. Every man on the crew got to know the comforting, pulsating rhythm of those power plants.

The B-17G also was the model we trained in back in the states. And that was only nine years after its prototype 299 made its initial flight at Boeing Field in Seattle on July 28, 1935. That and subsequent early models were created in the defensive posture. The outbreak of World War II changed all that. The alphabetical maze of improvements through the Cs, and Ds didn't affect its defensive mode until the model E came on the scene with self-sealing fuel tanks, improved armor protection and increased armament. Tail guns were featured in the model D, but it was the F model that would see the first chin turret under the bombardier's nose. Only a handful of aircraft were so fitted in the Fs in deference to the model G's imminent entrance. Head-on attacks against most Fs by enemy fighters were so telling that the chin turret was retained for the next model change. The Bendix chin turret with its twin .50 caliber machine guns and operated by remote control by the bombardier was one of two major innovations. The other was a new "Cheyenne" tail turret which was retrofitted into many G Fortresses.

One thing about the Flying Fortress that achieved international recognition--meaning easy recognition by friend and foe alike, was its silhouette. Nothing in the sky could come close to its conformation. Its dorsal fin in the the tail assembly was one its most pronounced features. Its chin turret forward completed its unmistakable look The sleek and thin--almost beautiful warplane, was a tribute to its designers. General Carl A. Spaatz has this to say about the big bird: "Without the B-17 we might have lost the war." Certainly its strategic contribution to the Allied war effort was incomparable.

We gave the British a chance at them first. In May, 1941 the first B-17Cs were ferried to England from the United States. In a period of four months of disappointing efforts with them, RAF quit daylight bombing. After 22 missions eight of its 20 Fortresses had been lost. No. 90 squadron of the RAF reverted to its Sterling bombers to continue the war. The poor showing of B-17s in the hands of the British had a deterring affect even on American brass. It took General "Hap" Arnold and Gen. Eaker to convince Prime Minister Winston Churchill that strategic daylight bombing was indeed the most positive and practical approach in the conduct of the war. Churchill agreed to let the fledgling 8th Air Force "prove" itself. And they did.

Incidently, I was to receive a certificate of commendation signed by General Arnold, Commanding General, Army Air Forces and my Commanding General, Brig. General Yantis H. Taylor. I think a lot of guys got that certificate--kind of a flattering "thank you" from the top brass to us guys who flew the heavies.

Our OTU lasted about three months and we shipped out of Gulfport on Sept. 30th and spent but four days at Hunter Field, Georgia before being sent to our port of embarkation. I wouldn't say the war was winding down, but by this time the Allies had landed in southern France, Belgian cities were being liberated and Russian troops had seized

Bucharest, the capital of Rumania, and took control of the embattled oil fields of Ploesti.

We shipped out of Camp Patrick Henry, Virginia on the French liner Athos II on Oct. 13th and arrived in Naples, Italy fifteen days later. V-2 rockets were hitting England and Humphrey Bogart was starring in the movie *To Have And To Have Not*. In St. Louis, the Cardinals in a 3 - 1 win over the Browns took the World Series in the sixth game. We off-loaded our troopship on the side of a sunken ship in Naples harbor and were immediately assigned to the 19th Replacement Battalion. It wasn't until Nov. 6th, a week later, after a cold and unpleasant ride in an Italian box car over the mountains, that we arrived at the plains of Foggia.

The first night they split our crew up as we sought temporary accommodations in tent city, our squadron area. My luck I draw a tent with five strangers. I was told the empty cot belonged to their flight engineer who'd lost his leg to flak on a mission that day. I had a fitful sleep, but the next morning they owned up to a poor joke on a rookie. The next day the six of us moved into our tent. It would become our home until the war ended.

I was promoted to sergeant three days before our first mission. Sergeants in POW camps got better treatment, I was told. Four days later I gained the rank of staff sergeant. It wasn't until April that I became a technical sergeant.

*   *   *

It was a bleak and trying time--that Christmas of 1944. Our Flying Fortress crew had received its baptism of fire. We'd only flown three missions, but the second one cemented our relations as a crew. The bonding affect it was to have as Christmas day approached was to become apparent.

That second mission saw our plane hit by flak and burning. We were 28,500 feet over the Austrian city of Linz. Marshalling yards were our target. The day was Dec. 15, 1944. We were hit five minutes after bombs away. What went on in the waist of the ship could have turned deadly, but for the courage under fire and the resourceful responses of our waist gunners Don Power and Elmer Nelson.

Probably the most difficult position, if not as dangerous, on a B-17 is the lower ball turret. The man who flies in that position better be short in stature for ease in access and egress and to enjoy whatever comfort the minimal space allows. Hank Soriano fit that description. Once all curled up in his power turret, his left eye peering through the sight, he then controlled the movement of his twin fifties by hand and by foot pedals. He was the sole protection to the underbelly of our airplane.

When our ship was hit Hank rushed to bail out of his cramped position. He popped out of his escape hatch into the waist in such a hurry he broke his oxygen connection and passed out near the feet of Don and Elmer.

Meanwhile, up on the flight deck where I was, we had our own kind of problems. We needed that fire in No. 1 engine out and Bob Neely, our pilot, but flying co-pilot on this our second mission proceeded to do so. He cut the fuel flow at the tank with the fuel cut-off switch. Prop control was placed in high rpm and full throttle was applied. Bob then feathered the prop to cut the oil pressure. He then pulled the generator and cut the voltage regulator as a safety measure against an electrical fire which we knew it wasn't.

Don Power, 52 years later would tell me exactly what happened back there in the waist. We met at long last at a 99th Bomb Group reunion in September of 1997 in Baltimore. We had much to talk about, but he sure recalled this incident. This is what he told me:

"Hank came charging out of the ball turret. I gave him my oxygen. I got a walk-around bottle. Hank revived and then Elmer's mask froze up and he could not get oxygen. I broke the ice from his mask and he was O.K. I got disconnected from the intercom and did not know what was happening. When I got reconnected, the fire was out," he said.

Bullets and flak were only part of the terror we experienced in those alien skies. We fought the cold with temperatures as low as 60 degrees below zero. Life sustaining oxygen was a constant, fed to us through tubes into a mask at our face. We were wired for sound as well as wired into heated suits that kept us comparatively warm in that sub-freezing cold.

As a crew we were learning to fight together, but we also had to learn how to live together. When I speak of crew, I mean the six of us enlisted men who lived in those pyramid canvas tents we called home. Our four officers shared another tent in another area. But it was within the confines of our tent, depressing as it was, that my story of Christmas unfolds.

The package arrived maybe a week or ten days before Christmas. It was from mom. Not a very large parcel and over-wrapped and under-protected as she always did things like that. Lots of brown paper, string in abundance and perilously close to becoming undone when I picked it up at mail call.

That time of year there were more stand-downs because of the seemingly incessant bad weather day after day. We only flew four missions that December--all coming in the second half of the month. Our tent seemed immersed, surrounded in a sea of mud. Overcast skies and the day to day living in unbearable monotony had a lousy affect on our morale. In France at that time, the Battle of the Bulge was just getting under way. We had a tendency to get down on each other being grounded as we were and living in such close quarters. But really, as far as getting along, we fared as well as any of the other crews about us. And despite the few differences we might have had, our actions under fire were never in doubt.

The days to Christmas slipped slowly by. I kept the package under my cot. I would open it Christmas eve. At home we always waited to open our gifts on Christmas morning, but with us surviving in the sloppy plains of Foggia, who knew what the next day would bring. Half a 55-gallon drum served as a stove to keep us warm. It glowed a deep red in the murky tent interior as we sat around opening what gifts we'd received and saved for the moment. I don't remember anyone else's but mine. I was glad the naked bulb at the top of the center pole wasn't all that bright. I then opened the package. It contained a miniature Christmas tree with six tiny presents wrapped in white tissue and bound with more string. Mom had included a gift for each of us and at the moment it proved rather unsettling to me. For some reason I was embarrassed, almost ashamed, as I passed out these tiny objects under wraps. They couldn't be much because we didn't have much. I was alarmed for fear they'd laugh. Wouldn't there be a collective and derisive put-down?

This caused me suddenly to become upset with my mother. How could she. She really didn't know these guys. How could she embarrass me so? Messing in other folks lives, that's what this was all about, but it was too late for me to do anything about it. Turns out I had nothing to worry about and very much to be grateful for. The wee bit of yuletide spirit she brought to that dark tent and each of us inside had an immeasurable impact on all of us. I can't recall today a single item as the men opened their tiny gifts in turn. But I do remember the blinding glow of affection that seemed to fill the room.

I'm sure the gifts were of the five-and-ten cent store variety, Maybe a rabbits foot or the like. But the fellows even agreed that the tiny tree should be placed in a command position for all to see until Christmas day. The idea of those insignificant gifts did leave a warm feeling inside. We were better for the experience. The mud wasn't so thick and the rain wasn't so wet after that. And the sun, when it shined, was more brilliant after that Christmas experience. We became truly a family bonded in a common fear of death, but also wedded in the special language of love.

May, 1944
Back Home
in New York on
Furlough

Basic Training
July, 1943 / Keesler Field, Mississippi.

Soon after earning my gunner's wings

Photo Study of a Teenage Gunner

Most of my thirty missions were flown at the age of 19 even as these photos were taken. My station as an engineer/gunner was in the top turret. I climbed onto the wing to the turret for an outside shot. The closeup is a blowup of a photo used in USAAF identification card we always carried with us on raids.

U.S. ARMY AIR FORCE

IDENTIFICATION CARD

УДОСТОВЕРЕНИЕ ЛИЧНОСТИ

DOWOD OSOBISTY

LEGITIMACE

LEGITIMACIJA

SZEMÉLYAZONOSSÁGI IGAZOLVÁNY

LEGITIMATION

William F. Powers
SIGNATURE

I AM AN AMERICAN AIRMAN.
PLEASE TAKE ME TO YOUR COMMANDING OFFICER AND NOTIFY NEAREST
AMERICAN OR BRITISH MILITARY MISSION IN BELGRADE, BUCHAREST,
POLTAVA OR OTHER NEARBY PLACE. ALSO, PLEASE ARRANGE FOR TRANS-
PORTATION.

THANK YOU

SHOW THIS TO RUSSIANS:

Я АМЕРИКАНСКИЙ ЛЕТЧИК
ПОЖАЛУЙСТА ПРЕДСТАВТЕ МЕНЯ ВАШЕМУ КОМАНДИРУ
И УВЕДОМИТЕ БЛИЖАЙШУЮ АМЕРИКАНСКУЮ ИЛИ
БРИТАНСКУЮ ВОЕННУЮ МИССИЮ В БЕЛГРАДЕ,
БУХАРЕСТЕ, ПОЛТАВЕ ИЛИ В ДРУГОМ БЛИЖАЙШЕМ
МЕСТЕ. ТАКЖЕ РАСПОРЯДИТЕСЬ О ПЕРЕДВИЖЕНИИ.
БОЛЬШОЕ СПАСИБО !

My I.D. card with languages of the enemy countries we attacked, Russians, of course, the exception.

I AM AN AMERICAN.

PLEASE TAKE ME TO THE NEAREST AMERICAN OR BRITISH MISSION,
OR TO THE NEAREST RUSSIAN MILITARY AUTHORITY.

THANK YOU.

JESTEM AMERYKANIN.

PROSZE ODPROWADZIĆ MNIE DO NAJBLIŻSZEGO POSELSTWA
AMERYKAŃSKIEGO ALBO ANGIELSKIEGO, ALBO, DO NAJBLISZEGO
WLADZA ROSYJSKIEGO WOJSKA.

DZIĘKUJE SERDECZNIE.

POLAND

JÁ JSEM AMERIČAN!

PROSIM VÁS ZAVEĎTE MNE K NEJBLIŽŠÍ AMERICKÉ NEB BRITSKÉ
MISI, NEBO K NEJBLIŽŠÍMU RUSKÉMU VOJENSKEMU ÚŘADU.

DĚKUJI!

CZECHOSLOVAKIA

JA SAM AMERIKANAC.

MOLIM POVEDITE ME DO NAJBLIŽE AMERIKANSKI ILI ENGLESKE MISIJE,
ILI DO NAJBLIŽE RUSKE VOJNICKE VLASTI.

HVALA

YUGOSLAVIA

AMERIKAI VAGYOK

KÉREM KISÉRJEN EL A LEGKÖZELEBBI AMERIKAI VAGY ANGOL.
BIZOTTSÁGHOZ AVAGY A LEGKÖZELEBB LEVO OROSZ KATONAI
HATÓSAGHOZ.

KÖSZÖNÖM SZÉPEN

HUNGARY

ICH BIN AMERIKANER.

BITTE BRINGEN SIE MICH ZUR NÄCHSTEN AMERIKANISCHEN ODER
ENGLISCHEN MISSION ODER ZUR NÄCHSTEN RUSSISCHEN BEHÖRDE.

VIELEN DANK

AUSTRIA & GERMANY

*This is the reverse side of I.D. pictured on the preceding
page. I carried it on all missions.*

- 31 -

Cast Of Characters

Lt. Bob Neely* . . . . .Pilot

Lt. Jim Wyatt** . . . . .Copilot

Lt. Steve Kaplan* . . . . .Navigator

W/O John Thomas* . . . . .Bombardier

T/Sgt Bill Somers . . . . .Engineer/gunner

T/Sgt Alex Leitman* . . . . .Radio/gunner

S/Sgt Elmer Nelson* . . . . .Waist Gunner

S/Sgt Don Powers . . . . .Waist Gunner

S/Sgt Henry Soriano** . . . . .Ball Turret Gunner

S/Sgt John "Red" Patterson . . . . .Tailgunner

* Deceased
** Whereabouts unknown

Notes:

Alex Leitman died Feb. 16, 1986 at the age of 74 at his home in Birmingham, Alabama.

Elmer Nelson died April 7, 1990 at the age of 67.

Bob Neely died Jan. 8, 1987 at the age of 64. He served in Korea and Vietnam and earned the DFC. He attained the rank of Lt. Colonel.

Red Patterson was "found" 51 years later after the war ended alive and well living with his second wife, Donna, in Santa Barbara, California.

Fifty-two years later Don Power was "found" in his retirement community in Jensen Beach, Florida with his wife Fern.

My crew before overseas assignment in training at Gulfport, Mississippi. Front row, L to R: Thomas, Wyatt, Neely, Kaptain; Back row: Power, Patterson, Leitman, Somers, Nelson and Soriano.

Mission Targets

No.	Date	Airplane	Form 5	Target
1	11/18/44	164	8:00	.... Vienna, oil refineries
2	12/15/44	411	7:40	.... Linz, marshalling yards
3	12/20/44	987	7:40	.... Linz, alt. to Brux
4	12/26/44	665	8:05	.... Blechammer, oil ref.
5	12/28/44	418	7:45	.... Regensburg, oil ref.
6	1/19/45	664	5:45	.... Brod, R.R. yards
7	1/21/45	664	8:05	.... Vienna, oil refineries
8	1/31/45	413	7:45	.... Moosebierbaum
9	2/05/45	664	8:05	.... Regensburg
10	2/07/45	665	7:25	.... Vienna, oil refineries
11	2/13/45	664	7:00	.... Vienna, ordnance depot
12	2/14/45	376	7:55	.... Vienna, oil refineries
13	2/17/45	411	7:55	.... Linz, marshalling yards
14	2/18/45	867	8:30	.... Linz, marshalling yards
15	2/22/45	385	8:20	.... Lindau, marshalling yards
16	2/25/45	664	7:25	.... Linz, marshalling yards
17	2//27/45	665	7:40	.... Augsburg, R.R. yards
18	3/08/45	867	7:00	.... Hegyeshalon, oil refineries
19	3/09/45	385	7:05	.... Bruck, marshalling yds
20	3/13/45	704	7:30	.... Regensburg, R.R. yds
21	3/16/45	411	7:25	.... Vienna, oil refineries
22	3/21/45	164	7:55	.... Vienna, oil refineries
23	3/25/45	411	8:20	.... Prague, Czech. airfield
24	4/08/45	867	6:40	.... Bressanone, R. R. bridge
25	4/14/45	867	7:35	.... Avigliano ammo factory
26	4/18/45	754	6:00	.... Bologna, 5th Army
27	4/19/45	754	6:35	.... Rattenburg R.R. yds
28	4/20/45	664	7:25	.... Vipeteno R.R. yds
29	4/24/45	164	6:15	.... Obr Drauburg, bridge
30	4//25/45	704	7:00	.... Linz, marshalling yards

(Hours documented above in my Form 5 conflict with my actual diary entries)

It's relevant, I think, to note that I fly a dozen different airplanes during my 30-mission tour of duty. Dick Drain, author of "Fifth Bomb Wing - History of Aircraft Assigned," has researched the B-17s of the 99th bomb Group and the Fifth Wing as evidenced by his written work. Using Drain's printed research, my friend Vic Fabiniak traced the history of the fortresses I flew and mailed his findings to me. The B-17s were either destroyed in combat, salvaged overseas or flown to Kingman, Az. to be scrapped.

The Demise of Fortresses I Flew In Combat

The following aircraft are listed in the order I flew them with their complete serial numbers as provided by Drain and forwarded to me by Fabiniak:

44-8164 (missions 1, 22, 29): Assigned 8/29/44 (Pff a/c). Transferred to depot Yugoslavia 8/22/44. Returned to U.S. 6/15/45.

43-8411 (missions 2, 13, 21 and 23): Assigned 10/17/44. 650 hours on 5/20/45. Sent to U.S. and Kingman, Az. 11/26/45 .

42-106987 (mission 3): Transferred from 483rd B.G. 3/31/44. Transferred to depot 1/19/45. Declared excess 11/30/45 with 75 missions.

44-6665 (missions 4, 10, 17): Assigned 12/12/44. Sent to U.S. 6/27/45 and to Kingman 12/20/45.

43-8418 (mission 5): Nickname: "Glittering Gal" . Assigned 10/10/44 . M.I.A. 3/20/45 Kornenberg, Austria. Flak. Crashed near Krizevei. Crew members: Richard Urban, Pilot ; Turriso, Marilley, Bjustron, Welch, Wamser, Austrian, Whitley, Boorstein, Appleman. (Missing Aircraft and Crew Report--13054)

44-6664 (missions 6, 7, 9,11,16 and 28): Assigned 12/12/44. Transferred to Kingman 10/4/45.

44-6413 (mission 8) : Assigned 8/14/44 . Battle damage, Sienna, 2/21/45 . Direct hit in bomb-bay. Mallardi, and Swithers manage to dislodge bombs. Harnett crew: Goodwin, Walker, Stentzil, Miles, Mallardi, Heath, Burris, Swithers, Seaverns. Mallardi wounded. Aircraft salvaged overseas 2/22/45.

44-6376 "Fuddy Huckle" (mission 12): Assigned 8/13/44. 782 hours on 5/20/45 . To U.S. 6/18/45. To Kingman 12/17/45.

44-6867 (missions 14, 18, 24 and 25): Assigned 12/22/44 . Sent to U.S. 6/23/45. To Kingman 12/22/45.

44-6385 (missions 15 and 19): Assigned 8/26/44. To depot 3/15/45 . To U. S. 6/23/45 . To Kingman 12/17/45 .

44-6704 (missions 20 and 30): Transferred from 301st B. G. 2/24/45 . To Dep.t 3/16/45 . Salvaged overseas 3/28/46.

44-6754 (missions 26 and 27): Assigned 3/19/45. Salvaged overseas on 3/31/46

.

My 30-Mission Target Map

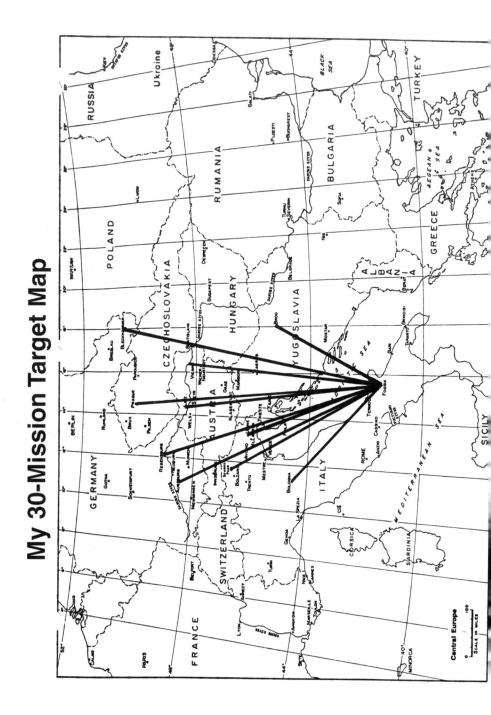

CHAPTER 2

Take No Prisoners

Hitler's war was winding down when I came on board in November of 1944. Unbeknown to me, of course, desperate measures were being taken by the Fuhrer and this last phase of the war became my war. And little did I know as my missions unfolded before me in the succeeding months ahead of the barbaric vengeance being played out on the ground below me. None of us knew. American flyers, particularly bomber crews forced to bail out, became the object of hateful derision and abuse from civilian and military captors. Resentful of the relentless bombing we had subjected them to for so long a period of time seemed just cause for their retribution. Germans threw away the book when it came to Allied air crews facing capture and their desperate measures in some instances turned to outright murder of hapless flyers, British and American.

"Crews which bail out are not to be protected against the population. These people only murder German women and children. It is unheard of that German soldiers should take measures to protect them against our population which is acting out of motives of justifiable hate. Why are my orders not carried out?" Hitler wanted to know, according to testimony given at the Nuremberg trials on June 8, 1946 by General Kurt Koller, Chief of Luftwaffe General Staff.

Speaking from his underground bunker of the Reich Chancellery in March, Hitler then turned to General Koller and said: "The reason why my orders are not carried out is only the cowardice of the Luftwaffe, because the gentlemen of the Luftwaffe are cowards and are afraid that something will happen to them too. The whole thing is nothing more than a cowardly pact between the Luftwaffe and the British and American airmen."

Hitler, obviously terribly disturbed, then exclaimed: "I hereby order that all bomber crews who bailed out in the last few months as well as all bomber crews bailing out in the future, are to be turned over immediately by the Luftwaffe to the SD (Sicherheits Dienst--Security Service), and are to be liquidated by the SD. Anyone failing to carry out my orders or taking action against the population, is liable to the death penalty and is to be shot."

Gen. Koller, in his testimony, said the Fuhrer became enraged when shown a notice taken from an Allied press reporter. An American combat crew, shot down over Germany a short time previously, (the middle of March), was overtaken by advancing American troops. They had declared that they were ill treated by enraged members of the population, threatened with death and probably would have been killed if German soldiers had not taken them under their protection.

Our air war had long taken its toll of German tactical and strategic targets. And innocent civilians living in close proximity to these targets suffered too. Our strategic bombing had been going on with increasing effectiveness for a long time. Having to endure the many months of sustained attacks while watching their own defenses crumble almost imperceptibly at first and then precipitously in the waning months of combat, had to have a resounding negative psychological impact on the people. These are the same people, swayed by the party line and the nobility of the Nazi cause, committed themselves to a German triumph, whatever the cost in Hitler's rise to power. Hadn't Hitler's propaganda chief Josef Goebels whipped his people into a frenzy of righteous indignation in the German conquests from Poland to France?

Blitzkrieg became a word synonymous with a German nation on the march. Is there any wonder the German people felt so secure, so unafraid, so superior? Hitler really sold his people a bill of goods they would live to regret. In the early days of the war they languished in German successes on land, at sea and in the air. His people were ecstatic. They were on a roll. They were promised a bomb would never fall on

Berlin--and then came Russia. The tide of battle began to change. And the days and weeks became months of setbacks from punishing Allied assaults from the air and on the ground.

Before I flew my first mission, the temper of Germany had changed dramatically. My first mission came on Nov. 18, 1944. I was nervous. I was anxious.

All the weeks and months of training were at an end. Flying practice missions in the states and in Italy constituted a demanding scenario of in-flight work as a crew. It also perfected our formation flying techniques. The day of reckoning had finally arrived. We were assigned to *The Old Lady,* ship No. 164. We were taken directly to the flight line in trucks. We drew our gear for the mission.

We also wore a shoulder holster with a loaded .45 caliber pistol. The gun could present a problem if we got shot down. Resisting armed captors could get you killed. On the other hand it could buy your freedom. Yugoslavian Partisans were friendly to us, but Chetniks were allied with Hitler. And Croatians, another of the fragmented peoples of a torn country at war with the Germans, would try to help you escape in a trade for the gun you carried.

That was the Balkans. A little different from what we could expect from the German military and civilians. Intelligence wouldn't dwell on the subject probably because they were as much in the dark about captured flyers as we were. We were vague about the use of the .45 pistol. Oh, we knew how to use it alright, but the wisdom to use it and under what circumstances was never really explained to us. It only added to unanswered questions that caused us increased concern before flying combat for the first time. Is there any wonder I might have been a little nervous, a little anxious about what was to unfold, not only for me, but for all of us.

Talk about anxieties. We were so innocent and scared. At least I was. Only one mission under our collective belts. Little did we know of the savage nature of the German beast. And probably a good thing we didn't.

It's important that we digress here because in this winter of '44 we see a German army on the ground and in the air with their backs to the wall. The Battle of the Bulge has begun far from our Italian base. Is it relative to what B-17 crewmen might expect? I think so. The enemy mindset became one of insensitivity out of what must have been for them a most frustrating turn of events in the change of the tide of battle since D-Day. Fortress Europa was collapsing all around them.

To what lengths were the Nazis prepared to go to stave off defeat? Was the Malmedy massacre which occurred Dec. 17th a window into their psyche? Remember, that was the 150 G.I.s from Battery B, 285th Field Artillery Observation Battalion of the 7th Armored Division that were scattered under an intense German armored probe into their sector. The Germans rounded up the surprised soldiers, parked a tank at either end of a snow covered field and proceeded to machine gun the American POWs. Seventy were to survive the massacre. When the dead were found, the shock electrified the American army from the lowest private to the highest general.

That savagery involved a large number of men. But now I would relate an incident involving the crew of a downed B-17 on the Austrian-Czechoslovakian border. Although only a few were involved, what happened is consistent with the mentality of the Malmedy massacre. It also serves to add credibility to the fears bomber crews like ours had to come to grips with as they prepared for another takeoff, another mission. Be it their first or their 49th, that unnamed fear would always be with them.

The 2nd Bomb Group were part of our 5th Wing. Charles Richards, in his book, *The Second Was First*, gives the heart rending account of the brutal slaying by two German officials of pilot Lt. Woodruff J. Warren and four of his crew. A fifth man, 2nd Lt. William Jolly, was shot and killed elsewhere by Josef Witzany. The other four became POWs.

Details of the tragedy were contained in a letter in October, 1995 from Mr. Karl Affenzeller, living in Freistadt, Austria to the crew's radio operator Warren Anderson. He wrote: "Now to the tragic event on December 9, 1944. Franz Strasser-Kreislerter in Kapliz and Captain Karl Lindemeyer, Chief of Police, murdered the following members: 1st Lt.

Warren, 1st Lt. Donald L. Hart, 2nd Lt. George D. Mayott, T/Sgt Frank Pinto and S/Sgt. Joseph A. Cox.

"Strasser was hanged by the Americans in December, 1945 (after a War Crimes Trial). Lindemeyer had died by reasons of suicide after World War II in Czechoslovakia."

Apart from the others, Affenzeller wrote: "Josef Witzany, Nazi-Ortsgruppenleiter and 'Volksturm-Chief' in the village of Oppolz (Ticha) was the murderer of 2nd Lt. William Jolly. Before the emergency landing took place, Lt. Jolly bailed out with his chute and landed safely nearby the pilgrimage 'Maria Schnee". A few minutes later he was shot by Josef Witzany. The murderer fled, possibly to Austria, at the end of the war. I don't know his fate." So concludes the Offenzeller letter.

What influenced these Germans to commit murder remains to be seen. A civilian population subjected to our intense and incessive bombardment has to play a role in their deportment. Here was a defiant and scared adversary. The heat of battle exposes the best and worst in men, in this case the latter. Civilized combat erases itself under these conditions. Two examples of barbarity in war, one as they sometimes affected American airmen, have now been offered to show the almost imperceptive color of war on fighting men on a psychological level. Hospital wards were filled with these mental casualties of aerial warfare.

That first morning we didn't attend briefing, but our officers did as did Alex. I met with the crew chief of the aircraft we were to fly and discussed its condition. No question the pride the man took in explaining their work on the ship before our arrival. He patiently reviewed everything for me which obviously I would, in turn, share with Neely. Meanwhile Hank and Alex, Red and Don and Elmer went to their stations to prepare for takeoff.

Yes, the work of months had lifted us to a point where we were as ready as we ever would be for our first mission. Our target that memorable first day would be oil refineries in Vienna, Austria. We would carry a 4,000-lb load of 500-lb bombs. It would be a long haul to the target--as it turned out we got eight hours of flying time in. Our altitude over the target was

26,500 feet. Guns started throwing flak soon after we crossed into Yugoslavia, From then until we hit the target we went through about six flak barrages. At Vienna the sky was full of flak. Bursts were close. You could hear tiny fragments against the aluminum frame of The Old Lady. A ship on our left wing had to feather a prop. We endured four more flak barrages on the way back to base. The two ounces of mission whiskey each one of us got helped our shattered nerves.

Our run to Linz on December 20th turned into a milk run. We carried 6000 pounds of bombs and posted a flying time of 7-1/2 hours. Altitude over the target was 24,500 feet. With three missions under our belts we felt like veterans--living, breathing human beings who had performed under fire and survived.

Interestingly, our chief opposition was not German fighters. It was flak from hundreds of gun emplacements in our target cities. The air war early on had virtually decimated the Nazi fighter force. Oh, on occasion, remnants of a once powerful defensive armada of fighters would rise to meet us in token resistance.

Oil refineries at Blechammer, Germany, were targeted for our fourth mission. It was a very long haul--eight hours at least. We bombed from an altitude of 27,000 feet. This mission proved to be the most frightening to date. As it turned out, it was the longest raid of my combat experience. I saw a B-17 go down--a first. The impact of war finally hit me. I didn't know the people in that stricken aircraft, but it told me the guys down below were playing for keeps. From my plexiglass enclosed top turret, visibility was perfect. From the beginning there was no question the plane was in trouble. It's engine was on fire and I kept watching, riveted in terrible fascination. The doomed plane continued in formation and I marvelled at its staying power. Then it veered off, went into a spin as it became engulfed in flames. Those of our crew in a position to observe the hapless bomber would call over intercom when a chute was seen. We agreed later we counted seven parachutes.

Enemy fighters appeared out of range and didn't attack us. We were at 15,000 feet about an hour after bombing Blechammer's oil refineries when we were caught in a wicked flak barrage. There were a few casualties among the bombers in our group, but all our planes returned safely to base.

Another time, same target, Mike Johns, an engineer gunner with the 347th squadron tells of his experience with a Nazi intruder. It was July 7, 1944 also on a mission to Blechammer. He was flying in the lead ship and just as they started the bomb run a B-17F appeared by the right wing of the plane on his right. He could see the pilot and copilot who were both wearing German uniforms. The B-17 appeared in olive drab paint with a swastika on its tail. It had a cross on its side. Johns even remembered the number on its tail. It was 124585. He wrote it down and years later found it as he was sorting some papers to put in his album.

The Nazi bomber opened its bomb bay doors on the bomb run in unison with other planes in the formation. They completed the bomb run with the rest of the formation but as the 99ers banked to the left, the Germans banked to the right. The German pilot waved off with a salute and disappeared. Johns said he kept his guns on the intruder until he left the formation. He had asked his pilot for permission to fire at it but he got a negative response.

When the Luftwaffe could get a B-17 it would repair and rebuild it and use it for a variety of purposes. Captured Fortresses were used in clandestine raids to drop spies. The Germans flew the bomber to learn its weaknesses and better train their fighter pilots in the art of its destruction. B-17s sometimes were kept in U. S. colors to shadow incoming bomber formations to vector fighters and flak batteries. The Luftwaffe was adept at placing its captured trophies at the right place and at the right time. Such moves were infrequent, however.

If the mission to Blechammer, our fourth, was frightening, our next one to bomb oil refineries at Regensburg was terrifying. We carried a 5,000 pound bomb load which would be released as an altitude of 23,000 feet. The only gratification from this raid was the Air Medal they awarded me and the rest of the guys on the crew. It was not for any heroics on our part. It was just an Air Force numbers game. Fly five missions and earn the Air Medal. They added two clusters to my medal by the time we were finished.

On this Regensburg raid we developed engine trouble just before hitting the target. We were flying at 27,000 feet, a bit higher than usual. But not for long. We couldn't maintain our position in formation and were forced to fall back. Number 2 engine was vibrating badly. We began to lose altitude--fast! We were now between the I.P. and the target. We dropped two bombs to lighten the load and maintain air speed. Waves of our own B-17s were passing directly over us. We were at the target and still losing altitude.

My view through the plexiglass of the top turret was perfect. But I wasn't happy with what I saw. I stared into open bomb bays with their doors wide open above me. Then bombs began to fall around us in strings seemingly close enough to touch. Yes, we were a single aircraft and alone beneath bombers dealing death from above. We were no longer with our squadron. More planes passed over us. More bombs fell around us. I had the best view of what was happening, but Red in the tail and Alex through his gunport in the radio room had ringside seats for the show too.

We salvoed our remaining bomb load after recovering at 18,000 feet and picked up fighter escort back to friendly territory. We were late in arriving back to base. We landed alone in the flight pattern. I was emotionally drained.

*　　*　　*

Probably one of the best narrative descriptions of what it was like to fly a high altitude combat mission is submitted here with the permission of its author, Les Hansen, navigator with the 347th squadron who flew this very same Blechammer mission as I did. His focus is not so much the combat action as it was how a B-17 crew managed to cope with extreme, abusive cold and their use of oxygen and other support systems to survive.

Hansen's "Cold War" Story As Reprinted
From the 99th Bomb Group Newsletter

H Hour! H Hour! The call echoed the length and breadth of the four or five acre tent city which housed the combat crewmen and a few of the support personnel of the 347th squadron. Everyone heard the call, but all but 71 of the approximately 420 men who heard it snuggled deeper into the olive drab blankets on their G.I. cots and immediately went back to sleep, knowing that at least for one more day they had been spared the ordeal of facing the cold war.

The 71 who were to be the stars of the day's drama rolled wearily from the warmth, if not the comfort, of their GI cots and began the long and arduous task of preparing for the cold. The hour was approximately 3 a.m. The place was the Plains of Foggia in southern Italy and it was the day after Christmas, 1944. What they knew, to the man, was the unrelenting cold they would be facing for the next several hours was their greatest enemy, and they prepared for it with the utmost care.

Each began by donning flannel long-john underwear. Next came a regulation uniform complete with proper insignia. This added little, if anything, to keeping out the cold, but rules of war at the time dictated that if you were shot down and captured without recognizable regulation uniform, you might very well be summarily executed as a spy. I personally wore an old set of summer khakis. I wore them without having them laundered until I could no longer tolerate the stench, then had them washed and immediately put them back into service.

Next came an F-2 heat suit. This is a comparatively simple rig constructed not unlike the inside of a toaster, except that the heating element wires were insulated and sewn to the cloth of the suit. The suit consisted of six pieces. First was a garment which looked just like the bib-overalls I wore as a kid (sic) growing up on a farm. The cord for plugging into the aircraft's electrical system protruded from the right hip and led to a jack which activated all the heating element wires in the second suit piece. This was a short bolero-like jacket which covered the arms and upper torso. At the end of each sleeve of the jacket was a plug into which the cord to each glove was inserted. Similarly, at the bottom of each trouser leg were plugs for each of the boots.

The gloves were rather thin, soft leather with the wire heating elements located only on the top of the hands, leaving the palms free for the sense of touch necessary to virtually every task a combat crewman was likely to perform. Inside the leather gloves, very thin silk insert gloves were worn to prevent the backs of the hands from being scorched by the heavy element wires.

The heated boots were made of light weight felt with the heating element wires located throughout the upper portion of the boot, but not on the sole. The whole shebang plugged into a 24 volt receptacle, at least two of which were located at every manned position on the aircraft.

The final outer garment consisted of fleece-lined leather trousers held up by suspenders. Over these came a long-sleeved fleece-lined leather jacket, zippered down the front. Fleece-lined zippered leather boots were slipped over the felt heated boots. While the boots were nice and warm, they would nearly always be jerked loose by the opening shock of the parachute in a bailout situation. Though the felt boots were held in place by their electrical cords, the soles of these were so thin that they wore through after they had been walked on for only a short distance.

Thus to give himself a chance to escape or evade capture after a bailout, one of every crewman's first acts after assignment to the squadron was a trip to the welder's shop where he had a thin, strong cable rig made which could be passed through the eyelets of his GI brogans and attached to his parachute harness. Life was complicated in those days.

(Because my duties as a flight engineer called for frequent trips through the aircraft, my GI shoes I placed at the base of my turret. Had a bailout situation occurred for me, I would simply use the shoe laces to tie them to my parachute harness at the last minute. This happened twice, but we recovered and a bailout was averted.)

Topping off the ensemble was a non-lined leather helmet with built-in earphones. *(Mine was simply a flak helmet which partially covered my ears, but was not fitted out with any hardware.)* The helmet was also equipped with the hardware necessary to accommodate an A-13 diluter demand oxygen mask. The diluter demand oxygen system was, simply stated, a system which automatically combined the pure oxygen carried aboard the aircraft with just the right amount of oxygen-lacking outside air to create a breathing atmosphere very similar to the normal air at or near sea level.

When finally suited up for the mission, the bomber crewman weighed about one-third more than his normal bodyweight and his physical reaction capability was just about half that of which he was capable in normal dress.

When finally dressed and ready, the crewman walked the relatively short distance to the squadron mess hall where they all gathered for transportation to the briefing room. Some of them ate a light breakfast and a few even drank a cup or two of coffee, but most simply waited to board the trucks for transport to the briefing room. The reason for this lack of interest in breakfast and early morning coffee will become apparent later as the actual flying of the mission is described.

It was not until we arrived at the briefing room that we found out where we were going that day. That is, of course, unless Axis Sally had told us on the radio the night before what our target was to be. She did this occasionally, and she was always right. (I'll go to my grave remembering the night she said, "I understand you boys in the Fifth Wing are going to make the longest overland mission in history tomorrow. All the way from Foggia to Berlin." We did too, but that's another story.)

Briefing, you understand, took place long before daybreak. *(In all my 30 missions, I never went to a briefing. Instead I was trucked directly to the flight line along with the other enlisted men of my crew so we could attend the ship we were assigned to fly that day.)* One of the first things you were handed after you took your seat was the photocopy of the map of the target. It's a simple thing. The intelligence people simply stretched and tacked a string of dark yarn over the route to be flown that day on a large map in Group Operations. It told you that your target for the day was Blechhammer, which, if you'd been in the outfit for more than a week, you knew it was an oil refinery in eastern Czechoslovakia that was defended by about a zillion 88mm and larger anti-aircraft weapons. Worst of all, it was more than 600 miles from home base. *(The target was the longest mission of all I flew and involved over eight hours of flying time.*) Briefing took about an hour, after which we were taken by truck to the hardstands where our aircraft were located. By then, daylight was with us, or only minutes away, and we started engines.

All four squadrons, of course, had to use the same runway and since we made every effort to space takeoffs no more than three minutes apart, it got a bit dicey at times. We took off by squadrons, and were generally in squadron formation while still at traffic pattern altitude of about 1,200 feet. From there on it got complicated.

Next came group formation. This for the 99th generally took place over the tip of a cape which extended some distance into the Adriatic Sea not far from home plate. Group rendezvous was usually planned for somewhere between 8,000 and 11,000 feet above ground level, and meant that, on a normal mission day, we were bringing 28 large aircraft into very close proximity in a comparatively small area (of sky). Surprisingly, I do not ever recall losing an aircraft during rendezvous. I am forced to conclude that someone was watching over us.

Wing rendezvous was next. The really hard part. This always, for us, took place over a lake not far from Foggia, and was usually set to take place at 17,000 feet. Wing rendezvous was always, to me, a near miraculous event. Here, on a normal mission day, you were bringing together 140 large, lumbering aircraft in a very small area, and within a very short time. (If you were more than a couple of minutes off rendezvous time, it might well be the last time you would ever lead your bomb group.) Rendezvous ulcers were not an uncommon disease among group and squadron lead pilots.

Now, you should understand that our flying machines, as magnificent as they were, and they truly were magnificent, were unpressurized and, in practical terms, unheated. I have been told on a hundred occasions that the Boeing B-17 had heaters. If this were true, I am undoubtedly the only man in history who flew 33 missions in B-17s whose heaters were not operating on those particular days. You should also understand our aircraft was loaded with bombs. Assuming an average day, this would be either twelve 500-lb general purpose bombs, or six 1,000-lb general purpose bombs. Either way, it works out to three tons of bombs. Compared to more modern machines, this is not a very impressive bomb load, but let me assure you that it was all the aircraft could lift to what was considered optimum bombing altitude, and in a very slow rate of climb at that.

By the time we reached Wing rendezvous at 17,000 feet, we had been on oxygen for something like an hour and temperature on the ground was 40 degrees at takeoff, it had fallen to 21 degrees below zero at Wing rendezvous. The bitter cold was already with us even before the air crews were out of sight of their home fields.

Once the Wing was formed, the long climb to the target began. At briefing, a target altitude was assigned. It was very rarely below 25,000 feet...the assigned altitude didn't really mean a whole lot. Every good wing, group or squadron commander would try to get just as high as possible before turning on the bomb run. The Germans were sighting their flak guns by radar, but it was primitive stuff, and the further away you could get from it, the less accurate it was. Hence, the higher the better.

When you are climbing approximately 140 fully-loaded aircraft, you climb, of course, at the best climb rate of the weakest aircraft in your formation, just as when you sailed in a convoy at sea, you maintain the speed of your slowest ship.

As you passed through 20,000 feet, again assuming standard conditions, the outside (and to hell with Boeing) and the inside temperature fell to just below 28 degrees below zero. At about this point in time, or perhaps even somewhat earlier, the moisture in your breath as you breathed through your oxygen mask, which you had been doing for something like a couple of hours, began to condense and water began to collect around your chin. This went on until, finally, it rose to the point where it began to run into the corners of your mouth. At this time, you pulled the lower part of the oxygen mask away from your chin and allowed the water to fall down the front of your flying gear. As this continues, and it does continue at an increasing pace as the temperature continues to fall, the entire front of your flying suit becomes a solid mass of ice.

There is really nothing you can do about this except tolerate it in the sure and certain knowledge that whether you survive the mission or not, you are for certain going to descend from altitude and it will eventually melt.

Now, if you have been indiscreet and have drunk, let us say, two or more cups of coffee that morning, the urge to urinate is becoming urgent. Let us say, for the purpose of illustration, that you are a bombardier on your first mission, and find yourself in this situation. You would, quite logically, elect to make your way to the nearest relief tube. Boeing, thoughtfully, put a number of these on the B-17. The closest one available to the bombardier, however, is located in the bomb bay. Measured in feet, this is no great distance from the bombardier, who is situated in the very forward part of the nose of the aircraft. Measured in terms of effort, it is just beyond the point on the moon where the Eagle landed.

Our suffering bombardier must first unplug his heat suit. At the moment this happens, he is about five minutes away from being cold beyond his wildest dreams. Next, he unplugs his oxygen mask from the aircraft oxygen system, but must immediately plug it into a walk-around cylinder of oxygen. This is a metal bottle, about 30 inches long, yellow in color, not terribly heavy, and equipped with a clip which will attach to the parachute harness. The clip, for reasons unknown, except to God, will not even begin to hold the weight of the walk-around bottle, and can be absolutely guaranteed to become disengaged from his chute harness before he has moved 10 inches.

Assuming he is now at 28,000 feet, he can remain conscious without oxygen for something like 45 seconds. He is, at best, in a perilous situation. He must make an immediate decision, however, because at this point he is in a condition which is urgent beyond safety considerations. But our bombardier is no fool. He holds his oxygen connection together by hand as he squeezes past the navigator, crawls up between the pilot and copilot on the flight deck, and works his way between the engineer-upper turret gunner's knees to the bomb bay.

As he enters the bomb bay, is is confronted with a catwalk approximately five inches wide on which he must stand. On either side of the catwalk is a rope he can hold to for support. He's been through combat crew training, so he knows that if he falls off the catwalk on the bomb bay doors, they will open immediately and he'll fall 28,000 feet as he left his chest chute in the nose because it was too bulky to bring with him. (The bomb bay doors were designed to open automatically with only a small amount of weight on them. This was done so that if a bomb were to come loose from its shackle, it would open the doors immediately and be released rather than rolling around on the floor of the bomb bay until it armed itself and blew the airplane all to hell.)

Finally, midway down the catwalk, our intrepid bombardier finds the relief tube. It is nothing more, really, than a funnel-shaped piece of plastic attached to a rubber hose which protrudes from the side of the aircraft. Here our man is faced with a major decision. He is faced with the urgent necessity of finding a small piece of flesh hidden beneath many layers of clothing, and find it in a minimum of time. The obvious answer is to take off his gloves and go for it in a hurry. But the answer is not that simple. If he removes his gloves and is unable to locate what he looking for in under one minute, he is very likely to suffer frostbite to his fingers and lose one or more of them to amputation as a result. So, our gallant warrior does the wise thing. He goes after it with his gloves on.

With a little luck he locates it after a couple of minutes. By this time, of course, this extremely delicate organ has been exposed to very intense cold for several seconds. Now, one need not be a physician to understand the effect of intense cold on this particular bit of flesh. Undaunted, however, he takes what he can find of it--and lets fly. But, he has forgotten an essential element--the ever-present, miserable, bloody damned cold. After no more than ten drops, the throat of the relief tube is frozen solid and our hero winds up urinating all over his glove and the bomb bay doors. But he's lucky in the end. He makes it back to his position in the nose of the aircraft without either perishing from oxygen starvation or suffering frostbite in ANY extremity. It is redundant to even mention it, but this is the ONLY trip our man will ever make to a relief tube on a high altitude combat mission.

From now on our bombardier will join the vast majority of his colleagues and follow one of two courses of action. Either he will drink no coffee in the morning and very little else the night before or he will carry with him a 50 caliber ammunition can to be used in emergencies. The latter course of action, though widely used, was not without its drawbacks. When you descended from altitude and things thawed out, it got pretty stinky. He will also realize, without being told, that defecation is not even a viable option, unless one is prepared to perform the act without removing any clothes, an event which, mercifully, occurred very rarely.

Although I am not in possession of the number of bomber crewmen lost to fighters and/or flak during the war in Europe, I am sure they are staggering as one direct hit on a B-17 erased either 10 or 11 good men. What I do know, however, is that toward the end of the war, when I was involved, most of our non-fatal casualties were losses of fingers or toes due to frostbite. But, enough of this, let us return to our day-after Christmas mission.

Presuming this was one of our good days and all our aircraft were performing well, we dropped our bombs from above 30,000 feet. *(On this raid to Blechammer, our 348th squadron altitude over the target was 27,000 feet. I did note in my diary that "flak was heaviest and most accurate I've seen yet. One fort flying high and to the right of us was hit and its No. 3 engine caught fire. Seven parachutes were seen." The doomed plane was from our group.)* At this altitude I have seen temperatures as low as 78 degrees below zero (F).

While the hardware was protected from the cold, this was not always the case with the crewmen. And the thing we worried about most was our hands. To begin with, glove heat elements burned out about three times as often as the boot elements which were the second most fragile part of the heat suit. Once the glove heating element went, as it all to frequently did, you had about two minutes to save your fingers if you were at, or near, maximum altitude. For most of the time I flew combat in Europe, there was no specific course of action in this situation.

Toward the end of the war a decision came down from on high that since the bomber crews were flying missions which generally lasted on the order of six to seven hours, they should be provided a lunch. *(I don't know about officers, but the enlisted men, at least in my crew on a combat mission, were provided with a K-Ration box. In it, as I recall, was a packet of two, maybe three cigarettes by Phillip Morris. Also a tin of cheese and a couple of crackers. There was some other stuff, but I can't remember what.)* Troop provisioning being what it was in those days, our lunch consisted of two slices of bread with a generous slab of cheese between them. No gourmet, to be sure, but perfectly acceptable to most crewmen. Now, since you donned your oxygen mask, generally, within 30 minutes after takeoff, you were a madman if you created even the remotest need for a bowel movement during the course of the mission. The lunch was universally saved until near the end of the flight.

This presented a problem, however. By the time you descended to about 14,000 feet or slightly less, you could safely remove your mask for at least a few minutes at a time. You had been in intense cold for hours. The cheese sandwich was frozen as solid as a rock and would remain so until long after you had landed. But our American airman is a person to whom any problem is merely a challenge, and that a solution is not possible is an idea completely alien to his nature. In the case of flight lunches, of course, the answer was duck soup. A muff was provided us which could be plugged into the second electric receptacle at each position. You simply inserted the frozen sandwich into the muff. Of course, the muffs still had to be used to save fingers when the heat gloves failed. After landing, it was always one hell of a chore getting the cheese and bread crumbs off your gloves. Everything has its price.

Once our bombs were away, we began to descend. Never mind that you were sick and tired of having your chin under water and a solid sheet of ice from your throat to your crotch. You were still in one piece and the noses of those gallant old birds were headed for home plate.

As we crossed the Adriatic coast from a target like Blechhammer, we were likely at an altitude of between 17,000 and 18,000 feet. Every smoker in the Fifth Wing realized that at this approximate altitude there was enough oxygen to light a match or cigarette lighter and they all lit up. They were still too high to leave their masks off, so they'd take a puff, put the mask back on for two or three breaths, then take another puff, etc. Because of the small amount of oxygen at this level, a cigarette lasted for something like a half hour.

If my memory serves me correctly after these more than 40 years, the 99th returned with 27 of its original 28 aircraft. The other was lost to flak over the target. This means we returned with 274 of the 284 men who had begun the mission. That's a loss rate of less than 4%. Not bad, but loss rates have never impressed me very much. If you were one of those lost, so far as you were personally concerned, the loss rate was 100%.

For those of us who survived, however, it was a day of victory. We had, once again, beaten the Kraut!--no mean adversary. We had also beaten that more insidious and dangerous sonofabitch, THE COLD!

CHAPTER 3

A Big Bird's Folly

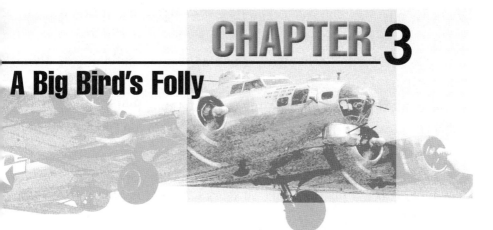

We didn't fly the next day after the Blechammer raid. It was a stand down, at least for us on Neely's crew. But I would be remiss if I didn't suggest even top brass can pull a boo-boo with prompt and unforgiving results. It's a story of poor judgment and inevitable failure of a combat mission. It occurred the next day, the day after I flew the Regensburg mission. In any branch of the military in time of war and in any rank there can be acts less than normal. The slapping incident of Gen. Patton can serve as an extreme in pointing to men under stress. What happened is not something we in the 99th are proud of, but it doesn't belong in the closet either. It's not a popular subject but it needn't be covered up either. Our 99th Bomb Group had not one, but two group commanders transferred out because of questionable actions. This is the story of one of them.

Marshaling yards and railroad shops at Castelfranco, Italy were the target of the men who flew December 29, 1944. Our group lead was being flown by the colonel.

The colonel, flying group lead, hadn't flown a mission in over two months. In fact he only flew four missions with the group. But he was deputy commander of the 99th Bomb Group that day that surely led credibility to the acronym SNAFU.

The colonel graduated from West Point. He completed his pilot training and was assigned to Hawaii in the years preceding Pearl Harbor and eventually assigned to a unit in England. Subsequently he was assigned to a 15th Air Force bomb group as Deputy C.O. in 1944 and flew about five missions with that group. He was transferred to the 99th and flew his four missions from the left seat.

According to Bernie Barr, group adjutant at the time, the colonel was considered combat ready to take over the 99th. Barr finished his fifty missions on December 27th, two days before the colonel's untimely raid. Actually, because Barr had finished a tour of duty in the South Pacific, he'd completed one hundred missions.

Barr's remarks were made when he prepared to present Colonel Ray Schwanbeck a plaque about 50 years later at a bomb group reunion. He said that Schwanbeck was not programmed to be the 99th commander, but through unusual circumstances he became boss on January 2, 1945. He then told about the colonel, as group commander, leading the mission to Innsbruck (actually Castlefranco). Then he remarked: "through some screw-up he got in the nose of the lead airplane of Al Schroeder's squadron to help the navigator and bombardier find the target and everything went wrong. (Barr then described the havoc and disaster of the mission and said "the next day the colonel was gone.")

The change of command was swift. The 99th needed a new commander. On January 2nd as he checked out to return home, Barr said he met Col. Schwanbeck as he checked in as the new commander of the 99th Bomb Group.

"We said hello," Barr said. He had known Ray Schwanbeck with the 19th Bomb Group in Australia in 1942. He had also been in Italy as vice commander of the 463rd Group for about four months and had flown several missions as group leader. He was able, available and qualified, according to Barr and he was called to report and he did.

On this fateful day four days after Christmas the colonel was not only appointed left seat in the lead aircraft of the 99th, but the whole 15th Air Force. It was the group's 324th mission of the war. The 99th would end the war with an impressive 395 wartime raids.

The colonel's crew was hand picked by Lt. John Plummer, a pilot from a small town in Pennsylvania. He not only picked the crew but he would fly with the colonel on a practice mission the day before.

Lt. Plummer was not only ordered to fly with the colonel on the practice mission, but flying as his copilot he was ordered not to instruct the colonel in any capacity whatsoever. There would be no briefing. As operations officer and squadron lead pilot of the 347th squadron, he was to concede later on that it was an order he would live to regret. It was an arrangement he couldn't help feeling a little guilty about. Lt. Plummer's first impression of the colonel was that he was a rather striking individual and soft spoken and who was neither rude or impolite. The lieutenant was not intimidated and he was not at all happy practice flying with the colonel. He speculated he might have drawn this duty because of his credible combat record of forty-eight missions.

Resigned that first lieutenants don't tell bird colonels anything unless they are asked and determined to follow the order "fly copilot only", the lieutenant's assessment of the practice mission and the colonel's skills left much to be desired. The practice was described as a "wild" flight and not consistent with veteran pilots. Nonetheless, Group Operations next ordered Lt. Plummer to pick a crew for the colonel.

The next day, without Plummer but into the mission, violent head winds create havoc as they entered the Brenner Pass. Heavy flak concentrations take a toll of his aircraft and the navigator, Norris Domangue is wounded--incapacitated. The colonel is now the blind leader of the pack of hundreds of bombers stretched out behind him. Stressed out, he abandons his cockpit seat. In an almost unprecedented move, he insists on navigating to the target. He's off course and formations behind him are beginning to fragment. He finally achieves Innsbruck where the 416th squadron splits to Udine, a secondary target some 120 miles to the southeast. The 348th, after a third unsuccessful pass over the target in heavy flak, hightails it back on a course south southeast from Innsbruck striking Castelfranco 120 miles away. The colonel tries to hit other targets to no avail and his last and final effort at Udine is unsuccessful. He failed to drop his bombs. His empty left seat was mute evidence to the frustrations incurred during the raid.

The colonel pulled another miscue on landing. His wounded navigator was in need of immediate attention. But instead of permitting a waiting ambulance to take him, he wasted valuable time by taxiing to his hardstand, ignoring the dangerous condition of Lt. Domangue.

The colonel was subsequently transferred out of the group to 5th Wing headquarters, never to fly again with the 99th. He was then transferred back to his former bomb group as deputy commanding officer.

Leadership in command of a missions should not be challenged. And when it fails to live up to the high standards demanded of combat lead pilots, there's going to be hell to pay. The colonel's indiscretions left in their wake men who had much to say about the mission. Lt. Plummer, for example, recalls, once the mission got underway, "the first inkling that things were amiss was when the "bombs away" message wasn't received in the communications section back at the base. And then we got a message that the group had broken up, a couple of planes down, a steep 360 degree turn over the target..." The lieutenant remembers being really shook up over these messages. He said he talked to a number of air crews who flew that day and concluded "it was obvious to me that we really did have a mad colonel aboard and that through his stupidity we could have really screwed up."

A real gung-ho leader of men, Lt. Plummer said of the mission: "it was very close to me. Part was *my* squadron. As operations officer it was my friends who I had ordered on the mission." And in a letter to me almost a half a century later he still seethes with anger and frustration over it. "Forty nine years hasn't changed a thing," he wrote.

Bill Calvin, the copilot relegated to the tail gunner's slot on the colonel's crew for this raid, tells all in a letter to Bernie Barr, editor of the 99th Bomb Group newsletter many years later. Charles E. Evans, Barr's regular pilot, flew copilot with the colonel. Calvin was ordered to fly in the tail gun position because the colonel wanted a commissioned officer to report on the formations behind them. This was not an unusual request of a pilot flying group lead. Lt. Calvin noted before takeoff that someone had handed him a large camera (like the old speed graphic newsmen used) and told him to get pictures over the target. Then, once in the air and over enemy territory, flying backwards in the tail he began taking pictures. And what was his opinion after it was all over flying in the tail gun spot? He felt like he was 200 yards from the nearest waist gun. There was no way of comparing the isolation in the tail to his regular cockpit seat.

That's when "things" began flying past his window--things he thought were parts from B-17s. "When I got my wits about me I realized it was chaff we were releasing. Meanwhile I was getting a great war movie played out in front of me. Planes were being hit and going down and chutes opening. I never did know if I got any of that on film. I was so shaken when I got back that I never thought to ask," he said.

"Among the multitude of things the colonel did wrong was in leading us up and down the Brenner Pass and all the valleys adjacent to Innsbruck. The flak was intense, very accurate, rocking the plane on every burst and still the colonel couldn't make up his mind. Our navigator, Lt. Norris Domangue, was hit in the leg with the first bursts, but we continued in the area going through seven flak areas while over the target area," Lt. Calvin asserted.

"Apparently we never got in a position to release bombs on Innsbruck and I could see that other groups were leaving us and going to secondary targets. How many passes were made I do not remember, but we got our rears shot up pretty good--good enough for all groups to leave us. We ended up with just a portion of our own group still with the colonel. He was violating the unwritten rule that with a wounded man on board you did not try to go back over a target again and again.

"We lost one plane completely and the rest of the group left us after the first flak area and we continued on with only seven planes. Of these, only two had bombs left, ours and the No. 4 ship. Finally, No. 4 left and still the colonel tried to hit targets, Udine being the last try. We finally headed home, lost all our wing men, brought the bombs back and a burned up No. 1 engine. The colonel wouldn't even feather it. It smoked all the way home and finally blazed up in the traffic pattern. It will be a warm day in the Antarctic before we go with him again," Lt. Calvin concluded.

It wasn't until they made the Adriatic Sea that Lt. Calvin was able to leave his station in the tail and move to the nose to attend the wounded Lt. Domangue. Once in the landing pattern a flare was fired to indicate wounded aboard. The colonel's landing, conceded Lt. Calvin, was "one of the best landings I experienced in a B-17, even with a full load of bombs."

"Good mission, men," exclaimed the colonel over the intercom upon switching off the last engine.

"We got back, but no thanks to you," the voice of an anonymous gunner was heard mired in sarcasm. After a moment of ominous silence, the colonel demanded, "who was that?" A very indignant sergeant bravely gave his name to the startled colonel who concluded meekly, "good to meet you, sergeant."

At debriefing following this Castlefranco turned Innsbruck mission the consensus of opinion among participating officers that the day had not gone well, to put it mildly. The officers, collectively, advised Major Al Schroeder to get out the courts martial papers. None of them, they resolved, would fly again if the colonel were to lead them.

Norris Domangue, the wounded navigator said after the raid, "the mission should have been worth four credits." Before being hit he recalls calculating and recalculating 135 mph winds and flying practically at right angles to the intended course, confirming others' reports of the variable winds through the pass.

The navigator recalled much later that it was Lt. Calvin from the tail who peeled back his blood soaked, shredded trouser leg of his heat suit to find the wound. "I remember the application of the sulfa powder, but resisted the morphine. With questionable flying skills suddenly manifesting themselves, I, like most of us on the crew at that time, felt that at least a bailout was a real possibility and I wanted to be as mentally alert as possible. A tourniquet was applied high on my thigh. My second biggest fear now was frostbite and ultimate amputation," Lt. Domangue concluded.

It was at this time that the colonel arrived in the nose to do Lt. Domangue's navigating. He would lead his formations of Flying Fortresses to the target while his navigator kept bleeding in the now overcrowded nose compartment of the ship.

It was to his credit, Lt. Domangue recalls, that the colonel, without his help, ultimately found the course home. They cruised 200 feet over the Adriatic with one engine totally out and a full bomb load. The colonel wanted to salvo the load of bombs into the sea but was reminded in doing so they would be over the impact zone and he would have succeeded where the German flak batteries had failed to end their mission. This error in judgment was pointed out to the colonel so they brought the bombs home.

"That proved to be my last mission," said Lt. Domangue. "I was rotated back to the states. Since I had been shot down and had to bail out over Yugoslavia on my 22nd mission and the colonel's mission was my 47th, they decided to waive the remaining three obligations and packed me off to Ellington AFB in the states," he added.

Observing from another plane in the 416th squadron, John B. Nevin had this to say of the mission: "It remains unforgettable to me. I was hit on that one and had my first test of panic," he said. He told of how his squadron separated from the group. His bombardier was hit and knocked out of action on the first run. They flew around the target three times, never out of the range of flak and never dropping their bombs. One by one their squadron mates left them and they completed the last circuit alone.

"Our engineer toggled out the bombs on the way to our secondary, which was Udine. Perhaps the only cool and considered action of the whole flight," Nevin said. "Near Udine we were jumped by five FW-190s and I thought we'd had it for sure, but like the 7th Cavalry, a lone Spitfire showed up and drove them away and then escorted us home," he added.

Flying with the 348th squadron that late December day was Clyde B. Tuttle. "On the pass over the target, the bombardier could not use the bomb sight because of 100 mph head wind. It could not compute that great wind force. After the second and third pass over the target in heavy flak, one squadron was sent down low and the rest of us went to secondary or third targets," he said, adding that they eventually dropped their bombs over the originally intended target, Castlefranco.

The only plane lost on the mission was that of 346 squadron leader Homer (Mac) McClanahan, whose story is told elsewhere in this book. His navigator had this to say about the mission: "As we approached the target I notified Mac that we were being led off course and were heading over a concentration of guns. We then sustained two hits which started fires in the bomb bay and in the left wing. Mac notified the formation and we pulled out."

Squadron leader McClanahan recalled Slesnik "screaming into the intercom that extreme danger was imminent," but it was his job to follow group lead. Mac believed the only reason they deviated from their chartered course was because the colonel, flying group lead, left his seat to tell the navigator how to navigate.

Once Mac's plane was hit and caught fire, everybody bailed out. Eight men were captured by the Germans while he and his waist gunner were picked up by Italian partisans, ex-Alpine troops. The two became separated after landing in different mountain ranges. Freedom for Mac came months later when Allied tanks pressed into the Po Valley.

Before the colonel's final departure from the 99th, Lt. Hansen of the 347th provided a little levity to the otherwise demoralizing incident. He said he didn't check into the group until just after Thanksgiving of 1944. He didn't fly the 29th, but what happened that day was the sole topic of the officer's club. His future suddenly became abruptly clouded when Lt. Plummer told him he had been selected to be the colonel's personal navigator. He was told the colonel was particularly interested in any bombardier or navigator who were recent arrivals and had flown only a few missions.

With the Castlefranco debacle having become common gossip and now Lt. Hansen chosen for the colonel's crew, both he and the bombardier candidate became quite uneasy and apprehensive. The colonel was to subject them to an unusual test. On the practice mission before his transfer out, a crew member came into the nose and blindfolded both him and the bombardier.At the end of an hour, the blindfolds were removed and they were given an aerial photo of a railroad junction with several buildings around it. They were also given six or seven sectional charts of southern Italy. They were timed trying to locate the target in the photo and pass the coordinates to the colonel. Lt. Hansen said he couldn't remember if they ever located on the charts what the colonel had in mind. It didn't matter because in a few days the colonel had disappeared. The lieutenant would not have to be the colonel's personal navigator after all.

OFFICIAL SQUADRON PHOTOS

*The photo below was given to me
by a 348th Bomb Squadron buddy, occurring during my duty tour
November 1944 - April 1945.*

*Through spinning props of camera ship, the focus
is on mortally wounded Flying Fortress with it's tail assembly in
shambles from enemy fire.*

A squadron Flying Fortress goes down in flames.

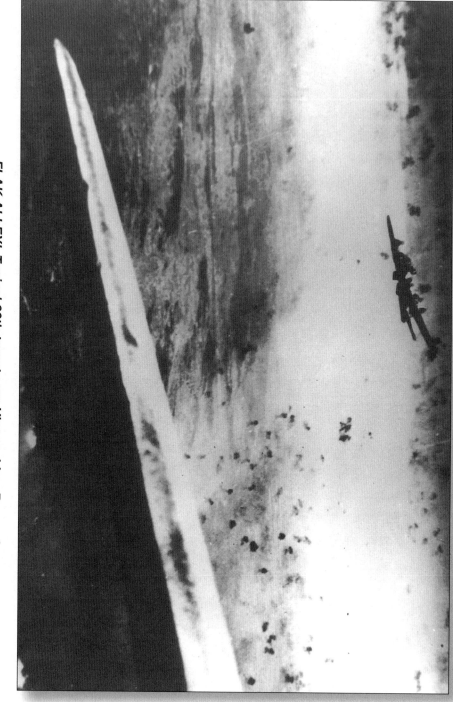

FLAK ALLEY! Typical 99th targets are Vienna, Linz, Regensburg

Black cloud of smoke from target signals a successful raid.

It's right wing enveloped in flames, B-17 plummets earthward

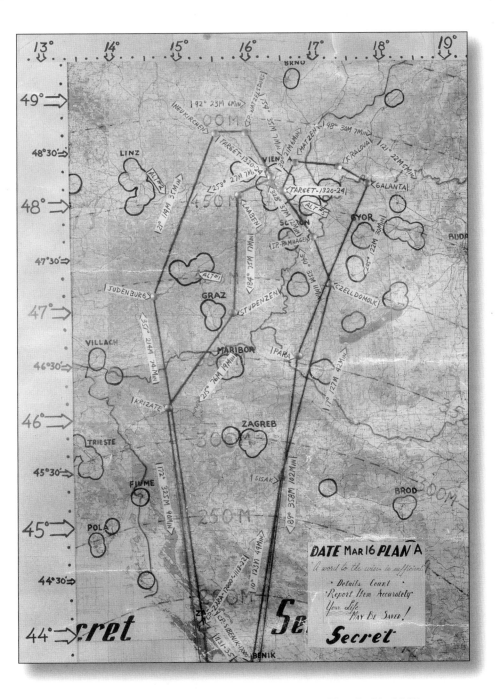

My 21st mission . Vienna . Flak Alley . March 16, 1945
Flying Time: 7 hours

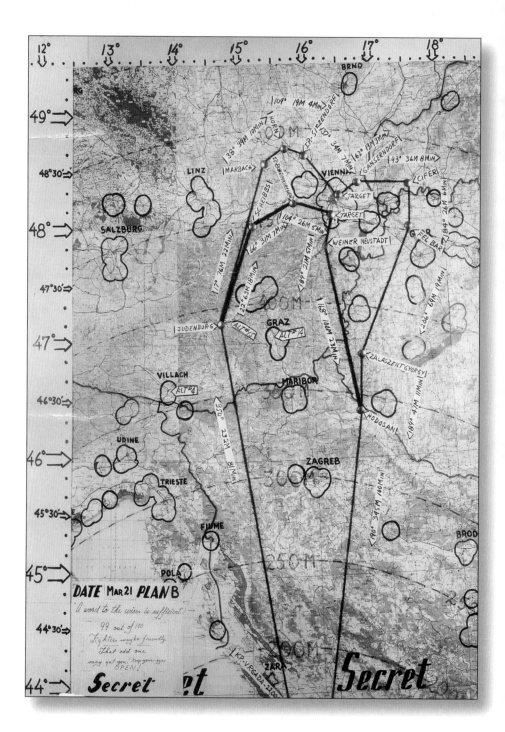

My 22nd mission . Again Vienna . -45º, 8 hours, 20 min. 3/21/45

CHAPTER 4

A Study in Flak

Our runways in Italy were different from the concrete runways used in Britain by the 8th Air Force primarily out of East Anglia where most of their bombers were dispatched from. Ours were steel matted and resilient to takeoffs, especially in bad weather. Takeoffs spelled trouble for every pilot using a mud-coated runway and directed by Sandfly tower. And that was the case for us on Neely's crew on our sixth mission to Brod, Yugoslavia.

The tower delayed our takeoff that morning of January 19th until 10:07--an unusually late start. Our runway was a sea of mud. Neely, Jim Wyatt, our copilot and me would have our hands full in the time it took to get off the ground.

As we taxied into position we knew the normal time between us and the plane ahead was maybe 30 seconds to a minute--depending on the bomb load and weather conditions. To get in the air and stay in the air with our 4,000 pound bomb load would mean we'd have to attain a ground speed of about 110 mph. Under those slippery conditions, it strained every nerve in our collective bodies. Spared this immediate anxiety were the rest of the crew braced in the radio room.

Takeoff procedure for Neely dictated a gradual application of power. He had to avoid over-control and he did admirably well under those trying conditions. His gloved right hand kept working the four throttles. He maintained excellent directional control with rudder and throttles while keeping the ailerons neutral.

I called off the increasing speed of the aircraft directly into his ear as I read the needle on the tachometer in the instrument panel just before us. I'm screaming 100 mph over the thunder of four engines as Neely walks the throttles, ever conscious of what seems to be a dismally slow pace. When we do hit 110 mph, Bob applies moderate back pressure to the control column and ship No. 664 lifts off--ever so slightly.

Wyatt watches the instruments for variations in manifold pressure, rpm and pressure and temperature gauges. Once clear of the ground and flying speed attained, he touches the brakes lightly to stop the wheels from spinning and raises the landing gear. Both Bob and Jim make a visual check and I check and report "tail wheel up." Jim places the gear switch into neutral and easily trims our ship. At 140 mph Bob orders Jim to reduce power and he does so, cutting back to 2300 rpm and we proceed to squadron and then group rendezvous. Jim adjusts cowl flaps to regulate cylinder head temperatures.

Our raid today was one of the shortest trips of all our missions. We hit the marshaling yards at Brod at 23,000 feet. Plan A this day called for a mission to Vienna, but heavy cloud cover shifted us to Brod, the alternate target. Hank from his ball turret and Red from his tail position reported excellent bombing results. We made a cross wind landing at about 14:55.

What was it about German flak gunners. They were slowly but surely being engulfed by advancing enemy forces from both directions but stubbornly stuck to their guns--us being their target. Orders are orders and in the German army that's the way the ball bounced. No questions asked. The German soldier was as brave and courageous as any other--especially with their backs to the wall. Their motivations were a mix of fear and resolve. The military juggernaut created by Hitler and his lieutenants was a demanding, authoritative instrument of power and will. Even in defeat, German esprit dictated a savage allegiance and dedication to orders. Their pride in their assigned units surmounted petty grievances. Discipline was really their unforgiving god which led them to feats of glory in victory as well as defeat.

So those flak gunners, mostly old men and 14 and 15-year old boys--and there were women in those towers too--kept to their guns. In order to confuse German radar, we dropped aluminum foil called window or chaff in bundles of about 100 strips each. It was Don or Elmer or both and sometimes even Alex who dispensed the chaff into the skies announcing our arrival.

As German air defense declined in late 1944 and 1945, we were told of their increasing emphasis on antiaircraft guns to beat off bomber raids especially on oil targets. By late fall of 1944, almost 1,000,000 Germans were involved in antiaircraft defense. Their 50,000 guns in place could collectively fire 5,000 tons of shells per minute. Flak batteries were placed in concentric circles around target cities. By year's end, the winter of 44-45, flak towers contained four to eight heavy guns, usually the potent eighty-eights. Their shells were time fused to explode effectively at 20,000 feet and a killing radius of 30 feet for each shell. When our planes came into range, all batteries fired at the same target at the same time. Flak guns were aimed visually or by radar. If visually aimed, the target was our squadron and group lead aircraft. The center of our formations were targeted by radar-aimed eighty-eights. This information I got from reading Thomas Childer's book, pages 87 and 88, entitled *Wings of Morning*.

Group and squadron lead plane pilots tried to know German flak patterns. Lt. Plummer of the 347th squadron, who was to be promoted to captain in the winter of 1945 and who earned two DFCs in 10 months of combat flying, having flown both leads, had this to say about flak:

"Krauts moved their flak batteries often and their flak gunners generally were a little anxious. Their first blasts were generally ahead of us in four or five large black bursts for each battery. If this happened we were in luck because we could take action to avoid the next series of bursts. The avoidance maneuver evolved as follows: if the initial bursts would be where you would have been had you not turned, the Krauts would have observed their error and would correct their next volley. If their initial blast was ahead and to your left, turn the group toward the left, straight toward the bursts, because their gunners would have calibrated their guns

Fifty Thousand Flak Guns

An estimated 50,000 ack ack guns in targeted European cities, manned by old men, women and children of a country in terminal death throes during the waning months of World War II, provided their awesome defensive and potent firepower. Our bomber crews viewed innocent black puffs, as depicted in the photo above, with relief, knowing what they saw couldn't hurt them. It was the unseen burst that rocked a plane, peppered it's coat, tore it's guts to maim and kill that engendered the torment of apprehension, that struck helpless terror in the hearts of the brave men who flew the dorsal finned answer to insane arrogance and hate.

This page is from the B-17 "Pilot Training Manual." Not only does the schematic precisely depict the engineer-gunner's station, but it affords an overall view of crew positions and their exit routes in dire emergency.

BAIL OUT
CREW ORDER AND EXITS

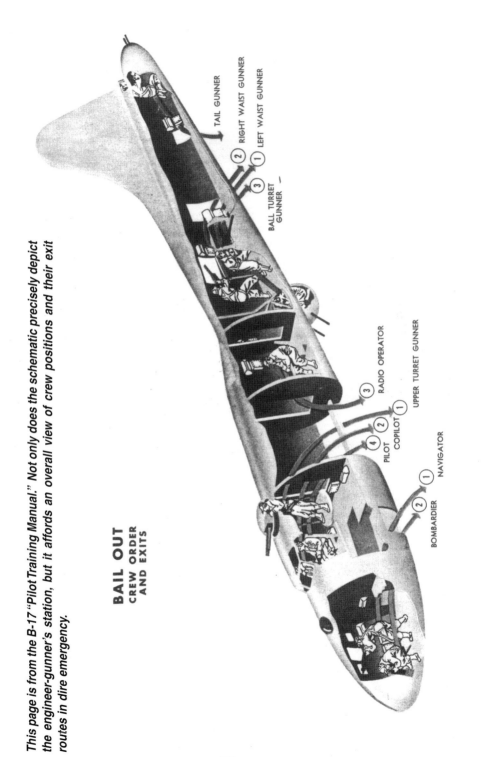

TAIL GUNNER

RIGHT WAIST GUNNER

LEFT WAIST GUNNER

BALL TURRET GUNNER

RADIO OPERATOR

UPPER TURRET GUNNER

PILOT

COPILOT

NAVIGATOR

BOMBARDIER

to aim at a point where you would have been if you hadn't turned and in most cases the flak missed the entire group.

"These flak avoidance procedures were not used on the bomb run," Plummer continued. "because on the bomb run the objective was to hit the target, not to avoid flak. If the Kraut's first flak bursts were right on you or nearly so, you were in deep trouble until you flew out of their range. This is what happened to me on my last mission. A shell exploded above and slightly ahead of No. 2 engine. It knocked out the engine, left window and my left ear. This was my last mission. My combat flying days were over," he concluded.

The second time in seven raids--this one to bomb oil refineries at Vienna--we experienced heavy hits by German flak. Maybe because we were the lead group over the target as Plummer pointed out. But no sooner had Thomas called "bombs away" when No. 2 engine was hit. We couldn't feather it because the oil was too cold and we soon lost oil pressure in that engine. The prop became a wind milling runaway. What happens if it should sheer off? Would it slice into the nose? I didn't know, but I wasn't taking any chances with the lives of our bombardier and navigator. After consulting with Neely, we agreed that Thomas and Kaptain should leave the nose for the radio room and its relative safety.

Even though we couldn't stop the errant propeller, what happened next justified the evacuation of the ship's nose section. Suddenly we took direct hits in the plexiglas nose, shattering it completely. Soon after flak destroyed the forward escape hatch near the navigator's station. The hits kept coming. We were to sustain heavy damage to our left wing and moderate damage in the waist. Knocked out of formation, we flew home alone without escort.

Our bomb load on our seventh mission was 6,000 pounds. Flying time was eight hours and 20 minutes and our altitude over the target was 27,500 feet. Our low temperature was -60 degrees. It was January 21, 1945.

My eighth mission to Moosbierbaum, Austria after ten days of down time, due mostly to inclement weather, was noteworthy only because I was permitted to sit in the copilot's seat for our landing at 1510 hours. A 75 knot head wind on our next raid added to minimal difficulties in reaching Regensburg on February 5th, bombing it from 26,000 feet in a temperature that hit -50 degrees.

I always sweat takeoffs, but this morning I though I'd need to sweat no more. Italian winter was really upon us. Again we faced a muddy runway. It's these kind of takeoffs I detest. When we finally got off the ground we were nose up and almost stalling out. Then we headed straight for the ground, but Bob leveled off just in time. It was my tenth mission, this time to Vienna again with a 6,000 pound bomb load and seven hours and 15 minutes of flying time.

Our No. 3 engine began detonating just before the target. We couldn't get maximum manifold pressure or rpm's so we eased out of the squadron formation, dropped our bombs prematurely and joined the 347th squadron flying below us. What happened next one never gets used to. I watched a ship off my right wing take a direct hit before its bombs were dropped. The plane simply blew up and vanished into bits and pieces of shards of metal. Its crew never had a chance. Erase ten young American flyers.

We weren't maintaining our speed and couldn't stay up with the 347th. And again, our own planes above us with open bomb bays intimidated us--at least me, with loads yet to be released. We strayed into the 2nd Bomb Group formation and returned to base with them.

An ordnance depot in Vienna was the target of our eleventh mission which was really a milk run and the only noteworthy episode of our next mission to oil refineries in Vienna was an oxygen leak that plagued us throughout the flight until I tracked it down to Alex's filler line. We got home with only 25 pounds in the ship's system. Oh yes, we were forced to make two bomb runs over Vienna with our 6,000 pound bomb load of twelve 500-pounders. It was February 14th.

Three days later they gave us Linz, Austria for a target. More specifically, its marshaling yards. We were to fly ship No. 411, a B-17 that survived the war intact and was retired to the scrap yards of Kingman,

Arizona. Our orders on this raid found us assigned as "spare" and to standby. It looked to be a maximum effort since 36 ships were being ordered up, according to the mimeographed plan of battle passed out at briefing before the mission. Our group lead pilot today would be Kane of the 346th squadron and Welborn would fly as lead bombardier. Our squadron leader would be Hemphill and Welchel was named lead bombardier for the 348th. Engine start was 0725 with taxiing to begin ten minutes later. Our crew was activated. Our group would see 360 men in action.

Besides Kane, other squadron leaders on this raid would be Caddock, 416th; Gockenbach, 416th; Koszarek, 348th and Wileman, 347th. Call sign for the 348th on this mission was FZG FORTNIGHT. Orders called for our group to rendezvous at 8,000 feet at 0907 hours. Wing rendezvous would be at 9,000 feet sixteen minutes later. We would hit the target at 25,000 feet at noon and then rally right to Aschach. Our ETA was 1445. As it turned out we logged ten more minutes than the seven hours called for, but we did bomb Linz at the prescribed 25,000 feet in temperatures of minus 40 degrees. Had we been forced to bomb alternate targets, they would have been Bruck and Salzburg, in that order.

"Bombs away, bombs all gone," came the familiar ring of Alex's excited voice over the intercom after we'd jettisoned our load over Linz. The bomb bay doors wouldn't close. My job then was to close them manually. That meant coming down from my battle station in the top turret, disconnect from the main oxygen system and clip on a walk-around bottle of oxygen--good for three minutes. Looking down from my cramped standing position on the narrow ten inch catwalk through the gaping hole created by the open doors was asking for it. Powerful black bursts with red centers exploded below me as I inserted the hand crank into the forward bulkhead of the bomb bay. No parachute with this job. Too bulky. Impossible to maneuver with it attached to my chest harness.The walk-around bottle was bad enough.

Our open bomb bay doors over the target created a tremendous drag and if I couldn't get the doors to close quickly, we'd be forced to leave our formation. Why the doors didn't shut baffled me. We hadn't sustained any real damage to that point. But flak bursts continued to dog us. I began to turn the crank and tired quickly. Alex passed me a second oxygen bottle. I was spread eagle as I worked the hand crank, one foot on the bulkhead, the other on the catwalk. The ship was being continuously rocked by concussions from nearby bursts. I pressed on, ever so slowly with the crank. I pulled it out to rest with the doors only partially closed. And just at that moment the doors began closing on their own. The switch was flipped from the cockpit. I think I saved myself a free fall to earth when I pulled the crank. Anyway we were able to maintain our position in the formation and returned to base without further incident.

Mission number 14 on February 18th, again to Linz, was another milk run, but four days later it was another story. It was the story of weather more than war, but the eight hour round trip to the marshaling yards of Landau, Germany saw us hitting instead, Udine, an alternate target because of the weather.

Much has been said and written about our illustrious comrades of the highly touted 8th Air Force based in England. They got the good press. We, who flew to targets in Europe's underbelly didn't score real big with the war correspondents of the day. I think they fancied the posh hotels of London more than the bombed out, non-English speaking accommodations in torn up Italy. The glamour boys of the Army Air Corps were those of the Mighty Eighth. They had their English channel and white cliffs of Dover. But we had the majestic but forbidding Alps. We had a less than benevolent natural obstacle under normal flying conditions, but when cloaked in storm, it could be a monster--a terribly awesome, intimidating and challenging monstrosity. And so it was this February 22nd.

I expect we were flirting with the peaks of the Italian Alps this day. Other days it could have been the Austrian Alps, even the Swiss Alps when seeking refuge. In any case we flew blind in a vicious snowstorm wing tip to wing tip. Out of sight of one another and we become lost from the formation, never to recover. Conditions were perfect for a midair collision as we slowly ascended over the groping peaks below. The enveloping snow continued as we tried to pierce its white curtain of hell. We continued to dog our way to the target only to find it concealed under 100 percent cloud cover. As we changed course our group came under attack by two German jet fighters. A top turret gunner near us was credited with one kill as it made a lightning pass from above. The ball turret gunner in that same plane was wounded. The weather closed in. Two squadrons dropped their bombs, but we didn't. We flew home with a full bomb load.

Mission number 16 to Linz on February 25th was uneventful for us, but crews in other ships sustained casualties. Flak hit the pilot in the lead ship of our element. I watched as someone bandaged his head. We made a visual run over the target with excellent results.

Terrifying as was the bursting flak, awesome were the guns that loosed it into us five miles up. Spewing murderous white hot nuts and bolts and jagged steel, the shells of an 88 could be fired maybe fifteen to twenty times in a minute. The guns' accuracy even exceeded the bombing altitudes we flew.

More deadly was the German 105mm anti-aircraft gun. This monster shot a shell containing up to fifty pounds of scrap iron. You could tell a 105mm exploding shell from an 88 because its smoke was gray while the 88s were black.

In these last months of the war, flak became the Germans' last powerful defensive weapon. Their fighters were all but gone, their subs all but sunk and their tanks decimated. As a gunner I felt wasted because the skies were virtually empty of the once proud and potent enemy fighter. But the continued concentration of flak guns over our target cities only added to my frustration--we couldn't fight back! We suffered through intimidating flak barrages ranging from a minute to fifteen minutes. Flak reduced our numbers, not fighters.

CHAPTER 5

Brutta Foggia

The other side of flying is supplying. Little glamour and lots of hard work. Bob Duffy, who was a lieutenant in command of the ordnance company serving the 99th Bomb Group from November 1943 to October, 1945, tells his insightful story of how the supply side of a bomb group operated. His people were responsible for loading each aircraft with the required bomb load for every mission. Duffy's is the rarely told story of ground armament people at work behind the scenes. Few medals were bestowed on these devoted and unheralded men who worked diligently under extreme weather conditions to ensure success at the target.

Bob Duffy made a 32-year career out of the Air Force and retired a Brigadier General. He was very active in developing guidance systems for International Ballistic Missiles and later as chief of ABRES (Advanced Ballistics Reentry Systems Development). He was very effective in matching intelligence service information to reentry systems requirements an development. After retirement Duffy was C.E.O. of the Draper Laboratories at MIT. He studied under professor Draper (Mister Gyroscope) while attending MIT.

I received written permission from Duffy on Aug. 2, 1997 to reprint his story as he had written it for our 99th Bomb Group newsletter. With humble appreciation for his efforts, we begin his first person story as it appeared in our newsletter, edited slightly.

Robert A. Duffy's Story

As my memoir of the year September '42 to November '43 with the 92nd Fighter Squadron, this discourse on the period November '43 through October '45, covering my time in the 99th Bombardment Group has been largely based on memory. These events occurred more than fifty years ago and I have no personal record covering the period because we were forbidden to keep diaries. Most of my chronology comes from the notes published by the 99th Bomb Group Historical Society and from a few letters home which were saved by my parents, now deceased.

The reminiscences come from the flyers who had the adventures and suffered the risks, wounds, and great discomforts attendant to the air operations with which we were associated. This history is meant to memorialize the work of keeping the group ready for the combat missions flown. It is also meant to leave my children with a record of that period of my life. Since my memory is imperfect, apologies would be made if this is not as precise as a historian would have it. Also, like most of us, I am apt to remember my own activities in a favorable light and the vertical pronoun "I" may be more pronounced in the telling.

My transition from the fighter world to that of the 99th Bomb Group was filled with dramatic events. The campaign for Sicily had been successfully concluded and the allies had invaded the European mainland. General Bernard Law Montgomery's 8th British (and Allied) Army had filtered across the Strait of Messina onto the toe of the Italian boot after their success in eastern Sicily. The western half of Sicily had been conquered by General George S. Patton's U.S. 7th Army. Six days after Monty's lodgement in Calabria, the U.S. 5th Army, led by General Mark Clark, followed with an assault on the shinbone of Italy at Salerno. Italy surrendered amid all of this, but Benito Mussolini, ejected and imprisoned by the newly formed Italian government, escaped and took the remnants of his Fascist government north to join his German allies. He formed a new administration to continue the war against Allied forces on the Italian mainland in strength from mid-September on.

British paratroops took the port of Tarot and, joined by Monty's rapidly advancing army, quickly took the Adriatic port of Bari. In short order the British captured the important airfield complex surrounding the city of Foggia. North of that area the going got rougher and the 8th Army slowed down. The left flank of the army was mired in the Apennine Mountains of Abbruzzsi where the American 5th Army joined them only to be stymied by a clever and determined German force. Aided by the miserable rugged terrain and the fall of winter rains, the Germans halted the advancing armies. A bitter, drawn-out mountain campaign ensued in vile weather. It was the worst winter in Italy's recent history.

The enormously important major ports: Naples, on the Tyrrhenian Sea, Taranto, on the Gulf of Taranto and Bari, on the Adriatic, were all in Allied hands by October 1, 1943. The airfield complex at Foggia served as the major operating base for the air war against the Axis from the south for the remainder of the war in Europe. Eventually about 2000 aircraft of the U.S. 15th and 12th Air Forces and the RAF's Desert Air Force were flying off these fields. Most of the 12th Air Force moved eventually to operate out of Italy's west coast and Sardinian and Corsican airfields where they supported the 5th Army and its allied ground forces. The RAF operated many of its planes out of Foggia through that winter of '43 an '44 until the 8th Army moved north.

Although this enormous concentration of air power on the Foggia plain was not a new phenomenon, it still was a strange transition. As a major, Fiorello LaGuardia, mayor of New York City, had, in World War I commanded a U.S. Flying Service pilot school here, and of course, the Germans and Italians had operated from the fields prior to their capture by the 8th Army. They had been bombed by our 99th Bomb Group during their tenure and we had taken casualties over the very fields from which our planes now flew.

This plain had been the granary of ancient Rome and Foggia had been a garrison camp during the pre-Christian era. In the perilous years when Hannibal challenged the Roman Empire, a great battle had been fought just south of Foggia (near the present city of Barletta, forty miles or so south) at Canne. It has been estimated that 50,000 men (our total in ten years of Vietnam warfare) were killed there in that battle.

In the Dark Ages, the area became a swamp, but the Fascist government in the 1930s reclaimed the land and established state farms making the former malarial wilderness again a productive agricultural enterprise. Our air operations disturbed, but did not completely disrupt that essential activity. Although we fed ourselves, not too lavishly, with what our strained logistics system supplied, there was a considerable civilian population to be fed. We did have a few lean months ourselves when German bombers sunk an ammunition ship in Bari harbor, damaging port facilities and disrupting the supply system.

The British town major in Foggia did not have an easy job. The Allied Military government, established immediately after the 8th Army moved through, had to police and maintain a cooperative, non hostile local populace or our operations would be threatened. I feel that they did an excellent job; I do not recall any incidents of sabotage on our field although there may have been some elsewhere as the armies moved north. From Foggia we could reach targets from southern France adjacent to the Spanish border to just south of Berlin and southern Poland to the Greek Islands to our east. We had no occasion to move our base north for the duration of the war. Some of our airmen (evadees shot down in the north) were exposed to hostile civilians in northern Italy, southern Germany, Austria and the Balkans. Those of us in Foggia escaped all that. We lacked comforts, and we had occasional air raid alerts, but our bivouac was a reasonably safe and secure home.

The 99th began operating immediately from Foggia No. 2, the Tortorella satellite field which had been used by the Luftwaffe JU-88s before the field was captured by the 8th Army. Our aviation engineers quickly restored runways with their small dozers and by laying down steel pierced planks. The field was ready for operations by early December.

By mid-December C-47s had taken most of the ground echelon to the new base and I, with the heavy equipment, followed in convoy aboard an LST which sailed into a bomb-damaged but useable Naples harbor well before Christmas. We trucked in convoy across the Italian peninsula (and its spine the Apennines represented) in pelting rain and through mud over miserable roads. Our campsite, just north of the airfield, was a hill-side on a farm which included a cup-like depression. This was the site where my company commander, 1st Lt. Ken Weidner, had established our bomb dump (wisely, I might add, since a munitions explosion would vent upward sparing our camp). An Italian family still occupied the farm we were on and there were aircraft not bomb-sheltered on the adjacent air-field. I was to remain there for the duration of the war.

We lived in pyramidal tents and eventually had all wooden flooring to keep us out of the mud. Almost immediately, we began constructing a semi-permanent building. We hired local Italian artisans who cut building blocks out of the live tufa (an adobe-like, dense, wet clay). They built these bricks into walls which we roofed with canvas first, creating a reasonably comfortable shack with two or three rooms. We had portable Briggs and Stratton gasoline driven generators for light. A substantial mess hall was quickly erected in similar fashion. An outdoor shower and open but ade-quate latrine were next. We hauled water in a standard Army tank trailer towed either by a 3/4-ton weapon's carrier or by one of our bomb-lift tow trucks.

Everyone dug a slit trench next to his quarters for air raid protec-tion. It was cold and windy. Aircraft fuel tanks, salvaged from derelicts, were filled with water, roof-mounted and served as solar-heat elements for "in-house" hot water. In time our camp (except for the almost ever-pres-ent mud in winter) became fairly comfortable. The flooring came from the dunnage timbers which braced our munitions during transit. Our chairs and stools were the metal crates which protected the bomb fins. The fuel was pressed paper soaked in used motor oil. This paper came from the rollers which encased each bomb to protect the welded lugs used to hang the bomb in the release shackles that were attached to the bomb racks of our B-17s. The pressed paper rings permitted the bombs to be rolled rather than lifted when moving the munitions.

The bomb we most frequently employed was the 500 pound general purpose munitions which required four strong men with lifting bars to move. With the rollers and the winch, two men could handle these 500 pounders--an important saving. The oil-soaked, pressed paper protective rings created a good hot fire for heating water to clean our mess gear, to warm our mess and sleeping quarters, and in time, our remarkable showers. Perhaps our greatest coup was the acquisition of a steam-driven Italian road roller. I never knew and did not attempt to learn where the roller came from, but its boiler supplied hot water for the camp.

Our bomb lift trucks looked somewhat like a wrecker with a fixed crane and hand-powered winch that lifted bombs to the surface of the low profile bomb trailers. They were hitched nose to tail and towed by the lift truck. Each trailer with bombs fit neatly under the bomb bay of the B-17s. An armorer assigned to that plane and our ordnance crewmen lifted the munitions (using a hand-cranked winch mounted in the aircraft to the bomb bay racks) where the bomb hung until released by the bombardier over the target.

Arming the bombs required insertion of a nose fuse and a tail fuse safetying the fuses with an arming wire that was held, with the bomb, in the aircraft-mounted shackle. If the bomb was dropped live over the enemy the arming wire remained in the bomb's shackle. If jettisoning over friendly territory, the wire, preventing the bomb from arming, was released with the bomb. The arming wire passed through the fuse propeller until the bomb was clear of the bomb bay doors. In free fall, the propeller in the fuse turned through a set number of turns to arm the munition. A safety pin fit over the release mechanism until the aircraft cleared friendly territory. Generally, the bombardier was responsible for removing this pin in flight prior to arrival over the target. At times the pilot, the aircraft commander could and did choose another crew member to do this. *(In the case of the Neely crew, Don Power, the waist gunner did this)* That enabled the bombardier (who had the least restricted view from his perch in the nose) to keep his eyes searching the sky for enemy fighters in front of the aircraft

One of the duties of the ordnance crew was to collect and count the pins after each sortie. *(Don Power kept a pin from each raid as a souvenir)*. Crewmen exposed to the enemy fire and the hazards of combat were not keen on dropping dud munitions and a quick ticket to the "dog house" came as a result of the unfortunate bombardier coming up short, or worse, empty-handed when the safety pins were counted. A friend of mine, now a vice president of the Aerospace Corporation, spent his early teen years in Vienna during our raids. He commented on the large number of dud bombs dropped and wondered why. That was a legitimate question.

Early in the game, the ordnance officer did all the fusing, but it soon became evident that this procedure would not work. A typical load was twelve 500 pound general purpose bombs. Twelve arming wires had to be inserted in twenty-four fuses and twenty-four Fhanstock clips had to be added to the ends of the arming wires to keep them from inadvertently slipping from between the fuse propeller blades. Six to ten aircraft per squadron flew on each mission. "Maximum effort" missions required that every flyable aircraft be launched and in that case, up to fifteen might be flown. Four squadrons had to be armed each night and we did not know until late in the afternoon which aircraft were to fly the next morning, what the munitions load would be (they varied with the target) and what the takeoff time would be. Eventually we worked out a system under which we would begin loading our trailers in the afternoon before we knew the exact load (betting that 500 pound bombs would be called for). If we were wrong, we had half of our trailers empty and could load those with the correct munition, unload the 500 pounders (previously loaded), and reuse the trailers after we had started filling bomb bays.

After discovering that there was not enough time or energy available for every fuse to be installed by the ordnance officer, the sergeant in charge would fuse the munitions and I or one of my colleagues would inspect the job. The whole procedure took most of the night, and if by chance, the target designation was changed for any number of reasons, all hell broke loose. Weather was the most likely reason for change, but the bomb load or fusing differences could also change the program. We had to unload and reload at times, just catching the last aircraft to taxi out of the hardstands where the airplanes parked for servicing. I don't recall one case in which we were unable to accommodate the operations people. It was exhausting duty so we did not see much daylight unless a "stand down" was declared by the 15th Air Force.

The 15th Air Force, the just organized American Strategic Air Force in the Mediterranean Theater, had moved its headquarters, under Jimmy Doolittle, to the city of Bari, south of Foggia on the Adriatic coast last in 1943. The B-17s, four groups at first, eventually were organized in six groups as the 5th Bombardment Wing, all based north of Bari, around Foggia. A B-24 wing was located at Cherignola midway between Foggia and Bari. Other B-24 wings were south of Bari toward the heel and instep of the Italian boot. The B-24s had a range advantage over our B-17s, but frequently they assembled in formation over or near and just east of Foggia particularly when targets were designated in central Europe or northern Italy.

The British Strategic Air contingents flew almost exclusively at night, but their operating airfields were scattered about the plain of Foggia. The RAF's Wellington (Wimpy) was a large, twin-engine, partially fabric covered aircraft and one squadron flew from our airfield. Adding the returning RAF to the mass of 15th Air Force planes, coupled with some 12th Air Force aircraft; and our wing of escort fighter aircraft, put many planes in the air in the early daylight hours. It takes only a minor stretch of the imagination to have the sky totally covered with expensive aluminum encasing many human beings. The din was remarkable! Traffic control must have been a nightmare. Very flares were used for emergency situations--an aircraft returning with wounded crew or a returning battle-damaged aircraft needing priority for our runway would fire a red flare triggering emergency vehicle deployment and causing shifts in the sequence of landing operations.

The aviation ordnance functions in the Mediterranean Theater had been reorganized in October of 1943 just before and during our move. The ordnance platoons of each combat squadron were withdrawn (on paper)

nd reassigned to a service group (the 324th in the case of the 99th Bomb
iroup) as aviation ordnance airdrome companies. Each company was
hen assigned to a combat group for duty. The net effect was that no phys-
cal changes occurred in work situations, but as the units moved to Italy in
ate '43, the four platoons assembled in one camp and operated one muni-
ions supply and service area (termed the "bomb dump" in our case).This
rouped resources much more efficiently (all, for instance, messed togeth-
r) and operated as one military unit. A group ordnance officer was des-
gnated, usually the senior department officer present. In our case, we
arely saw him because the duty station he selected was with group opera-
ions miles away from our camp. Our contact was by field telephone from
is office at group headquarters. Life was markedly different from my cozy
ittle fighter squadron. This was a big business.

The 99th Bomb Group had trained in the northern United States
Geiger Field near Spokane, WA., and Sioux City, IA.) and had been opera-
ional for six months in the Mediterranean Theater when I joined them at
)udna, near Tunis. They had established a strong presence in the 5th
3ombardment Wing, and it, with escorting fighters was absorbed into the
iewly designated 15th Air Force. The group's reputation was greatly
·nhanced by its effort in suppressing enemy opposition to the Allied inva-
ion of Sicily by bombing, in the face of fierce opposition, the airfields and
ransport to be used by German and Italian forces in countering Operation
lusky. A Distinguished Unit Citation (DUC) was awarded the group for
ieutralizing the airdrome complex at Gerbini, Sicily just prior to the allied
andings.

I arrived to assist in breaking camp for the move. On the 3rd of
)ecember most air crews and a few ground crewmen flew out of Oudna in
ainy weather destined for the new operating base. It did not take long to
ierceive the marked difference between the one of the fighter group and
hat of the bomber group. In the 92nd Squadron (a third of the strength of
ur fighter group) all of us knew each other intimately. Despite our loss-
·s, there was a lighthearted air about the unit. The cocky little fighter

pilots lifted everyone's spirits. We all shared the same rough discomfort of tent and dugout in the cold Tunisian winter of '43 and the searing heat of the desert fringe that summer near Orleansville in western Algeria. The highest surface temperature on earth had been registered near Orleansville, and in recent years, the city was leveled by an enormous earthquake. I'm not sure what the temperature reached in the summer of '43, but it was miserably hot.

The fighter squadron was divided into three flights for tactical deployment and the flyers did tend to group themselves informally by flight. The senior lieutenant or captain flight leader assigned his men to dugout or tent quarters, eight men to a tent or dugout for the enlisted men and half that number for officers. The nominal leader of the enlisted men was the master sergeant line chief rather than the first sergeant (one rank below the line chief), who was the administrator and disciplinarian. We few non-flyer technical officers tended to flock together, although this was not a hard and fast rule.

The bomb group was distinctly different since the flyers flew and socialized as crews. The four officer crewmen generally teamed up with another crew of officers to form a sleeping arrangement of eight to one pyramidal tent. The enlisted crew members, all gunners when in action, were bunked with other enlisted men at the direction of the squadron first sergeant and were exempt from most of the menial tasks performed by "rank and file" military men since time immemorial. I won't attempt to depict the hazardous existence these brave fighters experienced in combat aloft. There are, however, wonderful accounts extant written by the men who lived the tale. Our 99th Group Historical Society bulletin carries many of them. One of the very best I've read is Tomlin's Crew written by J. W. Smallwood, a 99th Bomb Group bombardier shot down over Germany in early 1944. The book was published in 1992 by the Sunflower University Press in Manhattan, Kansas.

Two cultures evolved in bomb group life. In one culture, life was tenuous and extremely uncomfortable and hazardous almost daily since we could launch missions at rapid intervals from the Italian airfields. In

he other culture, life was arduous, tedious and uncomfortable but generally safe. We worked every night to ready aircraft for the next day's mission.
The cultures crossed during "stand down" days. These non-operational
days were usually occasioned by bad weather at our primary target or, as
we experienced in '44, the Italian weather itself. March of 1944 was particularly odious. Occasionally the enroute weather was the cause for a
"stand down." We had the Alps between us and central Europe and the
Dalmatian Alps between us and eastern (Greece, the Balkans, etc.) targets.
Clearing the high peaks in these mountains with heavily laden aircraft was
an added hazard much complicated by bad weather.

Sports were the principal means for "cross cultural" contact and
our ordnance team did well in these. Liberty in town was another meeting
ground although "Bruta Foggia," as the locals referred to our nearby town,
lived up to its description. It was an ugly city.

Early on, the hot showers and baths provided through the American
Red Cross were a big drawing card. Their associated canteens gave the
men inexpensive coffee and donuts and the opportunity to see and talk with
the clean and lovely American women who served them. The Red Cross
took a bum rap because it charged for their refreshments while supported
by contributions from the American people. Turns out that Eisenhower did
it! The British Forces ran a canteen service they termed NAFFI that charged
their military a fee. The Brits convinced the Supreme Commander of the
Allied Forces that in fairness, U.S. troops should be similarly taxed.
Eisenhower complied as we thought he always did to his British allies' sug-
gestions. The charges were nominal in any case. The Red Cross operated a
similar service at most American bases. These mobile canteens, "clubmo-
biles", cruised the flight lines and brought hot coffee, donuts and this smiling "Donut Dolly" to the G.I.'s. In our rough and ready fighter existence (in
close support of the ground forces in Africa and Sicily), we never saw this
civilizing presence. Bomber service was distinctly better in this respect.

Despite the crossing of cultures at sports and social events, there
was a difference. It was not elitism on the part of the flyers because it was

they who were exposed; nor was it an inferiority complex on the part of us who were relatively safe. The difference occurred because we worked all night, the flyers all day; they went home (rightly, of course) after a set number of missions. We stayed on. They died, we lived and all of us were exhausted.

A long-standing friend of my wife is an artist whom I met for the first time recently at the Renwick Gallery of the Smithsonian Institution in Washington where his work was on display. At that time I learned that he had flown from Italy with a B-17 group. He had been an enlisted gunner and was now a recently retired professor of Ceramic Art. When I got around to asking him how many missions he had flown, he shyly answered "a half." He had been shot down on his first mission, had spent many months as a POW, had marched with his fellow prisoners west and south to evade "liberation" and perhaps further imprisonment from the advancing Soviet military.

When I first joined the 99th Bomb Group at Oudna, two veteran officers had just organized the 6632 Aviation Ordnance Airdrome Service Company out of the four platoons assigned to the squadrons of the 99th (346, 347, 348 and 416th squadrons). They were good, intelligent and competent soldiers who had worked with the group during its training at various bases, mostly in the northwestern United States. They had landed with the group's ground echelon in the spring of '43 at Arzew near Oran in western Algeria. Both had moved with the group to its early operating base at Navaron, south of Constantine, on the fringe of the Sahara Desert in eastern Algeria. The group's final North African base was at Oudna near Tunis after the Axis troops surrendered in Tunisia. From these African operating sites, the 99th Group had supported the landings in Sicily and the invasion of Italy.

The senior officer, Ken Weidner, became the first company commander. I believe he had been an engineer with Linkbelt, a power transmission company and mechanical manufacturer in the Midwest. Pat Vesey the other veteran officer in the newly established company, was a jovial Irishman having all the charm and chutzpa of the "ward heeling eastern politician, which he may well have been. They were both in their mid to late twenties, five to ten years older than I, and we were all mint-new first lieutenants, Ordnance Department, Army of the United States (AUS). The distinction was important because AUS officers held wartime rank not necessarily carried over to a peacetime military establishment. A more formal company arrangement would have had a captain as commander and lieutenants as leaders of the four platoons. The Army Air Forces at that time had probably 300,000 officers of which about 3,000 were ordnance--not enough to fill all of the needs for complete manning. I would guess further that of that total 300,000, about half were aeronautical rating holders (pilot, navigator, etc.) and all the rest of us were in business to support those flyers. Enlisted men who flew as gunners, flight engineers and communicators probably added another 150,000 fighting men. At peak the Army Air Forces numbered about 2,000,000 in World War II.

The two "old timers" (I had preceded them by six months in the theater by being a 92nd Fighter Squadron member in the invasion of Morocco in November of '42), left me at Tunis to clean up and move the heavy equipment by LST to Italy. I would give both Pat and Ken credit for organizing a solidly run well working company. Pat, very adept at looking out for "number one", arranged a transfer immediately after we got settled in Italy. Ken became the group ordnance officer as soon as that position was authorized and soon they were both captains. I and the successor officers in the company remained lieutenants throughout the war in the company which I now commanded.

An extremely competent and very much admired officer had led the 99th Group through its training and its introduction to combat. Colonel Fay Upthegrove taught our group the vital necessity for air discipline in tight formation flying for precision bombing and the tactics for defeating the interceptors they soon encountered. Shortly after our move to Italy, he was given command of a wing (a number of groups) of B-24s, based near us at Cerignola, a city south of Foggia and nearer to Bari, site of our 15th air force headquarters. Upthegrove was rewarded with the star of a brigadier general. A West Pointer, he served the peacetime Air Force gaining the rank of major general before retirement. He died Jan. 8, 1992 at his home in Bradford, Pennsylvania at the age of 86. It was to Upthegrove's new wing that Pat had himself transferred and I never saw him again. Of course, often saw Weidner, but most of our communication was by field phone when our bomb load was determined for the next day's mission. I became the official company commander on March 13, 1944.

Soon after arriving at our operating base, Foggia No.2, Tortorella, acquired two wonderful officers who did most of the line work of the loading areas at the aircraft hardstands of the flying field. Lt. Mike Vaccariello came first and he served as company executive officer (second in command) for the remainder of the war. Mike was an elegant, soft-spoken Californian--bright and responsive, he served well. Skip Rucinski, a tall and taciturn college basketball player from St. Bonaventure College in Olean, N.Y. (also a first lieutenant) joined us soon. He, too, was very competent, industrious and dedicated. Eventually we were joined by Al Clark, a sharp New Englander from Vermont with a marvelous sense of humor and a crackling Yankee accent. He worked well and fit beautifully into our operational routine as the fourth lieutenant we authorized. We had a harmonious tour of duty together.

When, in time, the bureaucrats gave up on the separate ordnance company idea and we were officially reassigned to operating groups, we all elected to remain together because we were more efficient that way. It was a seamless transfer of authority and no difference was discernible at the 99th Bomb Group headquarters nor at the bomb squadrons of the group. I credit Ken Weidner's acumen for that happy circumstance. He was politically astute and a very smooth operator. At the working level we loved our separate but equal existence in that slightly remote site. We were not ideal neighbors, so we got no complaints because we live with our cache of explosive ordnance instead of bringing our bombs up to the squadron bivouac areas. Incidentally, a terrible explosion at Navarin, in North Africa (in the bomb dump serving the 99th Group) killed 23 men when bomb being rolled off the open tailgate of a delivery vehicle detonated. They should have been individually hoisted out carefully and stacked using the bomb service truck, a system we insisted on during my tenure as boss.

I never saw any of these wonderful officers again after the war with the single exception of Al Clark, who somehow wandered into my den while I was a student at MIT in 1952. It was a brief contact that I lost shortly after leaving that school assignment.

The winter months of '43 and '44 were miserable early on. We did not fly daily in December and January because it rained so much with occasional snow falls. On the other hand, we were fully engaged just getting our quarters set up and learning the ropes of our new existence. Our flyers had to learn the idiosynchracies of the airfield which had an interesting ridge at the end of the single runway where a railroad crossed! We had several air raid alerts per night at first, and to our north and west there was a constant din of artillery fire. I was used to that because of my stint in Tunisia the previous winter, but it was all a bit scary for the uninitiated.

The Germans were certainly within earshot just to our north. Across the Adriatic in the Balkans a very large occupying force was engaged in battle with partisans. Some estimates put the size of the German occupation there at 300,000 to 350,000 troops.

In the previous fall an agreement on strategic priorities had been reached between the senior Allied commanders. It had been decided earlier between governments that the cross-channel invasion of Europe would occur in the spring of '44. The military leadership concluded that Germany's air force had to be target No. 1 if that invasion was to succeed. The decision makers who carried the day felt that the best strategy would be to fight the German air force in the factories before they flew. Their subsequent rationale said that since most Axis aircraft production was concentrated in south central Europe, both the British-based and the Italian-based Allied strategic air offense should aim for those assembly plants first.

The Foggia-based 15th Air Force became a major part of the a offense plan. The RAF would continue their night raids against the san targets. Our location permitted force projection from the south to threa en the highest priority targets, but the Italian campaign on the groun interfered often. Anzio, Cassino and the attacks against the German logi tics system in support of the Axis forces in Italy demanded our commi ment.

The British-based U.S. 8th Air Force had been carrying the brunt the daytime strategic air offensive. Their losses in late 1943 were bruta The RAF operating from Britain at night bombed with less precision an inflicted heavy civilian casualties which brought strong condemnation fc the Bomber Command leader, Air Marshall Arthur Harris, even from som citizens of his own country. Just as it seemed that the Italian-based strat gic air resources could be brought to bear to relieve the 8th and the RA Bomber Command, the two Allied armies in Italy ground to a halt. As consequence we became, for a while, a tactical-support force bombing ra transport and port facilities supplying the German defenders dug in acros the Italian boot. Stymied before Casino, the Allies concocted a surpris landing of a corps behind the German lines at a beach near Anzio. Ou group, the 99th, as a part of a much larger effort, attempted to isolate tha area. We got off quite a few missions despite our muddy field and the poo flying conditions.

In retrospect, I think we must admit that we were less than effec tive. The German commander, again Field Marshall Albert Kesselring, wa successful in transferring a reasonable large group of defenders fror within Italy and the Balkans. The Anzio beachhead was contained. Fou months later, in the middle of May, the VI Corps escaped from the killin ground it had established for itself. During those grim four months c entrapment, German artillery pummeled at will the beached Allied (large ly American) force, extracting a long list of casualties (60,000) as th butcher bill for our audacity. The 99th dropped antipersonnel munition on the besieging Axis troops.

We, the ground support for the 99th, got our workout keepin

aircraft ready for action on short turnaround sorties. Despite these tactical support mission, we did not completely neglect our more global responsibilities. On one mission to Piraeus Harbor in Greece, on the llth of January, the 5th Wing lost eight B-17s. Of that total, as many as six including one from the 99th, may have been lost due to a chain-reaction series of midair collisions in dense cloud cover over the target. In spite of our bad weather that winter, the air crews flew, died painfully, but carried out their missions.

In another effort to break the deadlock at Cassino the 99th and its companion groups found out about total war in a still controversial operation. Enormously expensive in human life, assaults on Monte Cassino by Americans, the French and finally by a New Zealand corps commander, Lt. Gen. Bernard Freyberg, after prodding by a deputy (British Maj. Gen. Francis Tuker, who did not want to attack with his infantry), fell for the argument that the Germans were using the monastery atop Monte Cassino as the observation and control center commanding their defense. General Tuker, commander of the Indian Division, was an intellectual who fancied himself the one truly knowledgeable practitioner in the art of modern warfare, and he demanded that "blockbuster" weapons be employed to obliterate the monastery if he must attack with his troops. Major General Mark Clark, the American commander, demurred and the British and American Air Force chiefs were reluctant. Sir Harold R.L.G. Alexander, the British field marshall in overall command (despite Vatican assurances that the Germans were not occupying the Benedictine abbey), ordered the monastery destroyed and we did.

When our crews returned we ground group support people learned of the destruction of the 1400-year-old shrine and we were troubled. I have read in the notes from our Historical Society about the reaction of the combat crewmen and the intelligence officers. J. W. Smallwood, a bombardier in our 346th squadron, flew that mission. He tells us of the reaction in the briefing room when the mission was described and ordered. I did not attend that briefing, so I have to depend on Smallwood's sobering account in his Tomlin's Crew - *A Bombardier's Story*. I know we all felt we had to do everything we could to help the poor damn infantry. Subsequent reports reveal that the German corps commander on the spot, a Roman Catholic general Frido von Zenger und Etterlin, Rhodes Scholar and lay member of the Order of St. Benedict, had forbidden his troops access to the monastery, and some reports indicate that Kesselring himself barred German troops from the abbey.

After the needless bombing, the ruins were occupied by the Germans (15 February, 1944) and no Allied troops ever won that peak. The Germans withdrew in an orderly fashion three months later when they retreated north of Rome and Polish soldiers of the Free Polish Corps under General Wiadyslaw Anders occupied the site.

I learned something about "heat of the moment" decisions from that experience. I have been reluctant to make quick judgments ever since. In fairness, the people responsible were under heavy pressure from all sides when the decision to bomb was made. Political considerations in the Allied countries, really humane concerns about losses in ground forces, and harsh, frustrated feelings toward the German forces contesting our advances on Rome combined to make the call a really tough one. Two hundred and fifty civilian refugees were killed inside the abbey, women and children included. In a month's time we were back over Cassino with our heavies, this time to level the ancient town of stone buildings itself. Again the 5th Army was further restrained because the defending Germans reoccupied the rubble and would not be dislodged. The 12th Air Force with its medium and fighter bombers inherited the problem. When Kesselring gave the order, the Germans retreated north of Rome, skirting the Allied ground troops at Anzio who were emerging from their confinement. The maneuver was skillfully planned and executed and the enemy escaped to fight another day--actually a year!

The major air offensive against the Luftwaffe finally got underway on the 20th of February, 1944. The Cassino monastery had been pulverized on the 15th and the 8th Air Force had begun five days later on to attack the aircraft production industry in Germany proper. We kicked off our maximum effort beginning on the 22nd, and the "big week" was underway.

The divided attacks from the west by the 8th and from the south by the 15th split the German fighter air defenses. Even so, that week we lost between the U.S. Army Air Forces, over two hundred heavy bombers with the ratio 3:2 for the 8th vs. 15th losses. The Germans lost many fighters and eventually that loss was telling--about 500 in all that week. Many analysts feel the loss of the experienced Luftwaffe pilots assured the subsequent success of the Allied air war. We took heavy losses on one raid, about 20 percent, on the final day of the all-out effort. The target was Regensburg--reachable from Foggia in Italy and from East Anglia in Great Britain--and the attack was coordinated between both forces. This time the Germans elected to concentrate their fighter strength in the south. Our 15th Air Force lost 32 heavy bombers that day. One of the aircraft lost was flown by the euphonious Tomlin's crew.

Ultimately the "Big Week" cost the combined 8th and 15th Air Forces about six percent of the employed bomber forces. The cost to the German arsenal was two month's production--a very significant impact because of its timing. Overall the Luftwaffe lost 800 day fighters in February and March of 1944 in countering the bomber offensive. As spring emerged in Europe after its worst winter in centuries, the U. S. Army Air Forces and their allies clearly dominated the skies. Mustang P-51 fighters could now escort into central Europe, even over Berlin, and the toll these superb fighters extracted made an enormous difference.

The whole coordinated press from that week through the following four months is a blur in my mind until Rome fell and the cross-channel invasion was launched two days later on June 6th. Our guys flew almost daily, and we worked the night through loading all our planes and on rare occasions unloading when last-minute cancellations or target switches necessitated different munitions. Air Forces resources were being augmented to match the pace of the war. Our wing was reinforced with two new B-17 groups of sixty planes each. Problem: no ground crews were available, and prepared airfields were behind schedule! The solution was to put two squadrons each of newcomers at the airfields of the veteran groups.

Now I had six squadrons to load every night instead of four. We would not have lasted if this backbreaking regimen had gone on for long. Eventually, the new groups consolidated on their own airfields and their respective ground complements arrived to handle the extra jobs we had taken on.

We amused ourselves (in our few resting hours) during those arduous days reading Ernie Pyle's stuff when we could get it and laughing at the plight of Bill Mauldin's "Willy and Joe" as he drew them sympathetically in our own newspaper, The Stars and Stripes. We cringed at the "Sad Sack's" predicaments in Yank magazine, A.J. Leibling's writings in the New Yorker, Hal Boyl's columns; when we could find them. They also realistically illuminated for us aspects of the war story we were living but which we could not experience first hand. We flew missions from Italy to support the Normandy landings, and even more surprising to us, we began a campaign to support Russian ground forces in eastern Europe.

By a fluke, the net of all this was blessed relief for us. Unknown to us and obviously to the Germans, a government-to-government agreement between the Soviet Union and the U.S. had established support activity in the Ukraine, manned and equipped by the United States, to permit an operation we called the "Shuttle". Aircraft from both Italy and Great Britain flew to three USSR air bases in the Ukraine, bombing targets jointly selected.

The 99th Bomb Group participated fully. For us ground crewmen, nothing could have been better. The group operated off our designated USSR field near Poltava in the Ukraine for several missions and then flew home to Foggia, again bombing targets of mutual interest to the Soviets and ourselves. The beauty of this for us was that the Ukranian field was manned by an alternate American contingent, not us, the ground element of the 99th. For security reasons we hadn't been informed or involved. In effect, at the peak of the ground war in Europe, we got about a week's vacation. Our air crewmen unfortunately did not. Still the electrifying news of the Normandy invasion and the fall of Rome raised spirits dramatically.

Elated, I gave everyone as much time off as I could and sent the maximum number allowable to rest camps for recuperation. Al Clark and I took a jeep, a knapsack apiece, our steel helmets and side arms and drove to Rome, nonstop. We got into the city after a pause at Cassino (I have a few pictures taken with Al's camera), and immediately became typical tourists.

As a Catholic soldier, I got to be part of an audience with the Pope. Escorted by a military chaplain, I met an American nun from a Polish religious order who's home was within a few miles of my own in the Pennsylvania coal fields. As an English-speaking nun, she was a guide and she sent a note to her parents by me to be posted home since she had been out of touch for three years. I no longer recall her name, but her family (enormously relieved to hear from her), asked if I could get food and clothing to her. I could and eventually did, but I've lost track of them all.

Al and I stayed at an exclusive hotel, the Excelsior, on the Via Venato. The Army had just commandeered it and now ran the hotel, one of Europe's most prestigious. I'm not sure what chicanery two lieutenants pulled to get billeted there. We had a magnificent time and, utterly broke and exhausted, left after three wonderful days. It took us 24 hours to drive back in time to prepare the outfit for the return of our bombers. Al and I had spent one evening with a recovering wounded infantry lieutenant in Rome, and we were deeply affected by the experience. He had been a platoon leader and was a part of the liberating force that entered Rome just the week before we got there.

Frustrated by the humdrum of our nightly "total" involvement, Al and I leaped at an opportunity that had just been announced when we got back "home". Paratroops were to be recruited and trained in the Mediterranean Theater! I still have the record of my physical exam and marvel at the 140 pound, 36-inch chest, 29-inch waist and 5-foot 8-inch height statistics--along with excellent and robust health comments. I am now thankful for the letter rejecting me because all recruiting had ceased after vacancies were rapidly filled by other probably equally frustrated officers in support jobs. I would probably have been killed.

The summer passed hot and dull and I was sent to Capri for a rest. Vesuvius was acting up and at one point one of our airfields in the Naples area was pelted with enough rock and ejecta to seriously damage a large number of airplanes. On the island, looking over the glorious harbor and the peninsula of Sorrento (jutting out of the Gulf of Napoli), one could forget the Foggia plain, but not the war. Everyone else on the island was a refugee in army uniform or a native catering to the soldiery. It was a change of pace and the setting unmatched for spectacular beauty. Hung over but refreshed, I gladly went back to work. Wartime-regimented vacation was not to my liking and I worried about my outfit. The only drink we could buy at our billet was a sickeningly sweet concoction of brandy (local--possibly one month old--and canned condensed milk remotely resembling a brandy Alexander.)

One night during the fall of '44 we either had a cancellation or got our airplanes loaded earlier than usual. Instead of returning to my company bivouac, I drove my jeep up to group headquarters and the officer's club. A crowd of flyers was grouped around a crap table. Occasionally we had beer shipped in those fake brown plastic bottles some bright chemist dreamed up. This happened to be one of the nights beer was available in lieu of vile bathtub gin and watery grape brandy which was shipped over from North Africa. I stayed to have "suds" and watch the action. The flyers gambled on anything and the stakes were usually well beyond my limit. I was standing at the end of the table (fingers stiff from the cold outdoors) and had just taken a beer in hand when the dice landed in front of me and someone said, "roll 'em". I picked them up, threw out a handful of lire (printed without backing as occupation currency grossly overrated at one lire per U.S. cent, when it was probably worth 1/100 that value) and let the pot ride when I made my point. The next roll was quickly covered by the flyers standing around the table. I rolled crap and quietly faded away from the betting. Before I could sneak off to my company several miles away, a big, handsome captain said to me, "You rolled that as badly as you blocked for Pottsville!"

I had been a high school blocking back (right halfback) on a single wing formation football team in Pennsylvania. The rugged captain had been a fullback in the anthracite coal country we both came from and more recently had played for Jim Crowley at Fordham University. Charlie Zalonka was on his second duty tour in B-17s, having flown with the 8th Air Force from England earlier before joining our 99th Bomb Group. Charley, much decorated, became our group lead bombardier and remained in the postwar Air Force, as I did, until he lost his life in the breakup of a B-36 in the fifties. Small world.

One nagging discomfort we all felt was not exactly hunger, but boredom with our food. Our cooks did a good job with what they had, and by spring of '44 we were actually getting fresh meat on occasion. There was a priority list and the combat units had precedence, but even they were sparsely provisioned. One of our guys noted on a local map a legend about a preserve or restricted-access area. The chart was Italian so we were not certain what we were reading, but we noted it was on the mountain just to our north. The spur on the Italian boot juts out into the Adriatic Sea crowned with something termed the Promentario del Gargano. Included was a small town labeled San Giovanni Rotondo, from which a winding road descended to within a very few miles of our camp.

It was autumn and our sharp-eyed informant opined that I was custodian of a small number of riot guns (shot guns loaded with double ought buckshot) which our sentries in the bomb dump carried on guard duty. The informant volunteered to take a friend or two on an armed reconnaissance. I told him to be careful but by all means to go. We had venison for dinner on several occasions after that. Turns out the Royal House of Savoy, the king of Italy, owned the preserve and it was well stocked--possibly because there was no attrition while the royals were away dodging the war.

A side effect of the hunt was a cognizance of the presence in San Giovanni Rotondo, the little mountain town, of a monk purported to carry the stigmata--the signs of the crucifixion on Christ's hands and feet. Padre Pio, the solidly built, brown-robed monk, was venerated locally as a saint. I'm not sure if the Catholic Church ever got around to recognizing or venerating the priest. He certainly was tucked in an out-of-the-way spot and it may be that this fact alone was significant. His hands were bandaged when I was offered one to kiss in the little church of his parish. He was tonsured and simply dressed in a heavy, rough robe held at his waist by a white cord. His only language was Italian and that in a very subdued voice as he was shy. I think I read somewhere that he had been moved from a much larger parish near Naples. He was not making headlines where we were.

The war was grinding us all down. We lost aircraft and crews but exacted a severe cost to our enemy. Late in the spring and just after the invasion the petrol oil and lubricants on which the German (and any other) military machine ran became a target second only to the aircraft production facilities. The Ploesti oil fields and refineries were a prime objective and the enemy defended his oil and lubricant lifeblood fiercely. The fighters would attack the bomber forces from the IP (initial point or setup start of the bomb run) to close the target. When the fighters broke from the attack, the antiaircraft artillery opened up. Between them the defenses took a terrible toll. The Vienna area and the synthetic fuel (coal processed to create liquid hydrocarbons) plants on the Polish/German border around Blechammer and Oswiecium (unknown to all of us but also the site of the infamous Auschwitz concentration camp) became primary objectives.

The major continuous oil attrition attacks did not start until the situation on the ground in Italy and on the continent (Normandy) permitted the release of bomber aircraft from the role the commanders had relegated them to, in support of the invasion and the breakthrough to Rome. March had been a dud because of the Italian weather. Although we regularly loaded most of our aircraft, they flew less than half the days of that month. This was no relief for us because we loaded, then unloaded daily. We got better as the weather improved that summer of '44; after the shuttle missions to Russia, we picked up the pace. Big raids were flown against communication/transportation targets in France in preparation for ANVIL, the invasion of southern France. This past summer my wife and I saw destroyed bridges across the Rhone River in Aries and Avignon, still memorializing after fifty years, the efforts of our group and others of the 12th and 15th Air Forces to isolate the invasion sites along the Cote d'Azure.

Some of our flyers parachuted into Germany and Austria after being shot down. Smallwood of Tomlin's Crew tells that tale excellently. Others were diverted into Switzerland where they were detained for the duration of the war. One of the men who worked in my laboratory at MIT after the war had that experience. The Swiss were strict in their neutrality but kind and understanding while sharing their food and facilitating the efforts of the international Red Cross to ease the plight of internees.

Others bailed out or ditched in the Adriatic, in Yugoslavia or in northern Italy. A number of our guys were recovered after walking down the length of the Italian boot--hard to believe, but they did it. William Orebaugh, who lives here in Naples, Florida, had been interned by the Italians when they occupied Monte Carlo in the beginning of their part of the war (1940). Orebaugh was a U.S. consular official relegated to an arrest status in the area around Perugia (southeast of Florence). Bored with the restrictions placed on his movement and communications, he contacted the local Italian partisans. He eventually ran a band of "paisans" who performed the role of rescuers and helped downed airmen make their way south to allied lines. We recovered some of our lost airmen through his efforts. He also arranged for specific missions to drop arms and ammunition and, most important, communication equipment. Several of our evadees have written accounts of their return to the 99th for our group Historical society newsletter. Through the letter and other sources, Smallwood, for instance, learned that he had been shot down by one of Germany's top aces.

In the fall of 1943, the MIT Radiation Laboratory back in Cambridge built a dozen H2X airborne radars--the pilot lot of their program as a part of the overall "Bombing Through the Overcast" project. the 8th Air Force got those sets to use in the Pathfinder lead aircraft. Philco and the Western Electric Company got drawings and specifications for quantity production of these first bombing radars. In the fall of '44 we got the production equipment for some of our aircraft. These we called "Mickey" ships. They operated as "Lone Wolf" raiders at first, but soon enough were available to equip lead ships for formations.

Now the enemy could expect their visitations around the clock and in any weather. We bomb-loaders and our aircraft ground crewmen could no longer enjoy "off time" due to weather such as those twenty days we could not fly in March of 1944. Bernie Barr, the past president and perennial spark plug for our Historical Society, (then the operations officer for the bombardment group), piloted the first 99th BG Mickey mission flying a 416th squadron airplane against the railroad marshaling yard at Innsbruck, Austria. That yard was used to assemble trains for the run through the Brenner Pass with material for German forces in Italy and the Balkans. It hurt the enemy to experience these raids--now at any time and in any weather.

An ironic side note is the fact that Professor Albert Hill was the head of the airborne components section at the Radiation Laboratory, MIT, during the time our Mickey gear was being developed. Thirty years after these events, Al Hill recruited me to come to MIT when the USAF no longer wanted me on its duty roster. Al still lives in the Boston area where he retired as VP and director of research at MIT, and from the C.S. Draper Laboratory, the place I served as president and director. Al was chairman of the board of that lab.

And so we all soldiered on, now flying missions day, night and even some in foul weather. Flyers rotated home after fifty missions. Some kind soul in the administrative line of our theater command structure felt it might be humane if a few of the ground people could be sent home for a thirty day leave. An elaborate scoring system was established to determine eligibility, but the heavy weighting went to time overseas.

I had been overseas on 7 December 1941, had gone home in May of '42 and had embarked for the invasion of French North Africa in October--I should not have been surprised that I was the first person I know about in our group to be selected for home recuperation leave. I boarded a large former Matson liner in late December. I landed in Boston a day before Christmas, 1944. When we left Naples, Vesuvius was acting sullen, glowering over the bay and fuming with occasional bright flashes of burning gases. It was hot!

Boston, on the other hand, was frigid. We boarded trains in the Boston Army Base and rode to Camp Miles Standish where we were given orders allowing us to go to our homes for thirty days. I did, to the tune of "Don't Fence Me In" which seemed to permeate the environment--on the soot filled trains, in the bars and on the radio at home. I'd never heard that tune or lyrics, but it seemed appropriate at the time. I nearly froze! Much to my surprise, on the old coal-fired train from Philadelphia up into the coal region, I ran into my brother-in-law on his way home--a few days late--on leave for the first time after a two year tour as a Marine corporal in the Pacific.

I spent four cold, snowy weeks at home on leave and saw very few of my old friends because , almost to a man, they were in the Pacific, Africa and the Mediterranean. Many were involved in a growing major battle in Europe. The Battle of the Bulge was underway. When I got back to Camp Patrick Henry, near Norfolk, Virginia I was given orders for two more weeks of leave as there was no transport available to take us back to Italy--everything went towards Brussels, Cherbourg or Liverpool.

At home I had borrowed my sister's car after her husband went back to the Marines at Camp LeJeun. I did get ration stamps for fuel and liquor, using very little of either because there was no one available to share. My sister was pleased when I finally departed and she was left with a full tank of gas and a bottle of Four Roses whiskey for the next time her husband got home. I believe I had another telegraphed extension for a final week making my total time on leave two months.

The raging Battle of the Bulge finally ended and the victorious Allied armies regrouped and entered Germany in pursuit of the beaten but still dangerous Wehrmacht. There was an especial sensitivity, which I felt keenly in Pottsville, because the 28th Division, the Pennsylvania National Guard outfit, had been overrun at the outset in the Hurtgen Forest. Casualty telegrams were arriving daily.

I got out of town feeling very uncomfortable and stopped in New York on my way to Norfolk to cheer up. It was a gay, colorful city, full of uniforms and I did not have to buy many drinks--in fact, I'm not sure I had to buy any. Soon I was on another crowded train sitting in an aisle on my B-4 bag enroute to Camp Patrick Henry. My life changed completely at that time. Our quarters, while we awaited transportation back to Italy were cold, breezy rectangular wooden temporary barracks. The coal heat was inadequate so we gathered nightly at the club because it was warm and lively. A few of my companions were returnees, but most were to be first-timers overseas. Again, I didn't have to buy drinks at the Officer's Club bar because the new guys wanted to know what it was like in Italy. We veterans spun great yarns and drank much of the newcomers' whiskey. The stories got better in the telling which reminds me a lot of our World War II reunions.

On one of those evenings awaiting our port call, I noticed three young women in Red Cross uniforms seated at the bar. All were attractive and several of my fellow officers and I engaged them in conversation.

There is an old vaudeville joke about three communities in southeastern Pennsylvania. Pottsville, Pottstown and Chambersburg were always referred to as the W.C. circuit. One of the girls was from Chambersburg. I came from Pottsville. By the time our ship reached Naples we were in love. We shared forty-five years of life together until a heart attack took her from us all. She died in 1989 while we vacationed in Italy. We were within a few kilometers of her first wartime field assignment with the Red Cross at Pontadera in Tuscany on the Arno.

I got back to the 99th Group and my ordnance company about the end of February. The air war, fought so successfully by the 15th Air Force, was tapering down in the late winter and spring of 1945. The cost was high. By the end of the campaign (8 May 1945), Mediterranean Allied air forces had suffered about 40,000 air casualties. I can't find the casualty count for the 99th Bomb Group, but they flew 395 missions, so a significant part of that casualty list was ours. A very high percentage of that total, some 28,000, will probably always be listed as MIA (missing in action) because of the grim nature of air warfare.

The unit was performing smoothly when I resumed command of our provisional company. I attributed this more to the dedication of the enlisted men, particularly the sergeants, than to anything we officers contributed. John Kavenagh, who acted as our first sergeant, was a superb leader. Tough, fair, taciturn and hardworking, he dominated the day-to-day conduct of our people. I'm not sure where he came from, but he had once been a longshoreman on the Baltimore waterfront. His fists were as big as my head and I don't know that he was ever challenged physically. Sergeants Price, McCabe, Trace and Ed Zawilla were most effective as platoon leaders. They were faithful to our responsibilities and maintained order and morale. We had only one court martial and that was more an illness--alcoholism--than a true dereliction of duty. The occasional "screw-up" perpetrator supplied the labor for latrine digging as "company punishment" but had a clear service record at the time of discharge after the war. I felt proud of them all and discipline was never a problem.

Late in the spring I had driven to the group headquarters on some errand when I noticed that the flag was lowered to half-mast. We had so many casualties that the flag was never lowered (to my knowledge). It was our first indication that President Franklin Roosevelt had died.

The effect of the news on us is hard to describe today after a half a century has passed. We were stunned and a sort of melancholia settled over us. We all went to special church services conducted by the chaplains. I thought deeply about how unfairly life treats us at times. This national leader, who had been so much a part of our young lives since our grade school years, deserved to taste the victory which we all felt was imminent. He led us in combating the grave economic depression which had blighted our youth. His wartime leadership was acclaimed by a great majority of our people and by much of the world's population. Now he was gone.

The "unconditional" surrender he and Churchill and Stalin demanded of Germany and Japan and its alleged prolongation of the war was the only criticism I felt had any validity.

In Italy, shortly after the President's death, German forces under Kesselring surrendered. Our group had an effect. The 15th Air Force laid "carpets" of bombs before Allied ground forces in the Po Valley. The 12th Air Force medium and fighter bombers made individual and precise attacks against the enemy positions. This support proved extremely helpful to the eventually triumphant 5th and 8th Armies. It was all over very quickly but not quite fast enough unfortunately for some of our valiant soldiers in that action. U.S. Senators Bob Dole of Kansas and Daniel Inouye of Hawaii were both severely injured in those battles. The access tunnel to Logan Airport in Boston reminds me of this every time I transit it and read the dedication to Lt. Callahan who served with the 10th Mountain Division and died of wounds in that action just days before the cease-fire.

One wonders today how many casualties were suffered on both sides while the bureaucrats haggled over terms and conditions. Before the end of the war in Italy, and unknown to us, but immediately evident at the end of the Mediterranean campaign, the shift of attention to the Pacific occurred.

Senior leaders were transferred quickly and quietly. Pilots and air crewmen found themselves with orders to transition training in the United States from B-17s to B-29s. We were alive with rumors about the transfer of B-17 groups to the Far East. In retrospect, we could have saved ourselves worry because I don't know where they could have been usefully based. The limited range of the B-17 was an enormous handicap. At any rate, a letdown was inevitable. The 15th Air Force, or perhaps just our group leadership, decided to give us all vacations at resort areas where possible or just time off for sports and recreation. Our group loaded B-17s with those of us who were "ground pounders" and flew us over all the target areas our flyers had attacked. I didn't get to Berlin or the northeastern German-Polish border targets, but I did over fly all the north Italy, southern German, Austrian, Hungarian, Romanian and Balkan target areas. The devastation was terrible.

We began to clear our munitions dump very soon after the armistice. The boxes of varied delay fuses, the stacked olive drab GP (one yellow encircling band), RDX or Composition "B" (two yellow bands) bombs from 100 through 2000 pound sizes in our dump, the clustered antipersonnel bombs--case after case of .50 caliber machine gun ammunition all had to be inventoried and packed for shipment. This was a lot of work, but we took it easy in scheduling the men so they could go to Capri or Naples for a real break.

A "point" system was established to determine priority for rotation home. Wounds, decorations, combat time, battle stars and months overseas were criteria used to accumulate points. Slowly we began to say "good-bye" to the old-timers. I outranked most of the people in the group on overseas time because of my fighter group time, but I had been home on leave so I was deferred for a while. Actually, I was in no hurry because there was that Red Cross girl living in the little town of Cacina next to the night fighter base at Pontedera. VE Day came and went and was no big shakes for us since it followed so closely the cessation of the campaign in Italy and the Balkans.

Our group was given a quota of a very few places in a rest camp at Cannes on the French Riviera. Maybe as a consolation prize, I was detailed to go. Tough duty! Two songs stick in my mind from those days. "Lilli Marlene", of course, but from an enchanting, tiny chanteuse in Cannes, "Symphony" haunts my memory. At any rate, very shortly I was aboard one of our B-17s on my return flight to our group at Foggia, "The Ugly." We were in the skies above northern Italy when the pilot turned to me (kneeling behind him for a better view of the Alps) and said, "The Japs surrendered." He had been listening to the Armed Forces Radio station. Seconds later the radio operator stuck his head and shoulders between us to tell the air crew that VJ Day was being broadcast as we flew!

The aircraft developed an acute illness requiring an immediate landing at the Milan, Italy airport. The pilot, perhaps overly exuberant, overran the short runway and our Flying Fortress became mud bound. A voltage regulator in a box of electronic gear under the pilot's seat was declared the culprit. Three days later we flew home to a mighty suspicious operations officer and returned his airplane.

We had heard the news of an "atomic" weapon being used twice and we attributed the cessation to those two events. Not one word of protest did I hear. My Red Cross lady in Cacina did not raise the roof but did arrive in time for us to go through the regulation process for marriage overseas. The Episcopal chaplain for the group performed the Army-authorized ceremony; but we had to repeat the process in the office of the mayor of the Commune of Foggia on the 19th of August. Satisfying both the law and the U.S. Army regulations and beginning a family of five children and their progeny started in the briefing room of the 99th Bombardment Group (H) with the group commander, Colonel Ray Schwanbeck, U.S. Army, giving away the bride. Ray had flown with the 19th Bombardment Group (H) in the Philippines when the Japanese began the Pacific War. The group executive officer kindly served as best man and made all the arrangements. We couldn't have been more beautifully accommodated. I was given two week's furlough and the use of a jeep. We toured northern Italy "on the economy"--not palatial, but not shabby either.

On our strictly G.I. honeymoon, I was fascinated when we climbed our jeep high above the city of Bolzano, just south of the Brenner Pass. Atop one of the peaks overlooking the southern entrance to the pass was a complete battery of 88 mm German antiaircraft guns. The guns could be depressed to fire down on aircraft flying through the pass.

We came home grateful to be alive. I was offered immediate discharge to civilian life, but elected to remain in the service where I served 32 years.

CHAPTER 6

Augsburg

This was my seventeenth mission. It could never have been told the way I've presented it without the help of two 346th squadron men--men who were shot down that 27th day of February, 1945. I watched as Dwight Reigert, ball turret gunner and the rest of his crew bailed out of his flaming plane only to become prisoners of war. Vic Fabiniak, in the other doomed aircraft, rode his ship down only to be interred by the Swiss for the duration. Not only were the Swiss able to reclaim the B-17G pathfinder, repaint it in full Swiss neutrality markings but it became part of the Swiss Air Force for training and radar trials. They even retained the 99th Bomb Group's Y insignia on the tail and the ship's serial number: 44-8187. And it was Vic, who more than 50 years later helped me in search of my crew and actually found Red Patterson, my tailgunner living in Santa Barbara, California.

There is a couple of things I always thought about prior to any mission. I was a trained aerial gunner fully prepared to protect my ship to the best of my ability and I was the aircraft's flight engineer, responsible for the maintenance of the B-17 in flight under all conditions. This is an awesome responsibility and whether on the flight deck behind the pilots or manning my turret immediately behind and above them, they were jobs not to be taken lightly.

A qualified engineer/gunner had to know his airplane. I worked closely with the pilots checking engine operation, fuel consumption and transfer and the operation of all other equipment on board. In addition,

I worked with John Thomas, the bombardier, who fully apprised me in how to cock, lock and load the bomb racks. A general knowledge of radio equipment was provided by Alex who showed me how to assist in tuning transmitters and receivers. No, Steve Kaptain didn't teach me how to navigate the ship.

I'm confident as we prepare for battle. We're not new to aerial combat any more. We're confident in our assigned roles and work effectively as a team of ten men, each with his job to do.

The klaxon horn sounded over the PA system loudspeaker at 3 a.m. It's H hour, time to rise and shine. You knew you were flying this day because Neely's crew was listed on the squadron bulletin board the night before. The early morning hours are cold, but the sky is clear as you don your long johns and cotton clothing--much easier on the skin than O.D.s. We'll pick up the rest of our gear at the personal equipment shack after breakfast, always mindful of the quantity of fluids I drink for fear of having to urinate in flight, in action, with all our flying equipment on at the most inopportune time. .

Five of us enlisted men are trucked to the line. Alex goes to briefing with the officers. We have yet to learn our target for the day. We draw our gear which includes parachute harness, parachute (chest type), heat suit, oxygen mask, flak suit and helmet, fleece-lined outer wear and pack it all into an A-2 bag.

We've been assigned to ship No. 665. At the hardstand I toss my gear up through the forward escape hatch and flip myself into the opening feet first. I crawl up to the flight deck and begin installing the barrels of my .50 caliber machine guns in their jackets and correctly set them. Once they are in place in the top turret I want to talk to the crew chief before our pilots arrive to preflight the engines. Always nice to know first hand if the airplane is acting up in any way prior to takeoff. I stack my chute on the flight deck along with my G.I. shoes--the two things I want to take with me in case of the necessity to bail out. Hours of flying in frigid 40, 50-degree below zero temperatures turn those shoes I've laid aside into refrigerated footwear which take an inordinate amount of time to thaw out after landing.

AUGSBURG R.R YARDS POUNDED
NINE PLANES LOST
99TH, 97TH GROUPS LOSE 2 EACH
FOUR B-24s, ONE B-25 ALSO DOWN

The Augsburg raid on this Feb. 27th afternoon in the year of 1945 cost the Americans nine aircraft, eight heavy bombers, one medium bomber. In addition to the four B-17s of the 99th and 97th, four B-24 Liberators and a single B-25 also went down, the crews of the last five aircraft being interned in Switzerland. Photos below and on the next pages are same day reconnaissance shots of the target area.

Railroad tracks end suddenly and railroad ties look like picket fences.

MORE AUGSBURG RECON PHOTOS

"Augsburg", sign under eaves, survives the raid. (See at bottom of photo)

Wreckage is everywhere as workers respond.

INTERROGATION FORM

INTERROGATION FORM
Nintey-Ninth Bombardment Group (H) AAF

DATE   27 February 1945   SQUADRON   348th A/C NO.   665   POSITION NO.

P	Neely, R.C. 2nd Lt.	LWG	Power, P.W. Sgt
CP	Wyatt, J.J. 2nd Lt.	RADIO	Leitman, A. Sgt
N	Kaptain, S.P. 2nd Lt.	BT	Limbaugh, D.F. Sgt
B	Gawronski, C.W. Pvt	RWG	Hickox, C.C. Sgt
TT	Somers, W.F. Sgt	TG	Nelson, E.E. Sgt

TIME OFF 08:51 TIME OVER TARGET 13:13 TIME DOWN 16:00

TARGET Augsberg M/Y.   ALTITUDE 22,000 HEADING 258°

TYPE OF BOMBS DROPPED 1000# FUSING ✓   NO. DROPPED 6

NO. JETTISONED ✓   NO. RETURNED ✓

IF MISSION NOT ACCOMPLISHED, REASON: ✓

A/C IN DISTRESS AND OTHER FLASH NEWS:
(Get time, place, heading etc......Was air-sea rescue notified?)

13:13 — 22,000 — B-17 from 346th Sq blew up over tgt - No chutes observed.

RESULTS OF OWN BOMBING M/Y looked to be well hit

RESULTS OF OTHERS BOMBING Same

NO. AND TYPE E/A OBSERVED NONE ENCOUNTERED

WHERE ENCOUNTERED?   WHAT TIME?   ALTITUDE

ENEMY MARKINGS AND TACTICS:

NAME, RANK, HOME AND STREET ADDRESS, GUNNERY POSITION, AND QUOTATIONS FROM MEN CLAIMING E/A DESTROYED:

(OVER)

HEADQUARTERS
SPECIAL NARRATIVE REPORT

HEADQUARTERS
NINETY-NINTH BOMBARDMENT GROUP (H) ARMY AIR FORCES
Office of the Intelligence Officer

SPECIAL NARRATIVE REPORT:
MISSION: 27 February, 1945 - AUGSBURG M/Y, GERMANY

I. ENEMY RESISTANCE

A. Fighters: No enemy aircraft were observed or encountered.

B. Flak: This group encountered intense, accurate, heavy flak over the target. The flak was predominately of the tracking type and was tracking very accurately. The flak started over the target and followed the formation off the target and during the rally. The flak was encountered for six to eight minutes.

The flak positions were located west of Augsburg and the flak followed ourrformation from the target to the rally. There was intense flak from the rally point at 48/27N, 10/34E. Eight (8) of our aircraft sustained major flak damage and seven (7) sustained minor flak damage.

II. SIGNIFICANT OBSERVATIONS

A. Flak Positions: Flak from 48/27N, 10/34E.

B. Land: 1415 - 20,000', L/S, 46/04N, 12/38E, 8 s/e E/A.
1144 - 18,600',A/D, 46/08N, 13/12E, 20 s/e E/A.
1320 - 24,000', A/D, 48/01N, 10/40E, 60 t/e and J/P E/A.
1409 - 22,000', 4 L/S at 46/05N, 12/40E, 3 t/e and 5 s/e E/A on field and 13 s/e E/A in revetments.

C. Air: 1319 - 22,000', 48/23N, 10/30E, A/C #698 hit in right wing, explode 6 chutes, 5 burning.
1340 - A/C #187 - 14,000', 47/30N, 11/20E, course 260 degrees, 2 engines feathered.

' D. Smoke Screen: 1318 - 23,400', Numerous smoke pots starting, attempting to cover large factory area at 48/27N, 10/34E.

III. CONCLUSION

A. Total Losses: From Flak: 2

B. Damage: From Flak: 15 (8 major - 7 minor)

C. Victories: None.

D. Corrections on Telephone Mission Report: None.

PHILIP M. PHILIPS,
Major, Air Corps,
S-2, 99th Bomb Gp (H).

ATTACK SHEET

ATTACK SHEET

(Complete this form in accordance with actual course of mission)

WING ___5th___   Date of Operation __27 Feb 45__

GROUP ___99th___

    1. Target Bombed __AUGSBURG M/Y__ . Was it the (underline one) primary, secondary or alternate?

    2. Method of bombing for each attack unit:
( ) visual, ( ) offset, (1,2,3) synchronous. (In the bracket, ( ), place the number of the attack unit which attacked by each method.

    3. Intervalometer setting (feet) ___150___ .

    4. Initial point (coordinates) __4845/1115__ .

    5. Auto-pilot or PDI run for each attack unit. (In the bracket, ( ) place the number of the attack unit led by each method.
        (1,2) auto-pilot, (3) PDI.

    6. Bombing Altitude (group lead box) __24,000__ .

    7. Bombing Airspeed (for each attack unit) 1st __215 TAS__ , 2nd __198 TAS__, 3rd __218 TAS__, 4th __MIA__ .

    8. How many range sightings took place in each attack unit?
1st ___1___ , 2nd ___1___ , 3rd ___1___ , 4th ___-___ .

    9. Was data pre-set in bombsight? (check one) (yes) no

    10. Was target material adequate? (check one) (yes) no

    11. Length of bomb run (seconds) ___280___ .

    12. Number of bombs salvoed on target __None__ .

    13. Was bomb run interfered with by other formations? (check one for each attack unit) 1st yes (no) 2nd yes (no) 3rd yes (no) 4th yes no.

    14. Was each attack unit flying tight, fair, or loose?
1st __Tight__ , 2nd __Tight__ , 3rd __Fair__ , 4th _____ .

    15. Dropping angle for each leader sighting:
a __.63__ , b __.58__ , c __.52__ , d _____ , e _____ , f _____ .

-1-

FIFTEENTH AIR FORCE LETTER TO MISS FABINIAK

FIFTEENTH AIR FORCE
Office of the Commanding General
A. P. O. 520

20 March 1945

Miss Blanch C. Fabinak
308 Merriman Place, SE
Canton, Ohio

Dear Miss Fabinak:

The War Department has notified you that since February 27, 1945, your brother, Staff Sergeant Victor A. Fabinak, 35233023, has been missing in action. Undoubtedly, your concern for his safety is very great. As I am unable to give you any assurance as to his fate, perhaps the few facts we have relative to his recent mission will be of interest to you.

Flying Fortresses of this command attacked important railroad yards in Augsburg, Germany, on the above date. Vic served as tail gunner aboard a bomber which was disabled when it was hit by flak over the target. Although two engines were seriously damaged, the plane was kept under control and it seemed to be maintaining altitude. The ship was last seen over Austria, as it left the formation and flew toward Switzerland.

Your brother's personal effects have been assembled and will be sent to the Effects Quartermaster, Army Effects Bureau, Kansas City, Missouri, from which point they will be forwarded to the designated beneficiary.

I share your pride in Vic's many accomplishments. He has been awarded the Air Medal with one Oak Leaf Cluster for meritorious service. Please rest assured that the War Department will notify you immediately should there be any change in your brother's status.

Very sincerely yours,

N. F. TWINING
Major General, USA
Commanding

HEADQUARTERS LETTER
TO MR. REIGERT

ADDRESS REPLY TO
COMMANDING GENERAL, ARMY AIR FORCES
WASHINGTON 25, D. C.

ATTENTION: **AFPPA-8**

HEADQUARTERS, ARMY AIR FORCES
WASHINGTON

FOR VICTORY
BUY
UNITED STATES
WAR
BONDS
AND
STAMPS

AAF-201 (12512) Reigert, Dwight G.
17198780

14 April 1945

Mr. John J. Reigert
1901 West 3rd Street
Sioux City, Iowa

Dear Mr. Reigert:

I am writing you with reference to your son, Staff Sergeant Dwight G.
Reigert, who was reported by The Adjutant General as missing in action
over Germany since 27 February 1945.

Additional information has been received indicating that Sergeant
Reigert was a radio operator on a B-17 (Flying Fortress) bomber which
departed from Italy on a bombardment mission to Augsburg, Germany, on
27 February 1945. The report reveals that during this mission about
1:20 p.m., your son's craft sustained damage from enemy antiaircraft
fire while over the target. The disabled bomber dropped out of formation,
and six parachutes were seen to emerge before it fell to the earth. It is
regretted that there is no other information available in this headquarters
relative to the whereabouts of Sergeant Reigert.

Believing you may wish to communicate with the families of the others
who were in the plane with your son, I am inclosing a list of these men
and the names and addresses of their next of kin.

Please be assured that a continuing search by land, sea, and air is
being made to discover the whereabouts of our missing personnel. As our
armies advance over enemy occupied territory, specail troops are assigned
to this task, and agencies of our government and allies frequently send in
details which aid us in bringing additonal information to you.

Very sincerely,

N. W. REED
Major, Air Corps
Acting Chief, Notification Branch
Personal Affairs Division
Assistant Chief of Air Staff, Personnel

1 Incl

Silk slippers plugged in to my heat suit adorn my sock protected feet and they in turn fill sheepskin-lined boots I'll wear throughout the mission. We've been warned about the very good possibility of losing these boots at the pop of an opening parachute and told to tie our shoes to our harness immediately prior to bailing out.

The officers and Alex arrive. Bob informs us our target will be the marshaling yards at Augsburg, Germany. No. 665 passes preflight admirably so I trade quips and some honest Injun concern as we move into line for takeoff. The early morning sun lends a sparkling brilliance to the ocean of pyramidal tents abounding in the squadron areas. I'm never ready for takeoff on those resilient steel matted runways, but it becomes a fact of life--if you're going to bomb a target, you have to, like it or not, take-off to do it. We're carrying six 1,000 pound bombs on this mission--an unusual bomb load when most raids they load us with 500 pounders.

We're in takeoff position. Jim locks the tail wheel and Bob sets the directional gyro. Brakes are released and we begin our ponderous pace down the runway. At least we've got fair weather to fly in. Way ahead at the end of the runway I see a B-17 lift off.

I'm standing between Neely and Wyatt and very soon my loud airspeed count dictated by the tachometer fills Bob's ear. I'm calling out 85, 90, 95, 100 mph--we need another 10 to lift off and the frightening specter of the end of the runway looms ahead. We need that 10 mph and we get it to ensure a safe departure from ground zero. We're also now at full power pulling 2550 rpm and 47 inches of manifold pressure on each engine. Bob eases the tail up slightly and it's lift off. Gear comes up and our airspeed increases dramatically before engine power is reduced by Wyatt. Our 28 planes should be in group rendezvous in the next 15 to 17 minutes and wing rendezvous shortly after that. Just before we go under oxygen Don in the waist pulls the pins and arms the bombs.

Flying group lead on this mission was Captain John Plummer of the 347th squadron. He was checked out by Col. Al Schroeder in January.

In all, he led the 99th in six missions of this, his second tour of duty. He explains the loss of two 346 squadron B-17s by speculating the Germans had one of their own aircraft or maybe even a captured B-17 at his altitude and radioed that altitude to flak batteries below.

"This loss has weighed on my spirit for the last forty nine years. Casualties are part of combat but if I had the group a couple of hundred feet higher or a degree or so to the right or left, there may not have been any casualties at all or there could have been many more. Such are the chances of war and its pressure of combat leadership," Plummer wrote 49 years later in his manuscript entitled *Hitting The Hun* .

Our target would be a little northeast of Munich and a bit south of the Danube River. It would take us, round trip, seven hours and 15 minutes of flying time. The city of Augsburg is the main East-West line from Vienna via Munich to the Rhine Valley and is joined by the main Berlin-Munich line which runs through Nuremberg. The railroad yards have a through capacity of 2000 box cars in a normal 24 hour period. Recent photo coverage of the target area showed 920 units in the marshaling yards.

The target is shaped like an inverted "Y" and is 3000 yards long and 600 yards across at its widest point. It's located on the southwest outskirts of the city. Outstanding natural features are the Lech and Wertach rivers which flow north on the eastern and western sides of the town, meeting at a point three miles north of the target. The yards are surrounded on all sides by closely built up areas.

Morning briefing indicates there is a possibility of harassing attacks by 15 to 20 enemy fighters and/or a few ME-262's from the Munich area. It is conceivable the enemy could move in effective fighters for the defense of this target should he so elect. Any of our stragglers are warned to be on constant alert for North Italian based fighters. The worst possible scenario is 65 to 70 enemy fighters.

Enemy ground defenses at the target is 88 heavy guns. Since our route back goes within 60 miles of the Swiss border, we are expected to honor Swiss neutrality. Therefore planes still with bombs on the return are ordered not to jettison them in Swiss territory but to return them to base.

The official intelligence report issued by Group after the mission described it in this fashion: The 99th encountered intense, accurate, heavy flak over the target. The flak was predominately of the tracking type and was tracking very accurately. The flak started over the target and followed the formation off the target and during the rally. The flak was encountered for six to eight minutes.

The report continued: flak positions were located west of Augsburg and the flak followed our formation from the target to the rallying point. There was intense flak at the rally. Eight of our aircraft sustained major flak damage and seven sustained minor damage. In all, we lost two planes to flak. Fifteen were damaged. Twenty men are missing.

I saw the two planes go down while we were under extremely heavy flak concentrations. However, I do believe we lost three planes that day. The third plane had to be that of Victor Fabiniak, a tailgunner from the 346th squadron who told me about the incident at a reunion of our group many years later. I never saw his plane leave the formation, but it did, accounting for the third downed aircraft. (This proved to be a false assumption on my part as I was to learn later.)

This is what the War Department wrote to Vic's sister as next of kin in announcing his MIA status: "Vic served as a tailgunner aboard a bomber which was disabled when it was hit by flak over the target. Although two engines were seriously damaged, the plane kept under control and it seemed to be maintaining altitude. The ship was last seen over Austria as it left the formation and flew toward Switzerland. Your brother's personal effects have been assembled and will be sent to... the designated beneficiary." Vic told me they lost a third engine on the way down and before they landed and were interred in Switzerland.

I watched as a second B-17 went down. It took a direct hit in its right wing between No. 3 and No. 4 engines. That ship caught fire and veered off and went down in flames. We saw six chutes, but some were already on fire. Our group bombed in trail formation with my friends who survived in the tail end Charlie squadron. Our bombing altitude over the target was 23,500 feet. We made a visual run over Augsburg.

Dwight Reigert was flying in the bomber that held formation for a while before it veered off and went down in flames. Watching them bail out reduced me to an astonishing realization that they could have been us. I met Dwight at the 99th's Rapid City reunion in 1992--the same time I met Vic. This is what the War Department wrote to Dwight's father when he was listed MIA:

"I am writing you with reference to your son, S/Sgt. Dwight G. Reigert, who was reported missing in action over Germany since 27 February 1945. Additional information has been received indicating that Sgt. Reigert was a radio operator on a B-17 bomber which departed from Italy on a bombardment mission to Augsburg, Germany on 27 February 1945. The report reveals that during this mission about 1:20 p.m. your son's craft sustained damage from enemy antiaircraft fire while over the target. The disabled bomber dropped out of formation and six parachutes were seen to emerge before it fell to earth. It is regretted that there is no other information available in this headquarters relative to the where-abouts of S/Sgt. Reigert."

I witnessed this incident from my top turret. The guys on our ship, including me, also counted six chutes plunging out of the burning plane. And too, I could have sworn some of them were on fire. But Dwight assured me all but the pilot got out safely from his stricken plane.

Meanwhile on our ship No. 2 supercharger began acting up but it corrected itself just before the bomb run. Flak was heavy for us too but concentrated just to the right of our flight path. Dwight told me he was taken to a bombed out police station in Augsburg after his capture. Both he and Vic provided me with photo copies of what the target looked like after our attack. They were P-38 reconnaissance photos taken soon after our visit. In all, our mission to Augsburg was a costly one for the 15th Air Force. Nine aircraft were shot down including the four B-17s from the 97th and 99th. Four B-24 Liberators also were lost, albeit their crews were interred in Switzerland. Finally, a medium bomber, a B-25, was shot down and its crew also interred. It's interesting to note that the Swiss had to shoot down a B-17 from the 97th that day after it was hit over the target and its crew bailed out to be taken prisoner by the Germans.

An interesting post script to this day's events. That B-17 shot down by the Swiss was flying Group Lead in the 97th. Ten minutes after it was hit the crew bailed out and the doomed craft was left on automatic pilot by its aircraft commander to fly its plotted course. It entered Swiss air space about an hour later and was intercepted by Swiss fighters and shot down when it didn't acknowledge Swiss signals.

The skies over Augsburg were indeed dark on my seventeenth mission. Our 99th Bomb Group by this time and on this date would record the loss of its seventy-first and its seventy-second B-17 since its first mission was flown back on March 31, 1943 out of Navarin Field, Algeria, North Africa.

CHAPTER 7

Last Mile From Hell

AMERICAN AND BRITISH POWs are greeted by their liberators, 104th Infantry Division troops, at the end of their 600 mile death march. Del Laudner, 348th squadron, can be seen in middle row of proud, happy but terribly exhausted and wasted airmen. For many POWs, the march did last 86 days. For Laudner it ended April 26, 1945, 78 days after evacuating Stalag Luft IV.

Even to this day the story of that brutal 86 day forced march of 6,000 enlisted British and American airmen guarded by German Volkstrum, including Del Laudner, a tailgunner of my very own 348th squadron, is little known. In the Bataan Death March, 26 percent of Americans perished in the Philippines early in the war at the hands of brutal Japanese captors. So insidious, so infamous was the Japanese treatment of American and Philippine soldiers that their fate has been

This photo is a blow-up of the picture on the previous page.

All photos in this sequence are courtesy of Del Laudner.

Behind and to the right of the smiling face in front of him is Del Laudner, 348th Squadron. (Photo is an enlargement of original above.)

told and retold to the American public to ensure its unhappy legacy in our history books.

The Japs planned on taking 25,000 prisoners with the fall of Bataan and were surprised they had captured 76,000 Americans and Filipinos. There were some on the Japanese general staff who considered they were in a racial war and the prisoners should be executed. Cooler and stubborn heads prevailed and at least this option for dealing with their prisoners was resolved. The numbers overwhelmed the Japanese in the first few days following the Americans' surrender. Their march to prison camps in suffocating and blistering heat saw American generals, unprecedented, forced to participate. Their rank earned them no favors. Our Gen. Jones compared their conditions to the infamous Confederate prison Andersonville during the Civil War. At one point in the march men were herded into boxcars similar to the 40 & 8's of World War I. As many as sixty five men were jammed into each car.

In the Death March endured by our airmen in the miserable winter of 1945, 23 percent of our men or approximately 1300 were lost. The incredible aspect of this terrible march is its secrecy or at least its relative absence of recognition--even at this late date--over fifty years after the fact. The P.R., the hype just never evolved. It's sad story has been buried in neglect. What these men were subject to easily equaled the unfortunate Bataan death march.

I'm indebted to men like Laudner and George W. Guderley and Joseph P. O'Donnell for their contributions to this piece. Without their reflections, printed and otherwise disseminated, the story of Del Laudner would be quite lacking in substance. Guderley, a retired U. S. Air Force major and former inmate of Stalag Luft IV and Death March participant, represented former inmates and the Air Force on September 4, 1992 when he spoke at the dedication of a memorial at the former site of the POW camp in northern Poland.

In a letter to me Guderley assured me the German treatment of POWs in accordance with the Geneva Convention was for the most part fiction. He said this was particularly true of Air Force POWs. They were

End of The Line

24th Infantry soldiers await the crossing of the Mulder River by Del Laudner and 250 other survivors of 78 days of death march hell.

Mulder River crossing to the American side provided by British engineers who built this makeshift bridge the last obstacle to POW freedom.

considered terrorists and labeled "Terror Fliegers" or "Luft Gangsters." Guderley, a 15th Air Force gunner shot down September 12, 1944, distinguished himself while a POW. He both evaded capture and escaped, but the Germans finally caught him on the Austrian-Swiss border after he had traveled 120 miles.

And again, he led the escape of 20 POWs from Stalag XIB, Fallingbostel, Germany. It was an extermination camp run by the SS. An estimated 35,000 to 40,000 Russian prisoners perished there and are buried in mass graves. A Canadian Combat Engineer Battalion and an armored spearhead of the British 2nd Army on April 18th liberated Guderley who had hidden out until their liberation. They were the first group of Allied fliers freed and were flown in RAF Dakotas (C-47s) to Brussels. The remaining portion of the prisoners continued "hiking" in a northeasterly direction until they were liberated by a British spearhead and a Russian force on or about May 3rd.

The American committee at the memorial dedication in Poland was headed by O'Donnell, another survivor of the atrocious 600 mile march and the author of "The Shoe Leather Express" a five volume account of the infamous march. O"Donnell was shot down in May of 1944 over Wiener Neustadt, Austria and landed in the Carpathian Mountains between Austria and Hungary. He was a ball turret gunner on the crew of "Patches". He roamed about the mountains for 24 hours before being captured by several German soldiers who spotted him through field glasses. On May 2, 1945 he was liberated by the Royal Dragoons of the British 8th Army. At that time he witnessed "thousands of POWs along the road on bicycles, carts and automobiles." One of those POWs could easily have included Del Laudner.

Laudner was shot down July 2, 1944 over Budapest on his 36th mission. He was captured by the Nazis and spent the next ten months as a POW, including being subjected to the Death March which ended for him on April 26, 1945. Del says he guessed he weighed 150 pounds before the march and experienced a weight drop to less than 100 pounds. German guards and their prisoners in the last days of the march fragmented into separate groups. Some held out the entire 86 days but others, like Del, were liberated a few days earlier.

Del was a replacement gunner on pilot Lt. Harry Reuse's crew. At the time of this ill-fated mission, Laudner speculated they had flown maybe thirteen missions. Del says his plane experienced engine trouble on their first run over the target. It was clouded over so they made a second run and still couldn't see the target. The group sought out its secondary target. Enroute Del's plane had to feather one engine which forced them out of the formation to become a sitting duck for enemy fighters.

Two ME-109s jumped them and shot out two more engines. They were subject to three passes by enemy fighters until their own escort came to their rescue. It was a little too late. Their plane was on fire and they had been given the order to jump. But for a few scratches, they all got out safely. They were captured by the Hungarian Home Guard in about an hour in a farming area with only a town hall nearby.

The officers were taken away in what Del figures was a 1936 Ford and he never saw them again. They were delivered to Stalag Luft III. The enlisted men were put in a horse drawn wagon and taken to a railroad station and put on a train for an all night trip to an army camp at Pecs, Hungary where they spent sixteen days. From there they were taken to a prison in Budapest and Del believes he was imprisoned there for maybe twenty days. It was Laudner's first meeting with a German soldier who just happened to be from New Jersey. He knew more about the 99th Bomb Group--even his 348th squadron--than Del, himself, did.

From the Budapest prison, Laudner was shipped by train to Stalag Luft IV along with twenty-four other prisoners and five guards. He recalls the numerous stops his train made to allow trains with more demanding priorities pass them by.

Doye O'Keefe was the radio operator on a B-24 in the 8th Air Force. He was shot down Sept. 27, 1944 by FW 190s. Three of his crew were killed, one wounded. He arrived at Stalag Luft IV in November. It's very possible Laudner and O'Keefe were together when their stalag was

German Captors became prisoners of American infantry rather than surrender to the Russians and the likelihood of being shot.

evacuated February 7, 1945 within view of bursting shells of advancing Russian troops. One thing for sure, they were liberated the same day on April 26th, 78 days from Day 1 of the march.

One must remember these POWs were airmen, not infantrymen. Hikes and marches were not part of their regular training. And certainly not in combat. They flew while the ground pounders walked, and walked and walked. Airmen not only were not physically up to a long march, their collective feet were sadly lacking in proper fitting footwear. Is there any wonder O'Keefe started getting blisters after three days into the march--a march that was supposed to have lasted only three days. Blistered feet got so bad for him that he could hardly walk Then, by accident, he met a soldier with shoes too big. Since O''Keefe's shoes were too small they made an instant trade and their mutual hurt was resolved for the better.

Death March stragglers at first consisted primarily of men with blisters, aching feet and tired muscles. These men suffered but they were expected to toughen up. The medics' slogan: Keep on marching and your blisters will turn into calluses and your aches into hard muscles. Sooner than later, however, straggling became more serious because the blisters became infected. The many abscesses that developed had to be opened. Mud and cold brought frostbite. Men collapsed from hunger, weakness, fear or pain.

It's quite probable that Laudner crossed the Oder River at the outset of the march. And during the entire march this group of men crossed and recrossed the Elbe River seven times to evade somebody's army--the English, the Russians or the Americans. It was past Swinemunde that they headed south to a large fenced in area with a large canvas tent near Magdeburg. They were strafed at other places by American planes in days that followed.

Two days before Laudner was liberated the POWs met with German officers and offered them a choice. There was no place for them to go. Get captured by the Russians and they would be shot, but if they surrendered to the Americans they would be treated as prisoners of war.

The next morning, April 26th, hours before their liberation, the entire German unit came out and turned over their weapons. Del's recollection was the Germans, scared to death of being captured by the Russians who were right behind them, surrendered their weapons to them the day he was liberated.

In this group there were 250 American POWs and after 78 days of hell, they were again on the march only this time the Yanks carried the weapons. They headed north to Highway 100 and then headed west, crossed the Elbe River and met up with a jeep with two Americans on patrol. Subsequently a rifle squad appeared and the German prisoners were released to them. The POWs were now free to walk the short distance to Bitterfeld, Germany and see liberation at last at the hands of the 104th Infantry. Six hundred miles of terror for the POWs would end in the small town of Bad Duben when they were greeted by the liberating infantrymen.

On that last day and as Laudner and his bedraggled survivors crossed the Mulde River to the American side, he said all hell broke loose. British engineers built a makeshift bridge to permit the Americans to cross. In their comparatively small group were some British airmen."Guys were all over the place," he said. "Two other guys and myself requisitioned some 10-in-1 rations, retired to a Hitler school, built a fire on the floor and ate all night."

Laudner joined the 99th Bomb Group in September, 1943 in North Africa as an extra gunner. He was one of 120 gunners sent overseas straight from gunnery school. He flew with several different crews before being shot down. One of those crews had Richard Hyle as its engineer gunner. Laudner says he flew quite a few missions with Hyle who was to receive the DFC for an extraordinary achievement. A veteran of 50 missions in which he shot down three German fighter planes, Hyle was cited for his action. He stuck with his ship after it was struck from above accidentally by eighteen frag bombs from another ship. Some of those bombs lodged in the wing and could have exploded, but he helped the pilot and copilot land their plane at a friendly field after other crew members had parachuted to safety. Hyle was decorated by Wing Commander Col. Charles W. Lawrence.

As a replacement gunner Laudner joined Hyle's crew when their tailgunner broke his back on that heroic mission. Del flew in that position with Hyle as engineer and top turret gunner until they completed their tour of duty and went home. Today Del lives in El Cajon, California.

Delbert Laudner's home town paper in Rockford, Iowa at the time ran a story entitled "Lest We Forget" and authored by John L. Frisbee, Col. USAF, retired, and assisted by George Guderley. It was the story of meandering columns of marchers who had exited Stalag Luft IV as the camp suddenly came within earshot of Russian artillery. It emptied in a hurry as guards moved the prisoners out from the exposed prison camp in northern Poland and ushered the men to various destinations in western Germany in one of the most intensely cold and disruptive winters experienced in central Europe in the 20th century.

Laudner was not immune to lice. The vermin affected all participants. The "body lice bastards", an appropriate term, were known to be the dreaded carrier of typhus fever. The men were perfectly aware of this potential health threat and that's why periodically they'd attempt to thwart infestation. Of course, the real motivation to rid themselves of the insidious pests was the incessant and constant annoyance they posed.

O'Donnell, in the first volume of his *"Shoe Leather Express"* had this to say about lice. "We as prisoners of war, were selected by the lice as warm blooded animals, since we bedded down either with the farm animals or bedded down in close proximity to the recently departed horse or cow resident. It was not uncommon for the farmer to protest the evacuation of his stock in order to make available accommodations for a lousy bunch of dirty POWs."

Further insight into the pesky mites is voiced by O'Donnell. "There were some sunny days, so we would gather to the leeward side of the barn and strip down to our waist for a lice removal detail. Our main concern was to remove the eggs. The eggs, about 1\64th" long, were usually found in the seams of our shirts or underwear and were neatly laid in a straight row of ten to fifteen in a cluster."

"There were two effective methods of removal," O'Donnell continued. "One was to pick the eggs out and crush them between the fingernails or to burn them out with a match. The latter usually resulted in burning the seams and the stitching of our shirts, and pants," he concluded.

*   *   *

"Lest We Forget" has been reprinted not only in the Air Force magazine, but the VFW magazine an the 99th newsletter. Guderley said the story has also appeared in the Congressional Record. The story below, reprinted from the 99th Bomb Group newsletter, has been edited slightly.

"Lest We Forget"
The American POW Death March From Stalag Luft IV
by Col. John L. Frisbe, (Ret.) and assisted by George W. Guderley

A prelude to the Death March unfortunately occurred in July of 1944 and set the tone for what was to follow. The ranks of prisoners already in Luft IV were swelled by 2500 POWs being transferred in mid-July 1944 from a camp near Memel, Lithuania. They were jammed into holds of two dilapidated coastal coal tramp steamers and spent five days en route to the German port of Swinemunde, thence by cattle car to a rail station near Stalag Luft IV.

The POWs shoes were taken from them. They were chained in pairs--many of them ill or wounded--then double timed three kilometers through a cordon of guards who used bayonets, rifle butts and dogs to keep them moving. Prisoners neither had food or water for five days. The next day they were given water and driven through a gauntlet of armed guards and guard dogs, then strip searched and had most of their clothing and possessions taken from them.

Early in 1945 the Soviet forces continued to advance. After the Reds' breakout at Leningrad, the Germans decided to evacuate Stalag Luft

IV. Some 3,000 of the POWs who were not physically able to walk were sent by train to Stalag Luft I, a camp further west. On February 6th with little notice, more than 6,000 U.S. and British airmen began a forced march west in subzero weather for which they were not adequately clothed or shod. Conditions on the march were shocking. There was a total lack of sanitary facilities. Coupled with that was a completely inadequate diet of about 700 calories per day contrasted to the 3,500 calories provided by the U. S. military services.

Red Cross food parcels added additional calories when and if the Germans decided to distribute them. As a result of the unsanitary conditions and near starvation diet, disease became rampant--typhus fever spread by body lice, dysentery that was suffered in some degree by everyone, pneumonia, diphtheria, pellagra and other diseases. A major problem was frostbite that in many cases resulted in the amputation of extremities. At night the men slept on frozen ground or, where available, in barns or any other shelter that could be found.

The five Allied doctors on the march were provided almost no medicines or help by the Germans. Those doctors and a British chaplain stood high in the ranks of the many heroes of the march. After walking all day with frequent pauses to care for stragglers, they spent the night caring for the ill, then marched again the next day. When no medication was available, their encouragement and good humor helped many a man who was on the verge of giving up.

Acts of heroism were virtually universal. The stronger helped the weaker. Those fortunate enough to have a coat shared it with others. Sometimes the Germans provided farm wagons for those unable to walk. There seldom were horses, so teams of POWs pulled the wagons through the snow. Captain (Dr.) Caplan, in his testimony to the War Crimes Commission, described it as "a domain of heroes."

The range of talents and experience among the men was almost unlimited. Those with medical experience helped the doctors. Others proved to be talented traders, swapping the contents of Red Cross parcels with local civilians for eggs and other food. The price for being caught at this was instant death on both sides of the deal. A few less Nazified guards could be bribed with cigarettes to round up small amounts of local food.

In a few instances, when Allied air attacks killed a cow or horse in the fields, the animal was butchered expertly to supplement the meager rations. In every way possible, the men took care of each other in an almost universal display of compassion. Accounts of personal heroism are legion.

Because of war damage, the inadequacy of the roads and the flow of battle, not all the POWs followed the same route west. It became a meandering passage over the northern part of Germany. As winter drew to a close, suffering from the cold abated. When the sound of Allied artillery grew closer, the German guards were less harsh in their treatment of the POWs.

The march finally came to an end when the main element of the column encountered Allied forces east of Hamburg on May 2, 1945. They had covered more than 600 miles in 87 never-to-be-forgotten days. Of those who started on the march, about 1,500 perished, either from disease, starvation or at the hands of German guards while attempting to escape. In terms of percentage of mortality, it came very close to the Bataan Death March. The heroism of these men stands as a legacy to the Air Force crewmen.

In 1992 the American survivors of the march funded and dedicated a memorial at the former site of Stalag Luft IV in Poland, the starting place of a march that is an important part of American ex-prisoner of war history. It should be widely recognized and its many heroes honored for their valor.

*   *   *

I flew my last mission of the war just the day before Laudner was liberated. As a combat crewman I was under no allusions about the Germans. They were and always have been a war prone people dating back to the Teutonic Vandals and Visigoths who ravaged Gaul, Spain and North Africa and sacked Rome in 455 A.D. Bismarck and Kaiser Wilhelm preceded Hitler in the art of war. Hitler went on to achieve unprecedented success and it took a half an armed world of people to finally contain him, then defeat him. I guess we'll never know how close we came to becoming slaves to the Aryan brotherhood bent on world domination.

I think the most startling aspect of the Death March is that it took place without our knowledge. It's also true that few of us were even aware of the ovens of destruction in the German concentration camps like Auschwitz and Dachau. We just continued to fly and bomb. Our lack of any information of the abrasive and inhuman suffering occurring below us might be considered a blessing in disguise to the men who flew the heavies. The added burden of such knowledge could only have heightened their stress of combat.

Can we possibly imagine the indignities of the march. The instances I cite are meant to convey what the Death March survivors had to contend with. On a night in April, 100 Kriegies were holed up in a barn with no food or water. Three of them slipped passed the guards (this was in farm country and small towns) stole some sausage in town and returned to the barn. The next morning all the POWs in the barn that night were herded outside. The German captain threatened to shoot every third G.I. if the thieves did not reveal themselves. They didn't. Nobody was shot, either, but it shows to what length the German guards would go to preserve a semblance of order.

It wasn't always the Germans that caused fear in the ranks. On a number of occasions Allied planes attacked the columns of marchers thinking they were the enemy. There was an instance of a P-51 pilot strafing them, not once, but twice. The second pass the Germans managed to mount a ground machine gun against the fighter pilot. There were no casualties. In another instance John Hargrove, an 8th Air Force gunner who suffered a broken leg after bailing out, said his group was mistaken for Germans and were strafed and bombed killing three POWs. On the long march there were days when POWs watched as P-47s strafed rail and locomotive traffic, viewed V-2s and submarines along with early jet fighters and rockets.

O'Donnell, 35 days into the march, had time to reflect. "From my roadside resting place, I saw my face for the first time in 35 days. I saw a harried, starved, unshaven and unbathed skeletons that once walked with pride and dignity as my companions. I now walked with animals, like myself, as companions. I now urinate and defecate in the woods like an animal with nothing more to wipe with but a leaf, some straw or my hand. I now urinate in the streets of small towns like a dog."

On the march the prisoners were forced into boxcars designed to accommodate 40 men or eight horses. Sixty-five POWs were pressed into each car. The doors were sealed shut. Overcrowding prevented all 65 from sitting down at the same time. The sick were allowed to lie down. Unbearable conditions prevailed and were aggravated by the filth and stench of human waste. Marshaling yards, especially with trains in them, were priority targets for Allied planes. In this case, the men having been sealed in boxcars in an area subject to Allied scrutiny, POWs considered their confinement as a diabolic and intentional plan by the German commandant to have them destroyed by their own air force. The Germans considered them "flying gangsters from Chicago."

The Death March of the American POWs was one thing. But at the same time from many different concentration camps, the Jews were being marched indiscriminately to anywhere so long as the Germans could avoid the advancing Soviets from the east and the British and Americans from the west. The Germans had their hands full but they really had a choice. They didn't have to march their prisoners to death. At practically every turn, they could have spared themselves as well as their prisoners. Their world was falling apart, the end was near, yet they persisted, even doubled their efforts to avoid the Allies when they could have chosen to remain in one place and spared their captives.

The final days of the war saw the Germans begin marches from many camps. Even as the American Death March was proceeding, the Germans launched a Flossenburg to Regensburg death march in April of 1945, a distance of 50 miles, but the senseless meandering accounted for 250 miles. Few Jews survived. Other marches instigated by the Nazis at that time were from Sachsenhausen, Neuengamme, Magdeburg, Mauthausen, Ravensbruck and satellite camps of Dachau. This is graphically illustrated by Daniel J. Goldhagen in his book about ordinary Germans and the Holocaust entitled *"Hitler's Willing Executioners"*.

George Guderley in his printed *"My Recollections"* addressed German hatred of Allied airmen almost matter of factly, citing "spotting two lynched British fliers and the ugly tempered German civilians." All this only enhanced the nasty aspects of the war few of us realized was actually occurring right under our noses.

As I write this it's fifty-five years since the dismal yet electrifying story of the POW Death March took place. A golfing buddy of mine, an engineer gunner who flew B-17s with the 8th Air Force, was astounded when I told him of the ugly drama that had unfolded under our very nose and we had no clue. He expressed his amazement at the extraordinary happening and the incredible time lapse that allowed it to be kept a virtual secret for so long.

CHAPTER 8

Voice of Tears

It was five days before the invasion of Sicily--July 5, 1943. The 99th Bomb Group had already flown 40 missions and the war was still very young. My 348th squadron, the outfit I was to join many months later, was to excel in an especially difficult raid on the Gerbini airdrome in Sicily and sustain a 50 percent loss of aircraft on the mission.

Gerbini was a Sicilian hornet's nest--headquarters of Luftwaffe Air Division III, one of the top Nazi fighter commands in all of Europe. These enemy planes guarded Sicily and the approaches to Italy. They had to be decisively vanquished and the airfield destroyed before the invasion was launched.

The 99th along with the 97th and 301st Bomb Groups would play a major part in setting the stage for the Allied invasion of Sicily. The 99th would be the lead group over the target with Col. Fay Upthegrove flying the lead Fortress. General Dwight E. Eisenhower, the Allied Commander- in-Chief, described the invasion as "the first page in the liberation of the European continent." The British Eighth Army under Field Marshal Bernard Montgomery would land in the southeast corner of the country and the American Seventh Army under George Patton would land on the southern coast.

The battle that ensued in skies over the Gerbini airdrome involved an estimated 110 enemy fighters, a formidable force that would decimate my 348th squadron. The three B-17s lost in the action carried crews known to be pals and buddies with Crew 19, in the Fortress "Patches"

They Brought Down 17 Nazi Planes

These gunners of a record-breaking Flying Fortress crew operating in the North Africa theater indicate number of enemy planes brought down. All sergeants from left: William M. Campble, Cuba, Ill.; Leo Robins, Los Angeles; E. R. Worthey, Eldon, Mo.; Benjamin F. Warmer, San Francisco; Edward Jackson, Boston, and Carlton McGee, Laurel, Del. They took part in the air battle over Gerbini, Sicily, when their group destroyed 35 planes in a day
(Associated Press Wirephoto)

COUNT FINGERS and you get a "Patches" Crew 19 with a kill total of 17 enemy planes, but for this remarkable raid on Gerbini, credit S/Sgt Emmet R. Worthey, third from left, with three kills and not four and S/Sgt Ben Warmer, fourth from left, seven kills, not nine although his total would be nine if he meant to include two kills on an earlier raid. Bombardier Lt. Edward J. Cadjer, not pictured, accounted for one enemy destroyed. The others, from left, all sergeants, are William Campbell, one; Leo Robbins, one; Worthery; Warmer; Edward Jackson, one and Carlton McGee, one. The air battle over the Sicilian air-drome cost the Germans 38 fighters destroyed, 11 probably destroyed and 20 on the ground destroyed. (Associated Press Wirephoto)

About The Ben Warmer Story

Information for the Ben Warmer Story is derived from three sources--all of which, at one time or another appeared in the 99th Bomb Group newsletter. I've copied a great deal of the newsletter's story by Edward Hymoff. He wrote for Impact, a publication no longer listed in the index of current publications. Woven into Hymoff's narrative is Warmer's own story of his actual shooting down of seven enemy planes.

Warmers was interviewed by the Associated Press about his incredible feat and the story appeared in newspapers across the United States.

Material that provides intimate insight into Crew 19 is provided by Genevieve S. McGee, wife of Carlton McGee. He participated in the raid with Warmer and died in 1991 of lung cancer.

that carried Ben Warmer--the waist gunner who would distinguish himself valiantly in one of the squadron's most critical and intense engagements of the war.

Headquarters Fifth Wing operating orders called for a bombing altitude for the 99th at 21,500 feet. It was to attack the south half of the Gerbini airdrome and its dispersal area. They would be provided a P-38 as well as an RAF escort. The enemy onslaught began as the 27 planes of the 99th neared the target. There were ME-109s, FW-190s and Macchi 202s as the Germans became persistently aggressive with determined attacks from all angles, singly and in groups.

Col. Upthegrove described an oddity in the tactics of the defenders. "As I got about 45 degrees in the turn at the IP (Initial Point), either nine or twelve fighters made a frontal attack at one or two thousand feet up and dropped bombs on us fused to explode in the air. Thanks to our turn the bombs fell to our left and exploded harmlessly. Then the battle began," Upthegrove said. The colonel was visibly shook after the intensity of the battle had receded somewhat and he received a call from Capt. Bob Elliott of the 348th. It was shortly after the turn for home when Elliott broke radio silence to inform his group lead commander in a quivering voice that he had only three planes left. Upthegrove said "keep coming, you can't do anything about it now."

Colonel Fay Upthegrove, died at the age of 86 a retired Major General in a Bradford, Pennsylvania hospital. A funeral service with full military honors was accorded him at St. Bonaventure Cemetery, Allegany, New York. He was born Jan. 28, 1905 in Port Allegany. In 1930 he married Martha Driscoll who died June 27, 1970. In Bradford, on Oct. 1, 1974, he married J. Elizabeth "Betty" Staley, who survived.

General Upthegrove graduated from the U.S. Military Academy at West Point, New York in 1927 where he was appointed second lieutenant in the infantry. But he went on to win his wings in San Antonio, Texas in 1928. His service career spanned three decades with duty assignments from the Far East to the North African and European Theaters of Operation during World War II. In April, 1942 he was appointed commander of the 99th Bomb Group and in February, 1943 he took the group to North Africa.

He flew more than 340 hours in B-17s, participating in 58 combat missions over North Africa, Italy and southern Europe. He was chosen to command the lead plane in the first Army Air Force "Hundred Bomber Attack" on enemy territory and he led his bomb wing in the first bombing of Rome. A year later he became commanding general of the 304th Bomb Wing of the 15th Air Force in Italy.

Among Gen. Upthegrove's numerous awards and decorations were the Distinguished Service Medal; the Silver Star, the Distinguished Flying Cross with one oak leaf cluster and the Air Medal with 10 clusters. He was rated a command pilot, command observer and senior aircraft observer.

Joseph C. Kenney, a radio operator in the 346th squadron and popular chaplain and founding member of the 99th Bomb Group Historical Society, had this to say about the general: "I recall clearly his insistence on flying close formation and, although I was just a radio operator, those wings tucked in tight like that were mighty impressive. Looking back in my diary, a number of entries relate to time when German fighters began an attack on us only to break off and press their attacks on other bomber groups flying a looser formation. Here is clear evidence that Col. Upthegrove's discipline imposed on our pilots unquestionably helped considerably to reduce our casualties."

Joe also noted, "I was told that Gen. Upthegrove was the actual author of the box formation along with the impressive company front maneuvers. Both of these served us well. I also agree the general had the ability to speak easily with any person under his command--all the way down to the greenest of aerial gunners."

It was the next month, a hot sunny day under the African sun in August that Lt. Gen. Carl A. Spaatz, commander of the Northwest African Air Force, fingered the medal, second only to the Medal of Honor, that was destined for the chest of S/Sgt. Ben Warmer. An aide read from

General Orders No.69. Maj. Gen. Jimmy Doolittle was standing by as Warmer, at rigid attention, stood ready to receive the Distinguished Service Cross for his incredible feat-- the shooting down of seven enemy planes over Gerbini.

Who was this Warmer fellow, anyway?

For one thing, he was one hulk of a man with his six foot, four inch frame weighing in at 220 pounds. This grand day on the tarmac of the 99th air base in North Africa saw a nervous Ben Warmer, in the company of two important generals. He listened to their tributes and then Gen. Spaatz pinned the DSC on him.

Before entering the service, Warmer played varsity football at UCLA. After he graduated from college in 1937 he was at loose ends. The world was in turmoil and Ben, rejecting his father's advice to become a lawyer, instead became a Secret Service agent. His father, a Superior Court Judge in Los Angeles, helped his son get an assignment as a bodyguard to Secretary of the Treasury Henry Morgenthau.

Ben Warmer enlisted in April, 1942, five months after America went to war. He wanted to fight. Most of his friends were in combat units. All he had to show for the few months he had already served was a letter of commendation telling him what a great physical education instructor he was.

The Battle of North Africa was in full swing in March of 1943 and more crews were being rushed to the war zone. Warmer was on one of those crews, having been relieved of his gunnery instructor assignment. He considered that transfer to a combat crew a very welcome assignment.

Crew 19 got their first airplane in January, 1943 at Salina, Kansas. On Feb. 4, 1943 Capt. Davis rolled the "Gremlin Castle" down the runway and off to the wars. Four days later only 700 feet over the jungle and through torrential rain they collided with another B-17 in midair. Sgt. Campbell, the engineer, was to notify the captain as he looked to the rear of the aircraft from his top turret, "Captain, we've lost our tail." Slightly above the treetops of the Brazilian jungle, Capt. Davis regained control of the ship and flew perilously for two more hours to Belem, Brazil where he landed the plane safely. For two months Crew 19 remained in Belem sweating out a new fin and rudder assembly. A superstitious crew re-christened the airplane "Borrowed Time". It wasn't until April 20, 1943 that they reached their final African destination.

It was two weeks before Ben Warmer's crew made its first mission... a raid on shipping in Bizerte harbor. That mission would cost them "Borrowed Time." Returning from the target the group ran into bad weather... so bad the crew had to bail out as the plane ran out of gas in the air looking for a place to land. Warmer's chute hung on a cliff and when he cut himself loose he dropped more than 30 feet breaking five ribs.

Bailing out under those extremely adverse weather conditions was just a matter of time. It was just before they jumped when Ed Jackson, radio operator on "Borrowed Time", signaled Warmer he was having trouble with his chute giving further insight into Warmer's unselfish and caring manner.

"It was Ben who wired my chute so it would fit as I prepared to jump on our first mission. He was also instrumental on changing the feed belts on the waist guns so that they would feed from overhead instead of from the side--it prevented jams," Jackson said in a 1987 edition of the 99th newsletter.

It was ten days before they had another plane to fly in. It was their fourth mission over Messina that they came back so badly shot up that Crew 19 decided to name their new ship "Patches". Warmer and his Crew 19 had participated in about 24 missions before they were scheduled to fly July 5th to Gerbini. It was on that mission that it was decided that Lt. Flake Casto, second in command under Capt. Max Davis, would fly as pilot. Capt. Davis remained behind. Casto, of Los Angeles, California, was a newlywed who tormented himself over having to leave his wife when he went to war. Turned out Casto proved to be an exceptionally adept copilot, proven in combat and subsequently rewarded with his own combat crew and airplane. Casto piloted the plane that let the others do the killing.

Who were the other brave men on Ben Warmer's crew that fateful day in July?

S/Sgt Carlton McGee of Laurel, Delaware normally shared the same waist space in "Patches" as did Warmer. But on this raid S/Sgt Emmett R.Worthey, normally the lower ball turret gunner, traded McGee for the position and McGee took up another position in the ship. He would die of lung cancer in 1991. Worthey, of Elcon, Missouri, bumped rear ends with Warmer. It wasn't until the model Gs came out that the waist guns were staggered. "Patches" was an F model with one of its attending faults being the inevitable tangle with each other's butt that waist gunners had to put up with under fire. This unseemly positioning of the waist guns was corrected in a subsequent model of the B-17.

Worthey may have been the musician on the crew but McGee was known to his comrades as a kind of self appointed morale booster who always harbored a positive attitude and a sense of humor. Worthey, on the other hand, actually wanted to steal a page out of Nero's book and fiddle while Rome burned. Whether guitar and violin playing Worthey actually did this on their August 13th raid to Rome is not known, but what is known is that the ball gunner turned waist gunner accounted for three enemy aircraft over Gerbini making him an ace when you count two previous kills. McGee was credited with one German plane destroyed in addition to two probables and two damaged.

The so-called "guiding light" of the crew was Lt. Vernon F. Schoedinger of Miami, Florida. As navigator he was responsible for steering the pilot and Crew 19 over South American jungles and the trackless Atlantic to their base at Navarin Field, near Constantine in Algeria.

They called him "Eagle Eye Cadjer". Edward J. Cadjer of Patterson, New Jersey, was of the firm belief that the only reason the B-17 was built was to carry him, the bombardier, personally, over the target for the sole purpose of loosing his load of destruction on the enemy below. He was credited with one enemy aircraft destroyed.

Six enlisted men comprised the rest of the crew. The engineer and top turret gunner was T/Sgt. William M. Campbell of Cuba, Illinois. In the eyes of his crew, he was the best flight engineer in the business. He'd proved his expertise after the midair collision over a Brazilian jungle when their sorely damaged ship was repaired and rebuilt to fly again. Campbell shot down one enemy plane at Gerbini and claimed one probable and one or two damaged.

Radio operator and center gunner T/Sgt. Edward Jackson of Boston, Massachusetts, 33, was the oldest man on the crew. His sole ambition was to own a bar back in Boston after the war ended. He also was credited with one, his first kill in the July 5th mission.

Tailgunner S/Sgt. Leo E. Robin of Los Angeles, California was a shy individual who was reluctant to claim his own aerial victories. More than once the men of Crew 19 had to brow beat him into claiming an enemy fighter shot down. In the case of Gerbini, he was credited with one, his second kill.

Warmer of San Francisco, California, had been an attorney in civilian life and a former Secret Service agent. He was the armament and turret specialist of the crew. It was his job to see that the guns and turrets were operational in all missions.

H hour was a few hours old as the men of Crew 19 were trucked to the hardstand. Each gunner methodically began checking his position and his gun station or turret. Warmer first checked his side of "Patches" from the outside. His field of fire was clear. He then pulled his ponderous frame through the escape hatch in the waist, happy to be aboard. Then Warmer began checking off the items that would mean life and death in the air: oxygen mask, radio headphones and the electric leads of his heat suit, to name a few. Temperatures up there could plunge to 50 and 60 degrees below zero. Death lurked in seconds without oxygen and frostbite was a constant threat at the high altitudes the bombers flew to strike their targets. The penalty for touching metal after shedding a glove, for whatever reason, could mean severe skin impairment.

Warmer checked his gun. He slammed the bolt back and forth a few times and its well oiled track and easy movement sounded satisfying as its gun swiveled easily on its mount. Then he carefully checked the ammo boxes and the neatly folded belts of cartridges that snuggled inside the wooden boxes. Soon the props were turned through, the engines coughed to a start and "Patches" joined others in a line for takeoff.

A routine check began for the crew as they attained 10,000 feet enroute to the target. At Luftwaffe headquarters in Gerbini, radar and sensitive microphones had spotted the B-17s. On the landing strips in nearby valleys, gray uniformed flight officers acknowledged the orders to scramble. In pairs and in groups of three and four, the black-crossed fighters revved up and then took off, turning south toward the approaching Fortresses. Luftwaffe Division III was out to smash the 99th.

The clouds lay far below the bombers and the pilots on "Patches" soon spotted the glob of brown that slowly enlarged into Sicily. Casto ordered all guns to be test fired. Warmer dipped the nose of his machine gun at the pale blue waters of the Mediterranean Sea below and fired a couple of short bursts.

"Starboard gun O.K." Warmer called into the interphone. The other gunners opened up and the sound of machine gun fire thundered above the steady drone of the engines. The coast of Sicily came beneath them. Someone in the flight of bombers had spotted the enemy fighters and relayed the news to Lt. Casto.

"We've got 'em at two o'clock high and nine o'clock low," Casto warned over the intercom. A moment later he called out "we've now got 'em at six o'clock high. Germans flying a hundred fighters were all over the place. In a matter of minutes, 22 enemy fighters had been knocked out of the sky. But there was still the bomb run and ten minutes to go before they would sight the target. Meanwhile, two B-17s were lost.

At this point Ben Warmer tells his own story as reported in an Associated Press dispatch the next day.

About five minutes off the target we ran into a howling antiaircraft barrage and coming up through their own flak were more enemy pursuit planes than we had ever seen. It had been their habit to lay outside their flak until it was over, but today they came right into their own fire.

The first plane I got a shot at came in at the start--a Messerschmitt peeled off from our right and leveled straight at us with his guns winking.

I winked back until the German was fifty yards away and then I saw him burst into flames and plow down under our Fortress. I signaled the left waist gunner to look out of his window and see if the plane went down. He nodded yes.

Number two and number three were daisies. Two ME-109s made a run together at the Fortress. I got one on the way in. He peeled off in a roll. The other came on but broke his run at about fifty yards and I opened up on his belly when he exposed it in a turn. The first plane slid off to the right for approximately one thousand yards and the pilot bailed out. The second plane went down and the pilot also left it. Meantime one of our own Fortresses had been set on fire.

The next two victories I didn't even intend to claim, but the gunners in some other bombers saw them parachuting down. There was a Messerschmitt making a run at our Fortress and I picked him up as he started his bank, held the trigger down until the plane began to smoke and he started out of control like a leaf floating in the breeze. The other one was making a run on a ship in our squadron, the one that was in trouble. The enemy had to pass within fifty yards of me, so I put approximately 200 rounds into him and the last I saw of him he was in a vertical dive and burning.

I got two more fighters but didn't have time to identify them positively. They were both making passes at a Fortress behind us and as they banked to make a run on her they had to pass me. One first tried dodging tactics when he saw my tracers, but he was too close for me to miss and he went down before he got to the plane he was after. The other one was doing the same thing. He was just under our tail and below us and shooting at the ship behind us when one of my incendiaries made him explode in the air. He was number seven. (End of AP dispatch)

The record achievement of Warmer and his crew included not only Warmer's seven downed enemy planes, but the crew's combined total of fifteen enemy fighters destroyed on that mission. So brilliant was their performance that Crew 19 attracted instant world wide attention through press, newsreels and radio. Warmer was asked to do the famous radio show "Army Hour". Publicity resulted in the wives and parents of crew members being showered with telephone calls and press interviews.

Warmer, five weeks before Gerbini, on a raid to Naples was credited with two ME-109s. Africa's ace enlisted man gunner finished his required 50 missions and was returned home from his 99th Bomb Group air base in North Africa on Oct. 15th with nine kills to his credit.

Ben died Dec. 6, 1977 in his family home in Riverside, California as a result of a massive heart attack. He was buried in the Warmer family plot in an Ontario, California cemetery, the final resting place of his parents and grandparents. He is survived by his wife, Helen Warmer and one son, Michael.

As a post script listing aerial enlisted aces, another of the 99th Bomb Group's top gunners with seven enemy planes to his credit--four of them destroyed in one day, was S/Sgt. Jack D. Guerard, 31, of Beaufort, South Carolina.

Guerard, a pint-size tailgunner, had his best day Sept. 8, 1943 over Fracatti, the city proper, in Italy. Most of his enemy attacks came from the rear of his ship. His ship was singled out after it had fallen out of formation with an engine damaged by flak and a riddled nose. Pumping better than 1200 rounds of .50 caliber ammo, Guerard blasted out of the sky a brace of ME-109s, an FW-190 and an Italian Regianne 2001. Three of his targets literally blew apart in the air. The only ace tailgunner in the 8th Air Force is reported to be Shorty Squires, credited with downing six enemy planes.

CHAPTER 9
Victory in Europe - V.E. Day

The missions I was flying ended as the war ended. The Germans finally threw in the towel with their unconditional surrender on May 7, 1945. All battlefields but those in Czechoslovakia lie silent. At 12:03 on the morning of May 8th the boys in our squadron were still celebrating. The drinks were on the house. Red, yellow, orange and green flares turned a beautiful night into day.

Our crew was somewhat subdued. Red, Hank and I went to the movies earlier that evening to see "Strike Up the Band" with Mickey Rooney and Judy Garland. When we got back to our tent we found Elmer and Don in their sacks asleep. Alex was still up. I dug out the last can of tuna fish. Hank produced some American Kraft cheese and Alex and Red furnished some stale slices of bread at least a week old. We enjoyed a sumptuous feast.

By 12:15 a.m. the flares had stopped going up. Red and Hank fell off to sleep, Alex was reading as I attended my diary. Rumors have been flying thick and fast the past few days. Naturally we're all wondering how and when we're going home. The hottest rumor is that the old crews, meaning us, will leave by plane on May 14th for home. Too good to be true and almost worse than sweating out a mission. Tomorrow they'll be wanting us to fly a gunnery mission and shoot up our overstocked bins of ammunition.

But getting back to the business at hand my 18th, 19th and 20th missions March 8, 9 and 13 to Hegyeshalon, Hungary, Bruck, Austria and Regensburg, Germany were relatively easy. The trip to Hungary saw me flying the left waist gun position on the John Harris crew along with Hank and Don. Sorenson was the flight engineer. While we were in the air on this date, the U.S. 1st Army crossed the Rhine between Cologne and Coblenz.

On the raid to Bruck our regular crew lacked Elmer who was in rest camp and Jim Wyatt and Steve Kaptain, copilot and navigator respectively. The guys who substituted for them were flying their first mission which was without incident. And the only notable thing about our 20th raid was the comparative warmth we experienced at our bombing altitude of 24,500 feet. The temperature was only 35 degrees below zero. Our ship, No. 704, on its next mission without us, was forced to crash land in Yugoslavia.

The 21st mission to Florisdorf oil refineries in Vienna had a different twist. It offered a sky full of belching flak over the target. General Patton, having defeated the Germans, saw them fleeing east to the Rhine in a mass retreat in the Saar Valley at the very moment concussions rocked our ship and flak penetrated the thin aluminum skin of our airplane from nose to tail. We flew tail-end Charlie and in this spot we were allowed a little more leeway--we could dodge to avoid a lot of shells bursting around us. While our wings were being ripped open, the two ships in our element ahead of us were experiencing their own difficulties and showed feathered props to prove it. We were in one flak barrage the longest I've ever been in one--a half hour it seemed, but actually only six or seven minutes. After we dropped our bombs on the oil refineries below the flak persisted. The heavy flak at our altitude might be attributable to the visual run we made on the target. Clear skies work both ways. We lost the two planes in our element, but they did manage to make their way back to home base.

Oil refineries again was a target on our 22nd mission on March 21st. We flew The Old Lady, ship No. 164, to the Kagran refineries in the Vienna environs. We only carried a 4,000 pound bomb load but we dropped it from 28,500 feet at minus 45 degree temperature. This was one of the longest raids of my tour lasting eight hours and twenty minutes.

Just before we hit the target No. 1 engine began running real rough. We dropped back from number six position to tail end Charlie. Elmer was flying as our toggolier and did a fine job dropping on the lead ship despite thick vapor trails which partially obscured his vision. Flak found us at our bombing altitude and caused it to pepper us uncomfortably close.

On the way back, about a half hour before we reached the Adriatic, Steve spotted an enemy aircraft at nine o'clock. I jumped into my turret in no seconds flat and had my guns bearing by the time he was at eight o'clock and gave him a short burst from both guns. The incoming FW-190 was at seven o'clock and closing from less than 1,000 yards out when Red, from the tail, Hank from the ball turret and me all opened up on him at once. Our red tracers filled the sky for a few seconds all converging on the enemy aircraft. This broke off his attack and he received a final burst from all three of our positions before he got out of range at six o'clock. Once we were over the Adriatic he disappeared.

Evidently we were the only ship in the whole formation who fired at the fighter. Ball turrets were stowed on the ships in front of us and probably its gunners and other gunners in the formation were entirely unaware of its presence.

We didn't fly the raids to Berlin and Ruhland the last few days, but those that did reported moderate opposition from German jet fighters. On March 25, 1945 we expected similar opposition since our target this time was the Kbely airdrome at Prague, Czechoslovakia--a mission that logged five minutes short of eight hours. Our bomb load was 3,400 pounds of fragmentation bombs--100 pounders to be dropped from 26,000 feet over a smoke covered target. There was some light flak and four fighters out of range attracted some of our fire until they were discovered to be P-51s, our own escort. Only two days before our run on Prague American tank units crossed the Rhine on the Ludendorff Bridge before it could be destroyed. This upset Hitler so much that he had a handful of top generals in this command shot for treason.

You wouldn't think a mere railroad bridge in Brenner Pass would cause us any trouble. This one did. Cy Diamond on the Harris crew flew copilot with us and we lost Alex to another crew to fly as panther operator. Elmer flew as toggalier. This being our 24th mission and April 8th on the calendar, we didn't expect things to be so rough because the Russians were penetrating three miles into Vienna as we flew. We knew it was only a matter of time and nobody wanted the celebrity attached to the last bomber to get shot down in the war.

The flight to and from the target was made on a beautiful day without a cloud in the sky. It was only a six hour trip. The valleys and mountains below us were peppered with small towns. But when it came time to make the bomb run and we opened our bomb bay doors, the flak began pounding us--tracking us all along the run. Flying in number two position, I could see the right wing of the lead ship catch a telling burst. Our bomb bay was rifled with shell fragments which also tore through the left side of the fuselage, some passing through completely to penetrate the other side of the ship. The exploding shell caused our plane to lurch and rock precipitously. The flight home was uneventful.

Two days earlier, April 12th to be exact, President Roosevelt, our 31st president, died at his Georgia retreat surprising many people.

An ammunition factory at Avigliano in northern Italy became our 25th target of the war. The date was April 14th. The Germans were supposed to surrender by now. They hadn't, of course. And we got hit in the leading edge of our left wing--not by flak or enemy bullets, but by, of all things, a flak helmet. Seems somebody up ahead of us and above us was peering through an open bomb bay only to lose his helmet. I'll take that kind of resistance any day.

Enemy troop concentrations came under our fire on our next raid to Bologna, Italy, my 26th mission. Let's pause a minute and consider what I just said. The mission was to be flown in support of 5th Army troops pressing the Germans in the Po Valley. We had to ask, why us? How does a lumbering giant of a bomber like a B-17 support ground troops effectively without blowing them up in the process?

Jim Peters is a friend of mine. Both of us served in the 348th squadron in the same time frame but never actually met until many years after the war. He flew similar type raids on April 9th and 10th and was privy to information that explains the method used to determine front lines.

Support missions like this probably affected the bombardier more than any other member of a bomber crew. He was put on notice that if even one of his bombs fell on the Allied lines in the course of the raid, he would be held accountable. Strike photos would unmask any culprit who deigned to miss his target. And woe be unto him should his release in error cause injury or death to those ground pounders. He would be dealt with harshly.

Peters, whose pilot was E. A. Scott, said in their approach from the Adriatic, they would get a signal set up on the shore from a marker beacon. It would be ground signal to the formation to turn inland to the west and flight crews should follow that beam until intersecting a second marker beacon positioned at right angles to their flight course. This would be the drop signal.

Not unlike my raid to Bologna, for Jim Peters, it was friendly flak some 5,000 feet below him, indicating front lines. He remembered enemy flak being on a horizontal plane. The navigator said their position was only 2-1/2 minutes from Bologna where the enemy flak was coming from. Further their bomb bay doors were opened over the Adriatic and were to be closed before they turned south over Allied lines. This was to prevent any delayed releases from hitting our own troops. Another red flag the bombardier had to concern himself with on a support mission of this type. And there was no room for compromise as the brass would sooner accept the loss of a bomber from a loose bomb in the bomb bay than the death of a single soldier on the ground.

Many years after the war when Peters, still in the service stationed in Alaska, had one of his men assigned to him reveal a bit of his past. He was in the infantry below when those support missions were flown. Yes, he was in the front lines and told Peters the Germans were in an orchard of apricot trees from whence the town was named. After the bombing all the foliage was stripped from the trees due to the proximity fuses that the frag clusters were armed with.

We carried 3,400 pounds of frag bombs to support Allied ground forces. To guide us in, soldiers of the American 5th Army shot up flak at 15,000 feet, indicating their front lines. Enemy flak was heavy and intense for a few minutes and then we were on our way home. Our mission called for the same safeguards to be in place as were with Peters in his earlier raids. But I flew our mission completely unaware of the constraints placed on John Thomas, our bombardier.

The next day we took on another railroad bridge located in Rattenburg, Germany. The temperature lofted to an acceptable minus 22 degrees below zero--so warm that I never plugged in my heated suit.

My twentieth birthday as we flew the next day to Vipeteno marshaling yards at the end of the Brenner Pass. April 20th is also Hitler's 56th birthday. In any case we've seen Berlin all but capitulate to the Russians with more than a quarter of the city under their control. And Vienna, a target that we were to hit seven times, had fallen to the Reds after several days of vicious street fighting. And here I am on my 28th mission on my birthday.

As we came in on the bomb run it was a beautiful sight to see. Formations of B-25s were hitting one target at about 12,000 feet, B-24s were hitting another and P-47s, P-38s and P-51s were strafing other objectives as we held to our bomb run. Smoke was issuing from every nook and corner of the Brenner Pass that I could see.

Kraut flak guns perched atop 10,000 foot mountain tops found our ships easy picking. Their fire was intense and accurate. Once again our squadron was lucky. Our lead squadron flying high and in front of us seemed to be getting hit bad. And the squadron behind us seemed to be in similar straits. Listening in on radio these planes were reporting men wounded and engines knocked out. A ship behind us could be seen crashing into a mountain side.

Bursts were close and we got knocked around by their concussions. I tuned on VHF and listened to reports of damage. ABLE squadron, for instance, had one ship with two engines out and a dead tailgunner. BAKER squadron was us and we were okay. CHARLIE and DOG squadrons had been roughed up and some pilots, knowing they couldn't stay in formation, were calling for fighter escort. On reaching home base I wasn't surprised to see two of our forts badly damaged resting just off the runway. And finally, to top off the day's excitement, I witnessed a show from the ground I'd never seen before.

A damaged B-17 with hydraulic system shot out evidently was making its second try for a landing. Its wheels touched and a parachute billowed out behind it and collapsed. A second one was released, but partially collapsed too. The aircraft was now off the end of the runway. It finally came to rest after turning two complete circles in a cloud of dust.

Scenes of horror had already unfolded before the eyes of American soldiers as they entered the Nazi death camp at Buchenwald earlier this month. And still the Germans struggled to survive. On April 24th we made a milk run to a bridge at Obr Drauburg in Austria in The Old Lady. We visited our target twice but there was no flak and no fighters to impede us. And Neely allowed me to fly the ship part of the way home.

The curtain is coming down all over the embattled continent. On the day of my thirtieth mission, April 25th, the Red army, having plunged into the heart of Berlin two days ago, is now beginning to savor victory. As far as we're concerned we've still got a job to do. We've been assigned to bomb the Hermann Goring works near Linz. We'll carry a 5000 pound bomb load and we'll hit the target from 25,900 feet.

When I got down to our ship this morning, No. 704, mechanics were working feverishly on No. 1 engine. Magneto trouble showed itself on preflight. Three times they thought they'd fixed the trouble. On the fourth try and just in time to fall in position on the taxi strip, the trouble was located and fixed properly. We had no trouble with the engine on the mission.

Today we would fly the No. 2 ship in the second element. Our squadron leader was Schuetz and Eber was the lead bombardier. Other

348th pilots on today's mission were Knox, Zenor, Scott, Mariconda and Gossman. The 347th flew to our left. ahead flew the 346th and 416th.

Engine start was 0835 hours. Taxi at 0845 and takeoff at 0855. Our group rendezvous was to be directly over Foggia at 6,500 feet. It would take a little less than an hour to accomplish this before we would rendezvous again 1,000 feet higher and eighteen minutes later over Termoli, just up the east coast of the Italian boot a few miles. Our key point would be Ledenice at 19,000 feet at 1126 hours. Initial point would be Wegscheid in trail and we would hit the target at 27,500 feet. Actually we bombed from 25,900 feet. Our ETA was 1555 hours. They were asking us for a seven hour mission but we did it nicely in six hours and fifteen minutes.

Nothing happened until we reached Linz and then all hell broke out. Flak was very accurate and very heavy. It was everywhere. Today our squadron took as much punishment as any of the others with us. Concussions rocked our ship and flak knocked out our secondary control cables and the interphone system in the tail. "Call" position on the jack box was knocked out throughout the ship. Fragments of flak went through our left wing and bomb bay doors. Our left waist gunner narrowly escaped injury when flak went through the sleeve of his jacket, just missing his arm. As far as the rest of our group was concerned, there was one ship that went down that I know of and two more are missing. Many planes lost engines and some reported casualties. What a way to end the war.

Just after we left the target I got a terrific attack of stomach cramps. They lasted until we descended to the 7,000 foot altitude and I felt well after that.

As this was our last mission of the war it also proved the undoing of Mussolini three days hence and Hitler five days later. The "Father of Italian Fascism" would die with his mistress and eleven others at the hands of Italian Partisans who caught, tried and executed them on April 28th. Hitler, meanwhile lived another two days in his Berlin bunker before committing suicide on April 30th.

*   *   *

Reflections

Four thousand men with broken wings,
Tired, wounded, crippled things,
We call ourselves men, and as men we try
To carry on our ideals held high.

We try to be happy,
We try to be gay,
We know in our hearts
That there will be peace some day.

We mustn't be bitter,
We mustn't have fear.
Tolerance, justice, love--
Yes, our way is so clear.

We return to God to renew our faith,
To ask for courage to carry on.
As they did in the oldest volume known
Beside the waters of Merman.

He won't let us down where e're we be,
He keeps his watch over us, for you see
We're tired, wounded, crippled things,
Four thousand men with broken wings.
                                    --Anonymous POW

Ralph Edwards, wounded and a prisoner of war, flew with the 2nd Bomb Group out of Foggia. His B-17 was in the last formation of raiders as they attacked Steyr, their target somewhere in Austria. His complete formation of seven planes was wiped out even before reaching the target. He was wounded in both arms before bailing out.

Edwards contributed to this book the preceding poem and the one that follows. He was also gracious enough to allow me to write his story which appeared in Sun Times, a retirement community newspaper in Mesa, Arizona of which I am the editor.

Untitled
by S/Sgt Frank Oettinger

All is quiet at the base,
Our combat men in slumber lay,
On the ramp the ground crews race
To load the bombers for the fray.

Hit the deck the C.Q.s cry,
You've a mission on today,
Over Steyr you're going to fly,
Make it snappy. On your way.

To our ships we rush in haste,
For the battle to prepare
Every gun from nose to waist,
Then we're off, in the air.

Steadily, we climb on high,
In formation, take our place.
Flying Forts high in the sky
Leaving far behind, our base.

Hostile lands we now are nearing,
Soon we'll tangle with the foe.
Through our sights we are now peering,
"Focke Wulfs coming from below."

Shells and bullets, tracers, flak
Show the fury of the fight.
"Watch the fighter, he'll attack,
Now he's diving out of sight."

Smoke and fire fill the sky,
Death rides high this winter's day.
While we all await the cry
From the nose, "bombs away!"

Now our duty we have done,
And for home we quickly turn.
But the fight has just begun
As the target starts to burn.

There's a fighter put to route,
But the others still come in.
"Wow! They got us, quick, bail out."
Guess you cannot always win.

Quickly, but with heart of woe,
We must bid our ship goodbye;
As we jump, we see her go,
A ball of fire in the sky.

Now all's quiet, we're alone,
Riding to the ground below.
Not a single engine's drone
Breaks the hush as down we go.

Minutes later we alight,
Jerry's waiting when we land,
PRISONERS! No more to fight
Gainst the Huns barbarian band.

Though our fight is over now,
Still our buddies carry on,
For we all have made a vow,
N'er to quit 'til Hitler's gone.

As in stalag we now dwell,
While our comrades ride on high,
All our spirits wish them well
Bombing Jerry from the sky.

When it's all over once again,
We'll return to those we love,
"Tis for them we sweat and strain,
Fighting, falling from above.

CHAPTER 10

Tailspin

There are all kinds of thrilling stories to be told of 99ers flying combat in World War II. If ever in the annals of 99th Bomb Group history there could be a story to emulate the fall and recovery of a B-17 in a tailspin I'd like to know about it because the man I'm about to write about, a pilot who in his time had flown squadron and group lead, has that story to tell. His miraculous, exciting and moving story spells out an episode that could easily have had a tragic end but instead his instinct and courage prevailed in face of almost certain disaster. John Plummer, on his 4th mission to Ploesti, August 18, 1944, is the quintessential bomber pilot, the likes of which movies are made.

Plummer is a sixth generation descendent of the original pioneer settlers in western Pennsylvania, Two of his ancestors were killed by Indians near Saxton, Pennsylvania in 1780. He enlisted in the Air Corps in 1942 and received his cadet pilot training at Santa Ana for preflight, Oxnard for primary (movie star Robert Cummings was his flight instructor); Chico for basic and Stockton for advanced--all in California. He received his Flying Fortress training in Roswell, New Mexico and Ardmore, Oklahoma. He flew a B-17G to Foggia and was assigned to the 347th squadron.

He completed his first combat tour in January of 1945 and began a second consecutive tour of duty until he was injured on a raid March 14th. He earned two Distinguished Flying Crosses. Highlight of his combat tours were the participation in four Ploesti missions and the invasion of southern France (Operation Dragoon, on August 15, 1944. John Plummer's greatest lifetime honor and thrill was successfully leading the 99th Bomb Group into combat against Germany. I flew the same mission to Augsburg on Feb. 27, 1945 that Plummer flew group lead.

He was to go on and distinguish himself in the service after the war ended. He was awarded a Regular Army commission in 1947. Among his varied assignments he was a B-29 aircraft commander on the first hydrogen bomb experiment in the Pacific in 1952. And at one time he was a VIP standby pilot for President John F. Kennedy at Otis AFB (Cape Cod) in 1962.

He and his wife Helen have four children and seven grandchildren. Seeing his son Stanley C. being graduated from West Point in 1976 was one of his proudest moments.

Seated around a table in the hospitality room of a Baltimore hotel in September of 1997 me and Don and Red met for the first time with Plummer, his navigator Norris Domangue and Al Schroeder, a 347th squadron commander who went on to become deputy group commander of the 99th. Plummer had a great deal of respect for both these men when they were flying combat. I had known of Plummer for years through correspondence and he was kind enough to send me his manuscript entitled "Hitting the Hun" after I sent him a tentative manuscript entitled "My War". This gathering of war birds, however, afforded my first opportunity to meet and visit with these stellar 99ers.

Ploesti became the definitive scourge of American bomber pilots from the very beginning. Rising to attack 13 oil refineries, pumping stations and storage tanks around Ploesti on August 1, 1943, 178 B-24 Liberator bombers from Bengazi, Lybia were subject to awesome losses, yet managed to curtail German production for six months by their imaginative low level raid. It was America's first big target of the war, but it cost 55 bombers destroyed of which only 33 of the original 178 planes came through to fly again. The Germans exacted a terrible toll. Of the 1,733 airmen involved in the raid, 446 were killed, 108 became prisoners of war.

Eight months after the initial assault on Ploesti was made, the 15th

Air Force decided that that oil target was important enough to be singled out again and again for further attacks. The 99th struck Ploesti for the first time April 5, 1944. The 15th Air Force was to record a total loss of 223 bombers in its 19 separate combat missions to this location. Ploesti was to receive top priority for the strategic Allied bombers striking Germany until the Russians swept in from the east in their rout of German troops and terminated the need for continued aerial attacks.

Plummer's fourth mission on August 18th was the last of the 99th's nine mission assault on Ploesti. And that brings us to that moment of truth. Imagine a Flying Fortress with two engines out and in a free fall, then a spin. Imagine yourself the pilot of that stricken aircraft as the plunge from just above 20,000 feet begins. Are you ready to signal the crew to bail out? Or has the centrifugal force already diminished that avenue of escape completely? Do you have the skill, the expertise and the confidence in what you're doing to recover from the spin? So sure are enemy fighters that you've bought the proverbial farm, that they abandon you to your fate.

He was a lieutenant then. But leading up to the frightening incident, Plummer, at the outset of the mission, his thirteenth, had foreboding premonitions. They'd be flying a man short. A shortage of navigators meant that their bombardier would navigate too. And further, morning engine start gave him some cause for concern. No. 4 engine was acting up but proved to be within acceptable limits. Perhaps it was the target itself that permeated his thoughts--knowing it to be one of the most formidable in all of Europe.

As they began to climb to 28,000 feet, No. 4 engine oil pressure was still a little low and the oil and cylinder head temperatures were higher than the other three engines. Plummer decided not to abort the mission even as the oil leak persisted. He had his reasons. For one, they'd be leaving the group short 13 guns and, maybe the most important, the psychological effect of "turning back"from a mission to Ploesti was a stigma that inferred yellow (coward). He sure didn't want that attached to his name.

Plummer Describes the Action

About ten minutes short of the IP at 28,000 feet, things began to happen badly for us. We had already taken some flak hits and one of the fragments apparently struck one of the electric bomb door motors because it caught fire. The flight engineer put it out. By the time he returned from the bomb bay where the fire was, No. 4 was pumping oil all over the engine nacelle and its oil pressure had gone below the red line mark of 40 psi. According to tech orders, I should have shut No. 4 down right then and feathered its prop because oil pressure was required to feather. If I had done so I could not have maintained our position in the bomber formation and we would have fallen behind and the Kraut fighters would have been on us quickly. So we hung in their with the firm instructions for Todd (Henry Todd, copilot) to shut No. 4 engine down when its oil pressure fell to 20 psi.

Shortly after turning on the bomb run at the IP we all got a big surprise. No. 2 engine quit with no prior warning of any type. It was probably internal engine failure as the ball turret gunner did not report any flak hits on the under side of the wing in the vicinity of No. 2 engine and I could see no damage on the top side.

Good old "on the ball" Todd immediately feathered the propeller on No. 2 and I applied nearly full power on engines one, three and four, knowing full well that No.4 engine was going to fail shortly. When I had dropped back sufficiently far to be even with number seven, we sort of traded places. He moved up into my abandoned number six position and I descended to his number seven position. This was a proper switch, ensuring a more precise squadron bomb pattern. I had traded altitude for airspeed and slowly descended below number seven's position, which permitted me to maintain a vertical position within the formation, ensuring that our bombs would be within the squadron's bomb pattern.

Within one minute after "bombs away" No. 4 engine caught fire. Todd immediately feathered the prop on No. 4 engine and extinguished the fire. While he was attending to the engine fire, I was busy flying the airplane. We now had only two engines operating, #'s 1 and 3, and I knew we were in big trouble.

In an attempt to remain as close as possible to the protective cover of our squadron and group, I turned rather sharply to the right in an attempt to catch them as they rallied to the right after bombs away. This maneuver proved to be a near disaster, because with only two engines operating and the very thin air at this altitude, a very rapid loss of altitude resulted. I saw my squadron and group rapidly disappear. I was alone in a crippled aircraft , about 400 miles inside enemy territory with the finest combat crew in the entire USAAF, but at this time things looked very dim for us. Our work would be rather structured for the next few hours.

To enemy fighters our crippled Fort would be an easy kill. I called several times for escort fighter assistance--none responded--the only fighters to be seen were ME-109s. There wasn't a P-38 or P-51 to be seen anywhere. As a matter of fact, in all my 66 missions I do not recall seeing any friendly fighters after we had reached the IP inbound, prior to target, unless there were some clouds around and the fighters were lost and needed help navigating back to Italy.

To discourage enemy fighter attacks, I maneuvered the Fort in a series of steep turns, during which I encountered severe turbulence (probably prop wash) and the Fort stalled violently (it may have been a high speed stall) and entered a spin to the left. The enemy fighters apparently assumed another Fortress kill because we saw them no more. As Todd and I struggled to regain control of the spinning Fort, my forefinger, left hand, reached for the "bailout" switch. The lives of eight other fighting Americans depended on my judgment as to the proper bail out time. It is extremely difficult to bail out of a large spinning aircraft because centrifugal forces (forces moving outward from the center of a spinning body), if sufficiently strong, can prevent movement in any direction except outward, thus preventing movement to a bail out exit.

To the best of my knowledge no one had ever pulled a B-17 out of a spin, but since we had plenty of altitude, somewhere above 20,000 feet and nothing to lose, I decided to attempt a spin recovery. If successful, it would assure our crew an opportunity to bail out under much improved circumstances. The spin recovery technique learned from Joe Morall, my Lock Haven, Pennsylvania College flight instructor in a J-3 Piper Cub and my AAF flight instructor, movie star Robert Cummings, in a PT-17 at the Mira Loma Flight Academy at Oxnard, were utilized. Power off, elevator controls (stick) or in the B-17 the yoke, forward, hard opposite rudder until the spin rotation stops, then gently ease back on the yoke (elevator) and return to level flight. In the Cub at Lock Haven and the PT-17 at Oxnard this had been a simple and enjoyable maneuver. But in a spinning Fort, it was different.

With the power off on the two operating engines (numbers 1 and 3) and the other two engines (numbers 2 and 4) with their propellers feathered, the vertically spinning Fortress rushed earthward. (I would hit the bail out switch at 12,000 feet if the spin recovery technique was not effective). Both Todd and I took on the right rudder, while holding the yoke forward and throttles closed. After several rapid rotations, the Fort's rate of spin rotation began to slow and as we passed somewhere in the vicinity of 13,000 or 14,000 feet, going straight down, the spin rotation stopped and we began the recovery with the indicated air speed very high indeed--much in excess of the maximum red line placarded speed of 300 mph.

During the recovery from the vertical dive, the elevators would not move, so, we used the elevator trim tab and completed the recovery somewhere in the vicinity of 8,000 to 10,000 feet. But we still kept losing altitude slowly at about 300 feet a minute. Both of the operating engines had really cooled down during the long dive and spin from somewhere in excess of 20,000 feet. Each had to be warmed up before I could apply sufficient engine power to maintain near level flight. I would really need those engines before that day was over, so the extra care didn't cost anything but altitude.

While warming up the two operating engines (numbers 1 and 3) I trimmed the Fort for straight flight and took account of the situation.

There were no enemy aircraft in sight, so now the crew could bail out safely. If time permitted I planned to put the Fort on auto-pilot, establish a gentle turn, then inform the crew by interphone that bail out was imminent. I'd then hit the bail out switch and if lucky we would all land close together and perhaps be able to avoid the Hun and return through the underground to fly and fight again.

After several minutes I increased power to 42 inches of manifold pressure and 2450 rpm. This power setting permitted me to maintain an air speed of approximately 115 mph, but we continued to lose altitude. We were still in the general vicinity of the target, but things were not all that bad, so why bail out now when we might land in unfriendly hands. Better we get a little further from the target where we might receive kinder and more helpful treatment from the local inhabitants. A quick check of the maps revealed that we were about 50 miles west, northwest of the Rumanian city of Bucharest. It might be possible to nurse our wounded Fortress a little closer to the western boundary of Rumania and Bulgaria, perhaps even to the eastern foothills of the coastal mountain range of Yugoslavia where friendly Chetniks or Partisans might save us from POW fate.

By now our altitude was approximately 1,500 feet above the ground and I added maximum power on numbers 1 and 3 engines to maintain level flight, with the air speed only slightly above stall. A closer check of the maps revealed that the Fort would be required to climb at least 2,000 feet to cross the eastern foothills of the Coastal mountain range and at least 6,000 feet to cross the Coastal range itself. I knew this was impossible. Our two operating engines were long over-stressed and could fail at any time.

The moment of decision with respect to bail out, crash landing or continue the flight was rapidly approaching. I must decide before reaching the eastern foothills and within 30 minutes we would be at those foothills. In order to lighten the load I ordered the crew to throw overboard everything not absolutely necessary. With the decrease in weight, the Fort flew better. I knew that the engines could not withstand these high power settings indefinitely and, after evaluating all of the circumstances, it became painfully clear that the situation was hopeless. To continue the flight defied all logical and rational thought. My fighting spirit and will to win began to fade. I realized full well that when I activated the bail out switch, our contribution as a crew to the Allied victory in Europe would be over. We would become a liability to our country instead of an asset. How I hated that thought and the thought of becoming a POW of the Krauts.

During these moments of personal stress I am sure that I asked for divine guidance when the most unusual event I have ever experienced occurred--over my headset and I presume the headsets of the entire crew, we heard loud and clear..."O beautiful for spacious skies, for amber waves of grain..." As if by magic, my fighting spirit and will to win snapped back. I could feel the hair on the back of my neck bristle, then with tears of courage, pride and patriotism swelling my eyes I informed the crew that we were returning to our base in Italy. I have no recollection as to what altitude we reached as we passed over the crest of the Coastal mountain range as I was too busy keeping her flying. I know we just made it by the skin of our teeth.

On landing and prior to dismissing the crew I made the comment "wasn't that great music we heard over in Rumania?" To which they replied, "what music?". I am certain I heard it or had some power greater than all of us taken me by the hand and guided my every thought and act during those most stressful hours of my life? It was virtually impossible, from an engineering point of view, to climb over mountains and sustain flight for over four hours, pulling maximum power on only two engines.

*   *   *

Fear Of Death

John Plummer's story of his spectacular 12,000 foot fall enabled him to embrace a philosophy thought out under duress, but finalized in a compelling state of mind that I believe is a worthy addendum to his "Tailspin". The following is a rational observation of his emotional reaction to aerial combat in his own words. He begins:

Webster defines fear in many ways, none of which totally satisfies the fear experienced by a combat airman. His fears begin at the I.P. where the bomb run begins. The I.P. has the usual variable 90 degree turning point, either right or left, to confuse enemy ack ack. It's on the bomb run which lasts anywhere between five and eight minutes that fear sets in if it hasn't already.

Road map to the target from the I.P. usually is hundreds of flak bursts directly ahead. That's your bombing altitude and the enemy knows it. From experience you know a direct hit on a B-17 in your formation will kill ten men. Bursts of flak are not selective. A near miss can bounce the Fort around sending a shower of fragments in all directions. They clatter and clang as they strike and penetrate the aircraft. In my crew of ten there were six casualties (including myself), two serious.

Fear has a cumulative affect. It builds up mission after mission. When you arrive on the bomb run you are terrified. Great amounts of adrenaline pumps into the blood stream. As you continue inflexibly on the run, you function as though you were in a partial state of suspended animation. You are so up tight that if you were hit you probably wouldn't feel it at the moment.

Even though I loved the B-17 Flying Fortress, the name "fortress" is misleading. When you think of a fortress, your mind conjures up extensive and massive horizontal defensive structures. The defensive structure in our Flying Fortress, its outside surface, its skin, is made of an aluminum alloy about as thick as the cover of a book. Defensively, the fortresses of old had only one axis to protect. That was its horizontal axis. In the B-17, all approaches (top, bottom, side, above) were subject to attack. Imagine the waist gunners standing near upright and being shot at from below with nothing but a thin sheet of aluminum to protect their bottom side. My gunner got it. My bombardier, with nothing to protect him but the same thin aluminum and the plexiglas nose, got it. My top turret gunner in a greenhouse got it. My ball turret gunner, whose turret could get stuck when its electrical mechanism was hit and unable to get out, got it.

Vulnerable B-17 crew members to enemy action we've just discussed. But lead crews and their vulnerability is paramount to my premise that these people were subject to an added degree of that fear of death. Principal enemy targets were aircraft flying Group and Squadron lead. If the leads, especially the Group lead, got shot down, the effectiveness of the mission would be seriously compromised. The inevitable fear persists. All flyers know it, but a corner on the market of fear has to go to the lead crews--both Group and Squadron.

Fear of death in aerial combat is unique in that it doesn't occur on, or in the earth, where nature intends we humans to live and die. Fear of death does exist in the strange hostile environment of the upper atmosphere where temperatures and atmospheric pressures are low. Five miles up is a long way when you're forced to fall down. Fear of that long terminal descent in or out of an exploding aircraft is the bane of every airman's subconscious thought. Those who flew the bombers of World War II shared the apprehension and anxiety of this fear. Only they could know it and might or might not experience it during their combat tour of duty.

CHAPTER 11

Slice of History

It's best I trace the beginnings of my 348th squadron and the people who activated it. It's better yet to know the history of the 15th Air Force and its reason for being because it was their dictates that decided how the air war was to consume us. From Walla Walla, Washington where our squadron was born in 1942 to North Africa and Italy our small but significant input into the war effort is a given.

There's no better way to begin our history than to cite the people who started our 348th squadron. I sat with three of our squadron's original pilots at a 99th Bomb Group reunion business luncheon in San Diego, California in May of 1996. The first phase of training involved crews from Boise, Idaho in late September, 1942. My table companions were among those crews. They were Warren "Whit" Whitmore, Edward "Mac" McLaughlin and Earl Davis.

Whit worked a lot with General Doolittle and flew often as wing leader. He was instrumental in forming the squadron at Boise. On his 50th mission he got shot up over Foggia and managed to get his aircraft back to Tunis still leading the Group before finally having to bail out of his stricken B-17. Jules Horowitz on that September 7, 1943 was piloting a ship in Maj. Whitmore's element while Mac, who still to this day had vivid memories of the mission, led the second element behind Whit.

According to Horowitz, Whit's controls were so badly shot up that when they got back to Africa, Whit and his crew bailed out and the plane crashed. Horowitz's diary indicated they were attacked that day by some 40 to 60 fighters. "Our problem," he said, "was very accurate flak. My three plane element was clobbered. Our plane had over one hundred holes," he added. His navigator was hit in the chest and went into shock. The bombardier of No. 3 plane was killed.

But it was the July 5th raid to Sicily's Gerbini airdrome (already discussed in Chapter VIII) that would leave an indelible mark in the record books of the 348th squadron. The 99th was to earn its first of two Presidential Unit Citations. The first strike at Gerbini was actually scheduled for July 4th, but because of a navigational error, the mission was aborted. Whit checked Mac out on that aborted raid for subsequent squadron lead. He flew as Mac's copilot in Mac's plane with Mac's crew.

Earl Davis was a senior flight leader and, like Whit, was another of the 348th's original pilots out of Boise. The tactical importance of the Gerbini mission could not be minimized. Enemy aircraft needed to be neutralized to ensure a successful Sicilian invasion. The 348th squadron was a designated participant and nine of its Flying Fortresses would participate. Three would go down including Earl. It was his 32nd mission. He was captured in Sicily, moved as a POW to Italy as the Germans retreated and finally to Germany where he finished out the war.

Edward "Mac" McLaughlin was the third man at our table that day who shared many of the same experiences of his two companions. He was with the original 348th cadre and one of its first pilots. Mac spoke of his tenth mission as the 99th fanned out over the North African desert in an attempt to catch the Desert Fox, General Erwin Rommel, commander of the renowned Afrika Korps. All they managed to do was lose seven planes including his own when forced to bail out because of bad weather.

These three men played dramatic roles in the formation of the 348th squadron back in the states. On Feb. 20, 1943 the squadron moved to Oklahoma City and on March 19th left there for a staging area at Camp Kilmer, N. J. two days later. The squadron left Camp Kilmer on April 23rd and boarded ship in Brooklyn, New York for overseas duty. They were at sea on April 29th. The transport carrying the squadron personnel to their overseas destination lost its convoy because one of its two engines blew up. Nonetheless, Africa was sighted on May 11, 1943 and the squadron arrived in Oran, North Africa the next day. It joined with combat crews at Navarin on May 25th.

An overview of squadron history should take into account the 15th Air Force itself. Maj. General James H. Doolittle of the Tokyo raid fame served as the 15th's first commander. On May 9, 1943 the North African campaign had been successfully concluded with an Allied victory over the Axis powers. The 15th Air Force was constituted on October 30, 1943 and activated on November 1st at Tunis, Tunisia. Although the 15th Air Force was the newest numbered air force at the time, it was initially composed of veteran units such as the 97th and 301st Bomb Groups. Predating official formation of the 15th Air Force, the bomb groups above and others including the 99th flew under the command of Gen. Doolittle's 12th Air Force. The 15th started its existence late in 1943 with experienced heavy and medium bomber units of the 1942-43 period, with both 12th and 9th contributing groups. It was assigned four B-17 groups and two B-24 groups and for a brief time in the beginning included two B-25 groups and three B-26 groups. Attached fighter groups made the 15th Air Force second only in size to the Eighth Air Force among overseas air commands.

General Doolittle and Lord Tincher, British Air Commander, addressed the 99th at Navarin on June 14th. Later the squadron moved to a base at Oudna, Tunisia, near Tunis. There they fought the war until the outfit was moved to Foggia, Italy after the Allies had secured Sicily and the Italian boot.

Headquarters Fifteenth was able to close down officially and reopen for business the same day, December 1, 1943, 475 miles closer to its assigned targets across the Mediterranean at Bari, Italy. They occupied 200 rooms in a large, modern office building formerly occupied by the Italian Air Force as a zone headquarters. Existing air fields in the Bari/Foggia area were a mess from previous Allied bombings. Enormous engineering problems were involved. Steel mats had to be set in place to keep the bombers from bogging down in the spongy turf. Steady winter rains added to the misery of men and machines. Even an auxiliary road network had to be built.

My squadron flew its first mission from Foggia on Dec. 14th, two weeks after coming under the umbrella of the 15th. Their target was Athens, Greece and it was completed without casualties. It wasn't until five days later that the 348th suffered its first loss under heavy attack by 40 to 50 enemy aircraft defending Innsbruck, Austria.

One of the most controversial missions flown in the whole war was the raid on February 15, 1944 that targeted the historic Benedictine abbey of Monte Cassino. The assault, which also involved the 99th, was designed to end the Fifth Army's month-long stalemate before the Germans' Gustav Line south of Rome. Lt. Gen. Ira C. Eaker did not approve of the abbey bombing, contending it would serve no useful military purpose. Whether the Germans used it as an outpost is still a matter of dispute, but continued pressure from ground commanders caused Gen. Eaker to acquiesce. There were two raids on the mountain abbey. The second, March 15th, also joined in by the 99th, saw a mass saturation bombing designed to eliminate German resistance. The town was destroyed, but the Allies were unable to break through at the time which more or less validated Gen. Eaker's original position.

A postscript to Ploesti and the 99th's participation beginning April 5, 1944 would have it that despite the massive and crippling attack on August 1, 1943 the eleven remaining refineries still had a production capacity of eight million tons--a reduction of only one million as a result of that so-called surprise attack in August the year before.The B-24 Liberator attackers flew then under the banner of the Eighth Air Force. The 15th Air Force, at the time, didn't exist, but it did function the next year when it began a series of strikes beginning April 5th and lasting until August 24, 1944 when Russian land forces moved into the area. Our 99th Bomb Group participated in these difficult and dangerous series of raids.

The Flying Fortress was designated a heavy bomber and its primary effectiveness depended on its strategic capabilities. Ploesti was a good example of this. The bombing of Monte Cassino was an excellent example of its tactical deployment whether you agree with its morality or not. Blasting bridges in support of ground offensives was an infrequent occurrence, but there were times the heavies were called on to do just that.

The largest tactical operation ever undertaken by the 15th Air Force was "Operation Wowser". It began April 15, 1945 and was considered the air phase of Lt. Gen. Mark Clark's Fifth Army breakthrough at Bologna, Italy. That city had been the anchor of the Germans' Gothic Line since the previous September. Practically every flyable bomber--in all 1,235--bombed troop concentrations, gun emplacements and strong points. Three days after the operation began my squadron got a chance to participate. On April 18th, my twenty-sixth mission, our target was enemy troop concentrations at Bologna. We carried 3,000 pounds of frag bombs to the enemy concentrations. We made a visual run at 20,000 feet but I could look down and see burning buildings below, an indication of the heavy fighting underway.

After this, missions were directed at preventing German escape from Italy. Food drops to inhabitants of Northern Italy and the evacuation of POWs by B-17s converted to cargo and passenger carriers, signaled the beginning of the end. By VE Day, 5,998 people had been returned by air, surface vessels or on foot through enemy lines. In over 300 successful operations, men were brought back safely from Tunisia, Italy, France, Switzerland, Greece, Albania, Bulgaria, Rumania, Hungary, Yugoslavia, Poland, Czechoslovakia, Austria and Germany.

After the fall of Bologna on April 21st, the German forces in Italy surrendered on April 29th. Flying Fortresses of the 15th Air Force flew their last mission on May 1st against the main rail station and marshaling yards at Salzburg, Austria.

The mission we flew to Prague, Czechoslovakia on March 25th, where we targeted Kbely airdrome, is considered by Headquarters, 15th Air Force to be the last real strategic air assault. In this case it was airfields and tank plants in the Prague region and we of Neely's crew were a part of it. My last mission of the war could be said to have been strategic even though we flew it as late as April 25th to bomb the Herman Goring Works near Linz.

As far away from us as it actually was, we of the 99th were called on to support Americans trapped in the Battle of the Bulge. Our efforts, including our December 26th and 28th, 1944 missions to oil refineries at Blechammer, and Regensburg, Germany, effectively curtailed resurgent German oil production during that grim battle.

As German resistance crumpled and Allied armies approached the borders of the Third Reich, the 15th Air Force conducted its first assault against Berlin on March 24th, attacking the Daimler-Benz tank engine works. German jets shot down two B-17s, (none from the 99th) the last aircraft to be lost by the Fifteenth in World War II.

Combat operations for the 99th Bomb Group officially began on March 31, 1943 and ended April 26, 1945. During its two-year combat history, the men of the 348th squadron earned one Distinguished Service Cross (S/Sgt Ben Warmer), eight Silver Stars, 19 Bronze Stars, 96 DFCs, 1118 Air Medals and 4,329 oak leaf clusters to the Air Medal. Our squadron destroyed more than 150 enemy aircraft. Its campaigns included Air Offensive, Europe; Tunisia, Sicily, Naples-Foggia, Anzio, Rome-Arno, Southern France, North Appenines, Rhineland, Central Europe and Po Valley.

Credit the 15th Air Force with destroying fifty percent of all the fuel production capacity in Europe and about the same percentage of the German fighter productive capacity. Its combat personnel made 148,955 heavy bomber sorties against the enemy. It lost 3,364 aircraft during the war; 400 of which were fighters. There were 2,703 men killed in action, 12,359 missing in action, and 2,553 wounded in action. Enemy aircraft destroyed by 15th Air Force airmen numbered 1,946.

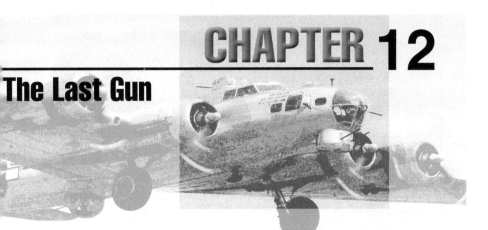

CHAPTER 12

The Last Gun

Jim Bruno is in his early eighties now; a happy husband to Merlyn, who he married in June, 1992. His first wife, Irene, died of cancer in 1985. Our first meeting was in the fall of 1993 at our bomb group's reunion in Ontario, California. Our correspondence was to continue over the years, because of the book he was writing entitled "Beyond Fighter Escort" and because of my desire to include one of his exploits in my manuscript. At opportune times Jim and me and our wives would continue to meet at other reunions. Also, Jim and Merlyn had a condo at Cape Canaveral, Florida. It was only a few blocks from my sister's condo. And in the spring of 1998 we saw each other on a couple of pleasant social get-togethers.

Gad, he was a handsome devil in that leather helmet, goggles, white scarf and leather jacket fifty-seven years ago. He really was a typical airplane jockey who lived and breathed flying probably from that August day in 1927 when he watched Charles Lindbergh fly over the family farm in his "Spirit of St. Louis". It wasn't until December, 1939, at the age of twenty-one, that he took his first flying lesson in a Piper Cub at Waukesha County Airport. The next year he and a friend decided to purchase a Curtis OX-5 Pheasant biplane. A short time later he bought his friend's share out.

He was a dashing cadet out of pilot training in 1942 who loved the girls as much as he loved flying. Orders sent him to Gowan Field, Boise, Idaho after graduating from advanced twin engine school at Roswell, New Mexico on September 29, 1942. The next day he married the love of his

Fifty dollars down earned Jim Bruno this OX-5 Curtiss Pheasant biplane in December, 1939. He subsequently came up with the $175 balance. In 1940 Bruno learned to fly alone after taking his first flying lesson the year before in a Piper Cub. That's Jim holding the right wing.

life, Irene in a ceremony conducted by a Protestant chaplain who married a Catholic and a Lutheran. Matrons and best man were Mormons. A purely ecumenical beginning.

Jim was ordered to Gowan Field, Boise, Idaho. It was there the 99th Bomb Group was being formed. The oldest man on their crew, a tailgunner, Jack Guerard, 35 years old, was to go on to become a gunner of distinction. In one day the South Carolina native would shoot down four enemy aircraft and by the time he'd completed his fifty missions he became an enlisted ace credited with seven destroyed. He died in 1992.

Captain Harry Burrell, Bruno's B-17 instructor, picked him for his copilot and they flew to North Africa in February of 1943 to begin and complete a 50 mission tour of duty with the 347th squadron. It was on the leg of their South American flight to Belem that they saw Crew 19's airborne but damaged airplane "Gremlin Castle" and its missing rudder and tail. That airplane carried the illustrious Ben Warmer who was to gain national attention as a waist gunner. The midair collision--destination North Africa, delayed Warmer and his crew for two months, but nobody was hurt in the incident.

The story I'm about to have Jim relate has to do with his wild mission to Messina, Sicily about six weeks before the invasion of that island off the Italian boot. The raid, flown on May 25, 1943, had H.B. (Bud) Bankhead as first pilot with Jim as copilot, ends with an extraordinary twist. After hitting his target and being hammered by hordes of Nazi fighters before and after the bomb run, losing his No. 4 engine to flak, a radioman mortally wounded, and controls shot out--he tells a frightful story of an extraordinary mission, one that was to earn him the DFC.

Entry into his log book that day told only half the story. He wrote: "Bombed oil dump; No. 4 engine hit; lost right aileron; Messerschmitt 210 attack." A cryptic account of the mission all right, but devoid of any enhancement, any expression. And this was so typical of the character of Jim Bruno, a jocular fellow then and a light hearted, fun-filled individual today.

He tells of a dogged and determined German pilot trying for a B-17 kill with repeated attacks on his crippled bomber--alone and virtually at the mercy of its antagonist. The savaged bomber crew dumped guns--everything they could to lighten the load. The wounded B-17E choked its way south above white caps, perilously close to the sea, as it tried to sustain flight back to its North African base. And then an incredible act of courage unfolds as Guerard, having moved back out of the tail and armed only with Bruno's .45 caliber pistol, begins firing through the open hatch over the radio room at the determined and menacing ME-210.

Bruno's graphic portrayal of this unlikely and desperate action depicts his frantic fight to survive against all odds. The crew's indomitable spirit under extreme duress prevails in a display of courage unsurpassed in the most trying circumstance. They had nothing to shoot back with except Bruno's .45 caliber pistol against a German fighter pilot aching for a Flying Fortress kill.

Bruno Tells His Story
In a chapter from his book "Beyond Fighter Escort"

Not very many bomber crews experienced a mission like this. Pilots at our base listened in disbelief as they heard how Bankhead, with his crippled bomber, outmaneuvered and out-fought the Nazis' best twin-engine fighter-bomber of the day.

This 25th day in May began with an early assembly of all crews in the briefing tent. We were eager to get the scoop on that day's mission. Our group itself had flown over twenty bombing missions with our crew having gone on 15 of them. And never had enemy planes or antiaircraft fire been a threat to our group. All our planes had survived every assault as our ground crews became accustomed to seeing all our B-17s return to base.

Conditions were bound to change--things were too easy and our lives were uneventful. Wars are not won or even lost this way. Someone has to pay the price. Something is bound to happen sooner or later.

Col. Upthegrove, speaking in his usual quiet voice, announced that this would be the longest mission to date. It would take us to the oil dumps of Messina, Sicily. Then he casually added: "Gentlemen, this mission is beyond fighter escort." It was to be beyond the fuel range of our P-38 fighter escort. We stirred in our seats and began to talk to each other in excited stage whispers.

The colonel pointed out the location of all enemy fighter bases along our route to the target. There were plenty of them. The odds were against us, but the job had to be done. To make matters worse, at the target we could expect enemy fighters to rise up from both Sicily and the mainland of Italy situated only a few miles across the Straits of Messina.

The round trip would be 1200 miles--a long grueling journey. This meant we would have to fight to conserve every gallon of gas. That is, we'd fight for every drop of fuel if we wanted to get back to home base. The flight engineers were instructed to "top off" all tanks after the engines were pre-flighted that morning. This procedure was to ensure that no one would run short of fuel. We'd have enough other worries during this seven and one-half hour mission.

We had been pampered long enough. Our previous flights had been of just half this planned distance with our stay over hostile territory being less than ten to twenty minutes in duration. Enemy fighters hadn't been too much of a problem, mainly because they were usually diverted to another target that was being struck about 15 minutes earlier by another American bomber group with considerable more missions to their credit.

That B-17 Bomb Group was the 98th. They had come to Africa from bombing out of England. These were veteran crews in the art in bringing destruction to the German war machine. We respected them. We were green at the art of bombing, having done practice missions in the past three months.

But now this was it! We were going to be tested. It was clear to us that each Fortress would have to depend on its gunners and their .50 caliber guns to get through the lengthy gauntlet--and get through twice.

"There will be a lot of antiaircraft fire coming at us during the bomb run," I muttered to Lt. Bankhead. "Batteries in both Sicily and Italy will be zeroing in on our formation."

The weather officer assured us of good flying conditions to the target and on the return trip. This seemed to infer to us we would all come back from what to us now seemed like projected suicide. The weather officer could be cheerful. He wasn't going. Then we went through his routine ritual of wishing us good luck--which meant it was time for me to leave and fulfill my assigned task of picking up the escape kits for the crew. The prospects of surviving capture so far from friendly territory seemed remote.

Lt. Bankhead broke the news about the mission to our gunners as we jumped from the jeep. To our surprise, they were enthusiastic. They immediately got to work, checking and rechecking both their weapons and the necessary ammunition.

"I want to see more action," said one of the youngsters, "we just haven't tangled enough with these Kraut-eaters yet," he added.

"I've got confidence in you fellows," I replied. Still in my own heart, I hated to think about those German Messerschmitts which soon would be boring into our formation from every angle to fire at us.

Out of the twenty-four planes in our group, Lt. Bankhead and I had the unenviable position of being the last plane over the target. We were in the last flight of the last squadron. The flak was always much more accurate, naturally, after the first wave had been measured for altitude. The enemy also had time on the ground to calculate your course. If you were unlucky enough to be crippled by flak--and had to lag behind, you'd be a sitting duck for the enemy fighters who always waited for that very thing to happen. They liked to engage single planes who couldn't keep up. They were outside the umbrella of safety afforded by a well armed formation.

Major Harry Burrell, our squadron commander, was not scheduled for the mission that day. Capt. William Clark would lead us. First lieutenant Dean Shields led the second element, which included our plane.

Soon we all became airborne and took a heading for the coast of Africa in the vicinity of Phillipeville. When the armada of 24 fortresses reached the Mediterranean, we were at an altitude of one thousand feet. We then dropped to five hundred feet over the water in hopes of escaping detection by enemy radar. As was my custom, I took a last yearning look back toward "home". This time, of course, there was no reassuring umbrella of fighters to escort us. Being in the last plane of the formation, I saw nothing but empty sky. In this theater of war, enemy fighters always concentrated their attacks on the last three planes over the target--if we were to get that far.

We were in a loose formation with over 200 miles of water to navigate before the scheduled climb to the bombing altitude of 23,000 feet. At that point some twenty Messerschmitts began their attack upon us. Apparently they were from Trapani Air Base in Sicily and they'd been warned of our approach. There we were with all that distance to go and we had plenty of trouble already. As we hadn't escaped radar detection, we were ordered to climb to our assigned altitude and close formation.

Now we had better fire power and fortunately for us all planes operated smoothly as the engines strained at full throttle to get us up to the planned altitude. Our gunners successfully fought off the first wave of Nazis with no damage being inflicted on our planes. After traveling another one hundred miles eastward, most enemy fighters rose to challenge us. They too broke off the attack after a bit of furious action. They returned to their bases without causing any damage to our planes. The enthusiasm of our gunners was paying off.

Our objective was the supply center for huge amounts of fuel which kept enemy airplanes, tanks, trucks and ships moving constantly against us. Our mission was three and a half nerve-straining hours old when we arrived at the target area. Enemy fighters, warned of our coming long in advance, were up high to meet us. Many diving attacks were made upon us before we could even start the bomb run. But our group would not be driven off. Our colonel stubbornly continued on.

We were seconds away from releasing our bombs when a large puff of black smoke below our right wing turned out to be an accurately exploding antiaircraft shell. No. 4 propeller spun wildly out of control. All efforts to feather it were in vain. The burst had struck the oil line at the governor. We managed to keep in formation until the bombs were away, but soon we had to face up to the fact that our wildly spinning propeller was creating a tremendous drag on the plane. We were in trouble. All efforts to stay beneath the group failed, and the widening gap was immediately noticed by a squadron of fighters waiting for just such a situation. The gunners reported eight fighters were attacking.

As the squadron of Messerschmitts singled out our plane for destruction, Joe, our navigator, excitedly got on the intercom asking for help. It was his feeling that they all were attacking at his area of fire. Lt. Bankhead told him to get off the intercom and let me direct the fire. I had already instructed the gunners to hold their fire until the German fighters were in range. We could not afford to waste ammunition. The men settled down and really gave that squadron plenty of lead from their .50 caliber machine guns. Sgt. May, our ball turret gunner, exploded one enemy plane, Joe claimed one and Jack, the tailgunner, had no trouble getting one. Our waist gunner and assistant engineer, Frank J. Kovac, got the fourth one. The battle was fought all the way from the bombing altitude of twenty-three thousand feet down to ten thousand feet. We were steadily losing precious altitude, but the remaining fighters had seen enough of us. They headed back to land, either low on gas or out of ammunition.

That helped, but by this time our formation was long out of sight. Another bomber from the 416th squadron had also been damaged and we heard the pilot report over the radio that his flight controls were hit. One of his wing men had dropped back to protect him. Now they would try to determine what could be done to regain control. Not one of our wing men, however, felt it was necessary to drop back to protect us. The flight leader ignored his tail gunner's suggestion to help us. "The are too far gone and won't make it," he told his gunner.

But our own problems were multiplying too. Our No. 4 propeller was vibrating the plane so violently that the engine cowlings flew off. Next, the propeller burned out the thrust bearing and pulled out the melting crankcase. As if this wasn't enough trouble, the prop slipped under the wing and severed the right aileron control cable. An order to bail out was readied at the height of the vibration, but this was soon changed with the order to prepare for a water landing (ditching).

It was at this time that me and other crew members feared the unknown. I could hear praying over the intercom. My whole life flashed before me. I glimpsed at the times I was not very nice to my mother and thought of the letter to my sister, Catherine, back at the tent to be mailed. Did I tell her I would be home soon? I had never experienced this feeling before or after. The missions had never left me apprehensive about not returning back to base. But this time as the prop was vibrating the plane as if to tear off the wing, I looked to the sun going down in the west and prayed to God to let me see just one more sunset. He was to answer my prayers. The rosary my parish priest had blessed and given me was always carried on my person, too.

Our tailgunner, Jack, did not hear the word "prepare". He only heard "bail out". He had jettisoned his exit door, then decided to crawl back to the waist compartment. No one had bailed out and he found the "prepare to bail out" had been changed to "prepare for a water landing." He was happy he was not out there over the blue Mediterranean dangling in his parachute while we continued on toward the coast of Africa.

We were forced to fly with full right rudder and full left aileron to keep from spinning out of control. The crew was instructed to lighten the plane and throw all loose equipment overboard to reduce the hazard of a water landing. Out went guns, ammunition, items of clothing and everything else that could be lifted from or torn away from the interior of our plane. Our waist gunner even through a pair of shoes out the window.

The impending prospect of ditching loomed as a singular problem to me as I had not learned to swim during the preparation for overseas transition. I had no one to blame for this unhappy predicament but myself. The swimming instructor had tried her best to teach me.

The Mediterranean looked calm and beautiful from ten thousand feet, but once we had dropped down to five hundred feet we saw that this was actually an angry sea, ready to swallow us and our entire B-17. We regarded the waves and swells as highly menacing to a plane with the little maneuverability we had.

I was calling off the dwindling air speed of our disabled plane and had lowered 20 degrees of flaps on instruction of Lt. Bankhead. Each second of time delayed the inevitable contact and the uncertain fate the sea had in store for us. Landing air speed of 90 mph found us still airborne and the plane refused to stall for a landing. We continued on, just above the water, with the greenish waves seeming to reach out for us and almost grab us. I could hardly bear to look at those cold waves. Instead, I glanced at Lt. Bankhead and read his face at once. We would not have to brave survival in the water after all! He inched the throttles forward and got the air speed up to 100 mph. The plane responded sluggishly to his efforts. Every time an engine missed our hearts skipped a beat.

Joe Boyle, our navigator, was called forward from the radio room where the crew had retreated for the ditching. "Give us a course for home," Lt. Bankhead said. "We're going to try to make it," he added. We had been flying due west from the ditching; now, we made a drastic turn to a southerly course.

Our engineer, also the top turret gunner, was instructed to pump the gas from the No. 4 engine to the tanks of the three other engines. To do this he had to pump the gas across to the left side of the plane, then transfer it back to the right tank of No. 3 engine. The transfer was begun, but soon our luck was to change.

We saw a twin engine plane that appeared to be coming to our rescue. No doubt our radio operator's "Mayday" signal was being answered. It looked to me like a Bristol Beaufighter. The English used them as fighters and bombers. The plane climbed several thousand feet above us. We saw it diving at us from the right side, the copilot's side. With his guns blazing at us, we soon found out it was the German's best fighter, the feared ME-210. It had cannons in the wing and guns that could shoot from the side of its fuselage. I fretted over the fact that the enemy plane could do 400 mph and determined I wasn't going to enjoy being this guy's clay pigeon. The thought of ditching in hopes that the enemy only wanted to claim our plane was quickly abandoned when his first pass came from one o'clock high with machine guns and wing cannon blazing at us.

"Thank God! I saved one box of ammo when we jettisoned everything else," said our bombardier. "Just one box. It's in the nose," he added. Our top turret gunner quickly loaded his guns and the enemy became more cautious in his attack after he almost absorbed a short burst from us. Each time the German fighter went into a dive, Lt. Bankhead would retard the throttles, dive to the water, call for 20 degree flaps and pull up while turning inside the fighter. This would cause our eager enemy to pull up as he began firing. His shots would go over us.

Our strategy couldn't work indefinitely. Common sense prevailed. The enemy soon found out that a pass from the tailgunner's position was effective since he wasn't firing. He had exhausted his ammo in preparation for the ditching. Also, the German pilot must have known a low pass at our tail would cause the upper turret guns to cut out while shooting. There was little defense against these devilish passes on the part of the enemy pilot and not much evasive action we could take. We were more or less trapped and he knew it.

A 20 mm cannon shell burst in the cockpit a few inches over my head. The pungent, choking smell of gun powder dried our throats. I saw blood spurt from Lt. Bankhead's throttle hand. I gestured to take over the controls. He shook his head and bit his lip a trifle harder and tightened his grasp on the throttle, refusing to be stopped by a handful of hot shrapnel.

The only casualty on my side of the cockpit was my wife's smiling photo. I had put it in the compass correction card in front of me and close to the windshield. Shrapnel shattered the photo and the aluminum frame. I was unscathed.

These attacks from behind us were hurting--although the enemy pilot had wasted much of his ammunition before discovering our weakness. A cannon shell struck our radio operator, Sgt. Fred Manship, a wonderful 19 year old from Pennsylvania. He was substituting for our regular radioman, Sgt. Kovac, who was ill. Fred had been busy sending out the "Mayday", "Mayday" distress signal while we were attempting to ditch. He had to repair the flak damaged radio wiring before he could send out the signals. And now, gravely wounded, our gunners attended him as the German strafed from the rear. Ironically, Fred's "Mayday" signal was answered by the German whose shell was to mortally wound him.

Our enemy was encountering problems, too. After 20 minutes of trying to cripple us beyond that which enemy flak had done, he ran out of cannon and machine gun ammunition. He made a bluffing frontal attack from my side again. We were surprised there was no fire.

Our tailgunner, sensing the fighter's ammo was exhausted, came into the cockpit from the radio room and pulled my .45 from my hip. He went back to the radio room which had the hatch open. We could see the

German pilot's red hair and grinning face covered with freckles as he thundered over the cockpit less than 15 feet overhead. Jack's heroic efforts were in vain as my gun misfired. I had cleaned it the day before and did not replace the firing pin in the correct position. Jack was sure he would have caused damage to the plane and pilot if the.45 had not misfired. We also felt a great opportunity was lost because of my inexperience with firearms.

We all breathed a sigh of relief as the enemy headed back toward the coast of Sicily. Lt. Bankhead again called our navigator forward to give us a course for the African coast. Having flown on a westerly course during the dog fight, it was now time to head south as we had passed the western tip of Sicily. There was over one hundred fifty miles of water between us and the African coast. Then another one hundred fifty miles to our base.

Before approaching the African coast our fuel indicators were showing the tanks dangerously low. The warning lights were close to lighting up.We knew that Tunis had fallen to the Allies about a week earlier. It was decided to land at the Tunis airfield with the warning lights blinking on two of our fuel tanks. We had the British to thank for capturing Tunis.

Fred, our wounded radioman, was still conscious and in good spirits when we touched down on the short grass runway. As the railroad embankment loomed ahead, Lt.Bankhead went for the brakes. The hydraulic lines had been damaged. He quickly went for the emergency handles above our heads and we stopped a few yards short of the tracks. The British, seeing the crippled condition of our plane, had an ambulance waiting when we taxied to the hangar area.

Our first thoughts were to get Fred into the ambulance. Three of us stood outside the waist gun window as other gunners lifted our wounded radio operator out of the plane. I reached out to support his back as two gunners took hold of his head and feet. The palm of my outstretched hand was hardly enough to cover the gaping hole in his back. The compress was saturated with blood, as was my right hand when we placed him on the stretcher.

Fred was cheerful. "Thanks for getting me back to the coast," he said. "I don't feel too bad. I think I've got a fighting chance to make it," he added. He was rushed to the hospital, but with the Nazis driven out of Tunis, there was little reason for the hospital staff to be on duty. It was four hours before army attendants could turn him over to a doctor.

After we received our quarters for the night, Lt. Bankhead went to the hospital to check on Fred's condition. He returned about midnight to give us the sad news that "Freddie" did not make it.

It was with heavy hearts that we were driven back to our base by an army truck the next day. The men could not believe their eyes as we pulled onto the base. We had been reported lost over the target and our next of kin were wired that we were "missing in action." Capt. Burrell was most happy to see us. He told me he would have dreaded having to write to my wife, Irene, if we had not returned. As for our flight leader who was also supply officer, he had taken Lt. Bankhead's and my air mattresses and given them to other officers. He sheepishly had them returned.

The enlisted men must have had reservations about me for the first 15 missions. The first thing they said to me after the ambulance left for the hospital was: "Bruno, you really came through!" I guess they never had any doubt about Lt. Bankhead, but I had to prove to them under fire that I could work as a team.

Lt. Bankhead was recommended for the Silver Star and the rest of the crew for the Distinguished Flying Cross. After only a month we were told that only Lt. Bankhead would get an award. It would be changed to the DFC. The rest would not get anything. None of the others were upset with the decision. We felt that Lt. Bankhead deserved the higher award.

The following week a crew of mechanics went to Tunis to survey our crippled B-17. They found an unexploded 20 mm cannon shell in the No. 2 fuel tank. It was given to Lt. Bankhead as a souvenir. I was given the picture of my wife, Irene, in the aluminum frame of the compass correction card.

James Bruno's story in which the bizarre episode of the hand gun versus the ME-210 was surely a highlight of his combat career, occurs comparatively early in the war. The 99th Bomb Group was only 22 missions into the war when Bruno flew his memorable 16th raid.

In a time perspective preceding Bruno's Messina mission, truly the world was at war and had been since the Germans invaded Poland in September of 1939. Ten months before Bruno's spectacular flight, our US Marines were battling the Japanese on Guadalcanal. Five months before his hair raising experience, the Russians had concluded the giant and bloody battle at Stalingrad which marked the turning point of the war. And closer to home, three months before Bruno's storied exploit, the Americans suffered their first defeat at the hands of the Germans at Kasserine Pass in North Africa.

I would be remiss if I didn't mention what happened only five days before his Messina mission--I joined the army on May 20, 1943.

After the war Jim Bruno became an insurance adjuster and remained at this work for 35 years. He made this interesting comment about his civilian job. "It was easier flying those missions than deal with angry policy holders who presented inflated claims and threatened to cancel their policies if they did not get their way."

The idea of writing a book came to him in 1968 when his job found him on tornado duty in Omaha, Nebraska. While in Omaha he called at the Harry Burrell residence and was told by Harry's mother that he died of cancer two years earlier.

The book was intended to clarify unsavory incidents in his life. For example, the FBI was reading his letters in 1944 over an 18 month span to the man who befriended him and gave him his blessings to make it in the Army Air Corps--he was Dr. D. H. Bruns, a German fighter ace in WWI, who lived in Milwaukee. Dr. Bruns was a doctor and CAA flight examiner who had given Jim his medical certificate for civilian flying. His frequent letters to Dr. Bruns were held suspect by the FBI until Jim was completely cleared of any wrong-doing in a personal letter to him written by J. Edgar Hoover. The FBI director wrote Jim: "The investigation was a part of our national security work and not in any manner a reflection on you."

Another reason for his book was to respond to mean-spirited criticism leveled by his civilian instructors. Before the war they hated him and openly told his pilot friends he would never make it. They were sixth grade dropouts, according to Jim, and hated him for passing the college test required of high school graduates going into the Flying Cadets. They failed him for his private license after he got a telegram to report for pilot training in California.

A postscript on Lt. Bankhead is in order here. He became one of Delta Airlines top one hundred pilots out of 4000 employed. He flew the L-1011 at the time of his mandatory retirement at the age of 60.

CHAPTER 13

A Gunner's Tribute

Memorial Day, since the watered down version came along a few years back, has been a troublesome annoyance to me. To accommodate a three day holiday weekend last year (1998), the real Memorial Day was on Saturday, May 30th, but it was observed on Monday, May 25th--five days earlier. The realignment of dates for the sake of a long holiday venue of picnics and parties has completely obliterated the original meaning and intent of this special day created in 1866, a long time ago. A tiny village in upstate New York, Waterloo, saw the first tears shed for the honored dead of the Civil War. It's where Memorial Day had its beginning. Two years later General John A. Logan, Commander in Chief of Union forces, suggested Memorial Day or Decoration Day be observed every year henceforth on this day in May.

That single day of remembrance was meant to include a moment of sadness and remorse--a day of mourning set aside for those who gave their lives for our country in battle. In the villages I grew up in they used to read the Lincoln Gettysburg address to be followed by a contingent of National Guard soldiers, an armored vehicle or two, a fire truck or two or three, firemen, Boy Scouts and Girl Scouts and whatever. Always an attentive crowd, respectful of the flag when it went by. Later taps would be blown at the village cemetery along with the appropriate 21 gun salute. It would take seven soldiers firing three volleys to accomplish this, but it was always a fitting tribute to the departed.

After the parade the crowds would invariably gather at the

American Legion building for the usual summer delight--hot dogs, soda pop, potato salad, corn on the cob to be followed by another speech or two from Legion officers. They flocked to the beer tent after, ever mindful, however of their recently commemorated fallen comrades.

These were the Memorial Days I remember. There's always been a special place in my heart for Memorial Day--even in its watered down three day weekend version. And it was so in the year 1999 when the essence of Decoration Day was spelled out by Red, my tailgunner, as he described his emotions in finally finding our pilot, Bob Neely. Yes, he was the first of us to visit our pilot's grave just north of his Santa Barbara, California home. So close, and yet so far. It's thoughts of him and so many others like him that demand a time--a single day, if you will--to observe the holiday as it was meant to be. My eyes were full after reading this letter from Red to Don, our waist gunner and me, probably the only survivors of our B-17 combat crew. A more fitting tribute to a man we all remembered and respected would be hard to come by.

Red's letter: "My trip north this time was on a beautiful early spring day. Atascadere is at the high end of the Salinas Valley where they have a much colder winter. His cemetery was showing off with early flowers and flowering trees.

"The office person at the cemetery was ill that day so I was helped by two young men in their early twenties. I told them who I was looking for and who that person had been to me by showing them the picture of the six of us in front of The Old Lady. Turned out that they were both wild about B-17s and learning about the air war and the men who flew them.

"They were so polite and interested and called me sir with every question. They wanted to know who each person in the picture was and what position they flew in. Their attitude was really quite moving.

"I followed the guide in my car to his office. He then gave me the location to Bob's grave. He then left me after asking: 'Is there anything else I can do for you today, sir?' So I stood there for a while and thought about Bob and how sorry I was that I did not know where he was living as I had passed by on Route 101 so many times.

"It did not look like anyone had been there for some time. No flowers and there was dirt and leaves in the flower holder. I cleaned it out and found a smooth white stone and put it there to show someone had visited.

"Then I came to attention and I saluted and said aloud: 'this is from Bill and Don and Red, dear sir. We held you in very high esteem.' And then I started to cry and got back in my car and drove back down the windy road wiping my eyes and crying all the way," Red's letter ends.

I had learned that Neely had died after a written query to the Veterans Administration in St. Louis, but they could offer little further information other than he remained in the service to participate in the Korean and Vietnam wars. At the time I also learned he earned the Distinguished Flying Cross and died of natural causes on Jan. 8, 1987, having advanced in rank from the lieutenant when we knew him to Lt. Colonel.

Fifty-one years after World War II ended and after a long search I located my tailgunner, Red, alive and well, in Santa Barbara. The next year Red "found" one of our waist gunners, Don Power, in Florida. Bob had been the object of a long search, first by me, then joined by Red. That search culminated in Red's visit to his grave.

It was fitting we located Neely when we did--before Memorial Day. But Bob was only one of 16,535,000 American participants in World War II in which 406,000 died. In 1998 there were still 6,319,000 living veterans of that war and they were dying at the rate of 1,000 a day. Those Americans who made the ultimate sacrifice are deserving of the tributes awarded them by their fellows. The freedoms we enjoy are sacrosanct and because of these brave men and women we continue to pursue a life which has to be the envy of others in every corner of the globe.

Memorial Days have a way of providing the opportunity of intruding into one's mind. I can't help but pause and reflect on the Flying Fortress bomber crews of the 8th and 15th Air Forces who had more than just Germans to contend with. The forces of nature also came into play (See "Fighting The Cold War" elsewhere). High altitude flying made temeratures of 50 and 60 degrees below zero commonplace. Frostbite took its toll of fingers and limbs, anoxia (lack of oxygen) oftentimes had damaging, if not fatal results. Wary combat crewmen had their hands full from the time they took off until they returned to base.

I guess we considered ourselves a special group of people, if not the chosen ones of the second World War. No, it was not that we were better or braver than the next guy. Nor were we more fit or more intelligent. We were just a special breed who fought the war differently from our ground and sea comrades. Airmen had to cope with an unlikely, unfriendly and unreal element. That element took tubes to breathe in and heatsuits and gloves to keep warm in. If we seemed overly proud and a smidge cocky, the truth is, we were.

After all we were flying a bomber that was only six years from inception when it received its first baptism of fire at Pearl Harbor. It came off the drawing boards in 1935 with the assumed number of 299, the prototype of the B-17. It got its nickname "Flying Fortress" from a Richard L. Williams who coined the term when he was a writer/editor for the Seattle Times. He had captioned a picture of the 299 for the paper and was so impressed, he wrote: "Declared to be the largest land plane ever built in America, this 15 ton Flying Fortress, built by Boeing Aircraft Co., under army specifications, today (July 17, 1935) was ready to test its wings..." Williams died in November, 1989. Little did he know at the time how apt and prophetic his two-word description of the legendary four engine bomber would turn out to be.

In July, 1935, Boeing turned out the Stealth bomber of its day. The five gun emplacements in the 299 and its size captivated the press corps and won for it its nickname. Although it would evolve with succeeding model changes, it wasn't until the "E" model appeared that one could really say the plane was designed for combat. It was initially designed as a defensive aircraft. And so it was as it did search and destroy sub patrols off both coasts. As an offensive weapon, however, it would prove itself in battle. It spoke to its potential from the very beginning and went on to ensure its place in world history as one of the greatest strategic weapons in the Allied arsenal in all of World War II.

With the British in the throes of near defeat waging seemingly hopeless night raids on German and German-occupied cities of western Europe, the American effort initially in their behalf was belittled. Our first attack inside Germany, to Wilhelmshaven, was flown by the 8th Air Force on Jan. 27, 1943. The British in the bleak winter of 1942-43 were quite skeptical of Americans' daylight bombing attempts. The 8th Air Force, at the time, had, of course, not had time to prove itself. The English were convinced that night bombing was the only sure way of carrying the war to Germany. In fact, so positive were the British, that Churchill in January of 1943, wanted an end to American daylight bombing.

Had it not been for the articulate rationale of Gen. Ira C. Eaker, commanding officer of the 8th Air force, the British might have prevailed. Instead, Churchill, although not convinced, conceded more time was necessary for the Americans to prove their case. Two months later, March 18th, the American raid on Vegesack, a primary German sub-building target, allowed a vindication of the B-17 in its own right. Innovative Yanks designed an automatic flight control system in the B-17. This provided a link between bombardier and the plane's automatic pilot and gave the bombardier control of the aircraft during the crucial bomb run. So successful was the mission, no further objections were heard from the British.

So the war progressed to the inevitable end, but only because neither the elements of politics could stay the mission of the B-17, America's Flying Fortress. In the decade between 1935 and 1945 as many as 12,731 B-17s were built. U.S. flyers paid dearly in their efforts to win the peace in Europe. About 4,750 Fortresses were lost on combat missions. The casualty toll of the combined 8th and 15th Air Forces was 24,288 killed, 18,804 wounded, 31,436 taken prisoner. and 18,699 listed as missing in action. More than 11,000 American aircraft from all (four) participating numbered Air Forces were lost in Europe during World War II.

I've only recited the World War II Air Force casualties in Europe. Since the Revolutionary War 1,090,000 Americans have died in the service of their country. I think these people are best recognized by an honorable tribute on a given day in May--that being May 30th--as Memorial Day was intended. Make that day, once again, a holiday, but a holiday of remembrance.

Our pilot Bob Neely served us well in life. We knew him as a more than competent aircraft commander with an easy personality and always a friendly grin. On July 10, 1999 I received a letter from one of Neely's best friends, first pilot, John Harris. We didn't get to know Bob on a personal basis because officers and enlisted men didn't mix. But Harris knew him and wrote of their friendship. His letter, dated July 10, 1999, follows:

"Bill, this is in response to your inquiry about Bob Neely and any impressions I had of him. I am saddened to learn of Bob's death--although it was 12 years after the fact. He was a great guy--a good friend and a darned good pilot.

"I really only knew Bob from the time we were in transition (learning to fly the B-17) through the end of World War II--and then through the mid-1950s, when we lost contact with one another.

"I suspect that his moves in the military and as well as my moves in the civilian sector had a lot to do with this, as well as our interest in our individual careers and what was going to happen next. Bob, as you know, was raised in Larchmont, New York. As I recall he had an older sister. I think her name may have been Ruth, but I am not certain. His dad was in the optical business either as an optician or an eye doctor, or perhaps both. I believe his mother died when he was a youngster and he never spoke of her.

"He attended private school. And I recall that it was the Rye Country Day School. He was a freshman at Yale prior to entering the service. As you can see he traveled with an affluent crowd and learned to handle himself well in any situation.

"Did he drink? He sure did! But I never knew him to mix flying with drinking. I never saw him drunk, but he sure was mellow on several occasions. He was not alone, however. I never knew Bob to go overboard with the ladies. He enjoyed their company--and he was always a gentleman.

"Was he religious? We never really discussed that. He was an Episcopalian. I recall this because while we were at Camp Patrick Henry, prior to leaving for Italy we secured passes and Bob, Red Davis and myself went into town (Norfolk). On our way home we decided to take communion at a nearby Episcopal church. Red was a Methodist, I am a Congregationalist and Bob was the Episcopalian. We often said this helped to get us through the war without a scratch.

"Did he enjoy a good time? You bet he did. We went to rest camp on Capri and also he and I went to rest camp in Rome--saw the sights and had a great time. Mary and I spent a long weekend in Larchmont with Bob, his wife-to-be, Dorothy Smith, and a group of their friends in late October, 1945 and had a great time.

"One of the attendees at the party was Angela Lansbury ("Murder She Wrote", etc.) who was a young English actress just beginning her career on Broadway. Little did we know that she would go on to fame and fortune, not only on Broadway, but in television, which was a new media.

"Dot and Bob were married in February, 1946. We did not attend their wedding because of another wedding commitment in my home town of Greenfield, Massachusetts on the same date. As a matter of interest, the groom had been a waist gunner in the 99th and was a member of the crew commanded by a pilot by the name of Fouts. This was the same Fouts with whom I flew my first two missions. His name was Clinton May and he died several years ago. It is indeed a small world. It is even smaller in that the girl he married was my wife's closest friend.

"These are memories of the Bob Neely I knew during and shortly after World War II. I am glad that I knew him. He was a true friend. (Signed) John N. Harris."

What can I say? Harris has provided me with even a better understanding of the man we all knew as our pilot.

About My Pilot...

Bob Neely fought the cockpit yolk with gloved hands invariably stained with sweat as beads of perspiration angled down his clean cut sideburns. This was the pilot I came to know and respect as a B-17 airplane commander.

He was awarded the DFC for getting our crippled ship torn by fire back to base safely.

Bob left the Air Force in 1945 soon after VJ Day but was recalled for Korea. Home again in '52. Decided on a military career. Flew B-52's in Vietnam. Flew Lear jets as a civilian for a charter outfit for 10 years and retired in Paso Robles, California in 1985. He died of cancer two years later and was buried in Atascadaro committed with a color guard, a 21 gun salute and a buglar's taps.

He is survived by his wife, two sons and a daughter.

My Pilot's California Grave

Bob Neely died of natural causes in 1987 and was buried in Atascadere, California. He was to remain in the service after World War II to participate in the Korean and Vietnam wars. He advanced in rank from the lieutenant we knew him to Lt. Colonel.

CHAPTER 14

Enemy Salute

In the early days of the air war over Europe, like when our 99ers began arriving in North Africa to do battle, young pilots in their early twenties were finding themselves struggling for identity. Purpose was theirs by virtue of the war itself and the job they'd trained for. Achieving that purpose, fulfilling their commitment as young fledgling bomber flyers, taxed their every talent. Their wings didn't come easy, but when they did their mind set was directed one way--their determination to pit their skills against the enemy, win out and come home in one piece.

Julius Horowitz, a Jewish pilot, was one of those men who flew the early tough missions out of North Africa and later, Italy. I only mention his religious affiliation because of the stark irony that occurred on his 25th mission to an enemy airdrome in Athens, Greece. He was flying the right seat that day checking out Jim Connally in the left seat.

"Today's trip was one of my worst,"Jules said. "I was in the copilot's seat and had nothing to do but watch," he added saying "we had pretty poor weather and had some pretty close flak from six to eight minutes. After bombs away we were hit by 30 fighters. They really came into our formation--what was left of it."

He then tells of a plane from his squadron going down and noted that morale seemed to be getting worse because of lack of equipment and planes. On this day of his 25th raid, October 10th, he noted his second wave was only seven "measly" planes and expressed the sentiment: "no wonder fighters were not bashful. Our gunners fired 6,000 rounds of ammo in the fight."

His tent mate Kermit Mack, squadron S-2, was in the habit of sending P.R. (public relations) pieces to hometown newspapers. Horowitz tells of reading about this mission in one of the New York papers. The story said that after bombs away and coming off the target in a company front, Horowitz's plane was on the extreme right side. An FW-190 was boring in on him from 4 o'clock. He was able to see 20 mm bursts coming closer and closer to his wing and cockpit.

Jules reached for the flare gun in the ceiling above him. He knew it contained a shell with the colors of the day. Desperate, he could shoot that at the attacking fighter. He reached up and tried to pull it down, but was frustrated in his efforts because he'd forgotten, in the heat of battle, it took a half turn to release the gun. At that very moment the enemy pilot broke off his attack and passed directly below him. He was no more than 40 feet away when he saw Jule's hand go up, figuring he was waving at him, so waved his hand in return as he passed out of sight.

The New York paper headlined the incident that took only 10 seconds: "Jewish and German Pilots Salute in Heat of Battle."

Julius Horowitz graduated in the class of 42K and received his wings Dec. 12, 1942. His primary school was in Camden, South Carolina. He took his basic flight instruction at Shaw Field, Sumter, S. C. and he took his advanced training at Moody Field, Valdosta, Georgia. From there it was B-17 transition at Sebring, Florida.

It was in February, 1943 in Salt Lake City that Jules picked up his crew. They proceeded to Boise, Idaho and Rapid City, South Dakota for phase training. From there he signed for a new B-17F, No 393, at Salina, Kansas early in June. They spent about a week checking out the instruments and "wringing" out the aircraft. Then on to Morrison Field, Palm Beach, Florida.

The next morning, June 11, 1943, he departed the United States as part of the Rice Provisional Group--five B-17s with full crews enroute to North Africa. They spent a night each in Puerto Rico; Georgetown, British Guinea; Belem and Natal, Brazil; Dakar, French Senegal; Marrakech, Morocco and finally to Sale Field, Rabat, Moroco.

Horowitz was a replacement waiting assignment to one of four operational groups. On his Atlantic crossing they left at 20 minute intervals, aiming for a point halfway between Dakar and Bathhurst, then flew up the coast to Dakar. He said they were briefed to ignore radio beams as they were put out by German subs. If the beams were followed they would parallel the coast out to sea and run out of fuel.

On July 13th Horowitz left Rabat for Navarin, Algeria where he was assigned to the 348th squadron. One of his tent mates was Stan Samuelson. After his tour, he returned to the states, married, was assigned to B-29s and was lost in the Pacific after 15 or 20 missions. Horowitz was assigned to Capt. Elliot's crew as copilot to get combat experience.

In those early days public relations played a big part in America's conduct of the war. There had been some American setbacks, but the successful invasion of Sicily a week before Horowitz's first mission on July 19th to Rome had public information officers focusing on 15th Air Force bomber command. What's more, targeting Rome, hitting military targets only and sparing the Holy City, would be big news back home if the raid came off as planned. It did.

Queenie was the bird they flew to Rome. And to add to the crew anxieties, they carried a correspondent from the International News Service and the author of the best seller "Guadalcanal Diary", Richard Tregaskis. He was to describe the Rome raid and the little opposition they met. Could be the story filed by Tregaskis and cabled back home might have been filled with more fiction than fact to please the folks back in the United States. But Horowitz would never know--he was too busy flying.

On August 26 Horowitz said his plane and crew were standby and didn't fly probably because Gen. Spaatz and Gen. Doolittle were at their base to present American's second highest military decoration, the DSC, to Sgt. Ben Warmer of his own 348th squadron. This was for the waist gunner's outstanding achievement July 5th over the Gerbini airdrome in Sicily when he was credited with downing a record seven enemy fighters in that one raid.

An enemy B-17 infiltrates Jule's raiding party to the Bologna marshaling yards on Sept. 2nd, his ninth mission. He tells what happens: "All was well until we got to the target area. We were at 24,000 feet in the second wave. Our leader then screwed up. There were several near collisions. Bombs were dropped at a 45 degree angle. Of course they were off target.

"Then, to make matters worse, besides enemy fighters, we saw the enemy B-17 and P-38. The Germans were known to use captured B-17s against us. They would close in with our attacking aircraft and radio position, altitude, numbers, etc. to their own command posts."

Five days later on his eleventh mission, this time to Foggia, the very airfields our own crews would fly out of months later, became a target. Jules would fly with his original crew and describe the mission "the roughest yet."

"My plane wasn't functioning too well," he said. "Then we were hit by forty to sixty fighters, but they didn't bother us too much. Our problem was very heavy accurate flak. My three plane element was clobbered. Our plane had over one hundred holes in it when we got back. Brooks, our navigator, was hit in the chest and went into shock. He is O.K. now but no more combat for him. The bombardier of the No. 3 plane was killed. Major Whitmore, our element leader, had his controls shot up so severely that when he got back to Africa they all bailed out and the plane crashed. The flak was so good today that sixteen planes are out of commission as of now."

Jules enlisted as an aviation cadet on December 8, 1941, the day after the "dastardly" attack on Pearl Harbor. He flew the southern route to North Africa. But what he remembers most had nothing to do with combat flying. He got lost in training on his first cross country flight in a basic BT-13. He landed in a very small field over telephone wires and ground looped to avoid going into the trees. The commandant of cadets came after him and cracked up his plane while an embarrassed Horowitz, his plane still intact, had to face the music. His instructor was sure he came in under the wires. But those wires were nothing to the flying impediments he would face as he continues to disclose more of his diary entries.

Mission No. 21, Bologna m/y, Sept. 25th:

After several canceled missions on account of bad weather and with B-24s flying alternate missions, finally got one today. It started badly. While climbing we entered mean looking clouds which scattered the formation--partly because the leader was climbing too fast.

As soon as we got clear of the clouds, we received heavy, accurate flak. Finally everyone got back in formation. I was tail-end Charlie again. We dropped our bombs but the turn off the target was not as briefed. We were then attacked by fighters who were with us for about a half hour. They came in pretty close. We had a number of 20 mm holes. Our left waist gunner claimed an ME-109.

Today I came home on three engines. I'm trying to get a No. 3 cylinder head changed. No luck. A number of planes were sweating out gas on the way home.

Brooks is getting grounded. I guess his nerves are shot since the time he was hit over Foggia.

Oct. 6th:

We were scheduled to fly today, but I refused to fly my 3-engine ship, No. 361. I wanted a four engine plane like everyone else. Another crew flew my plane. I was lucky to do what I did. Our group was hit by thirty to thirty-five fighters and two planes were lost. My replacement crew came back all shot up with several men wounded. They had a close call. If I went in my 3-engine plane I doubt if I would have made it back. No. 3 engine was burning eight gallons an hour. An engine has an oil capacity of forty gallons.

Mission No. 24, Salonika, Greece:

I still don't have a plane. I wasn't scheduled except that we were short of flight personnel. I flew with Ericsson. Shortly after crossing the coast the plane started having tantrums. Cliff decided to abort.

I didn't try to talk him out of it since today was Yom Kippur and I was quite uneasy about flying. Morale is getting pretty bad. The last two missions had about fifty percent aborts. We are not getting replacement parts and all new equipment is going to the 8th Air Force. There is also a shortage of flight personnel.

Mission No. 31, Weiner Neustadt ME factory, Nov. 2nd: I left early today with a full gas and bomb load. It was a long trip--1913 miles round-trip. The 97th and 301st were to lead us, but they didn't get to Foggia on time so we led the parade. We bombed at 24,500 feet. It sure was cold. My crew who saw what was happening--I was too busy keeping the plane in tight formation--said that it was the worst flak they had ever seen.

We were hit by about eighty fighters, Goering's best. Those enemy fighters were top notch. Our P-38s had their hands full. We were lucky that we had B-24s following us. The fighters gave them a very rough time. They weren't able to keep as tight a formation as us. The B-24s were better escorts for us than the P-38s because fighters sought B-24s out like bees to honey, virtually ignoring us.

Eight B-24s and four B-17s went down during the action. Two of my gunners each claimed an enemy plane and the Germans weren't even shooting at us. Their targets were the B-24s behind. We landed near Gela, Sicily after a 14 hour flight where we spent the night. I slept under the bomb bays. In the early morning we were refueled and the engines were preflighted. I never heard a sound although I was no more than 25 feet from the engines.

A No-Credit Mission, Dec. 9th

It was to be a sneak attack on deck over the water. Briefing was for a 4,000 foot bombing altitude. Between Genoa and Spezia one of my engines was on fire. Funny how the rest of the squadron quickly moved away from me, afraid that I would blow up. Some of the crew asked if they should bail out. I told them that since we were over water at a very low altitude and in enemy territory, they had better pray instead. It wouldn't hurt.

Of course, I turned back and hoped to make it back to base. Eventually the fire burned itself out. After landing I saw that the horizontal stabilizer was badly burned. Incidentally, the other planes turned back ten minutes later because of bad weather.

North Africa To Their New Base in Foggia, Italy, Dec. 11th:

The plane was all packed. I had 15 men. Ten crew and five ground crewmen and 15 dogs. Babe and Lady, our two terrier beagles who were from the same litter, both had pups prior to the move. When I joined the group, the two dogs already lived in my tent. They would go to all the briefings. I had to take them to Italy because they were family. As soon as we got our tent, we dug fox holes. Axis Sally was promising us presents from the sky immediately after our arrival.

R & R, The Isle of Capri, Dec. 19th:

Our crew left for rest camp early this morning. Went over the mountains on the steepest roads I've ever been on. After getting lost, our truck finally found the ferry for Capri. The boat trip took three hours. Sheehy and I went to the Aquisisana Hotel about 1,000 feet above sea level in Grand Marina. We spent a week having a good time touring the island and visiting the Blue Grotto.

One morning I was sitting in the large lobby off to one side. Another lieutenant sitting on the other side of the lobby when the front door opens and someone yells "attention!" We both pop to and in walks Gen. Eisenhower and a party of ten people heading for the dining room for an early lunch. He was on his way from Africa to England to head up SHAPE. On his way through the lobby he notices me off to one side. He turns and comes up to me and sticks out his hand and says, "I'm Eisenhower." I reply, "I'm Horowitz." He turns and walks across the lobby to the other lieutenant and repeats the procedure. He then walks into the dining room with his party. I consider him a great man who wasn't too big for his britches.

We left Capri a day early to check out Naples. Sheehy met two friends from home. One was a ranger. We found out later that he was killed at Anzio. The other was a front line medic, both just coming off the front lines.

On Dec. 28th we returned to base. I learned that my plane, No. 832, which was loaded for the mission that I was supposed to fly was shot down over Augsburg. The plane was flown by Cy Stidd and crew.

Mission No. 40, Wiener Neustadt, Jan. 7th, 1944:

I nearly crashed on takeoff. Part of the way down the runway I found the horizontal stabilizer rolled all the way back. It was O.K. when I preflighted the plane earlier.

On the way to the target we hit a heavy cloud layer. When I broke through the top of the clouds I saw only one other plane from the 99th. Our new squadron C.O. who was leading for the first time was not following standard or routine procedure.

A classmate of mine who was in another group was lost because of an incident similar to what I just mentioned. A group was entering heavy clouds. An element with an inexperienced leader turned 180 degrees and went into another group just arriving at the cloud layer. Their three planes took out five planes of the second group. Eight planes went down, my friend among them.

I saw the 2nd Bomb Group several miles ahead. I redlined the throttles in order to catch up with them before I met up with some undesirables. My bombardier wanted to salvo the bombs to lighten the plane, but I forbade him to do it. Lucky for me. When we got to their target it was covered with clouds, so the group dropped on the alternate target, Maribor airdrome. I stayed with the group until we got back to the 5th Wing area and then returned to my home base.

An interesting sidelight to this mission. My plane didn't have tail markings when I joined up with the 2nd Bomb Group. Since I was their guest, so to speak, and didn't have a specific position in the formation, I picked the safest spot to fly. I positioned my plane behind and below the colonel's lead plane. To me, everything was normal. when the group dropped their bombs, I followed suit.

A week later in town I met some buddies from the 2nd. Then I discovered how lucky I really was. I didn't know what radio channel they were using and since I kept radio silence, I wasn't privy to their excited radio chatter. They informed the lead plane of my positioning myself in the midst of their formation. They thought I might be an enemy B-17 because the Germans were known to give ground batteries course, speed and height in similar action. The C.O. told them to watch me. If I didn't drop bombs when they did to open fire and shoot me down.

I'm glad I didn't know about it at the time.

Mission No. 47, Marseilles, Jan. 27th:

I flew as squadron lead again. We had heavy, accurate flak. I took a hit in No. 4 oil cooler and lost all the oil before I could feather the engine. We had about thirty enemy planes in the area. They didn't bother me, maybe they didn't see me. When the enemy left and with my prop windmilling I knew that I wouldn't be able to keep up with our planes. I put my plane into a dive and pulled out about one hundred feet above the water. I flew about four hours with a windmilling prop and a frozen engine.

When I passed the bomb line I decided to land at Capodachino, Naples. I didn't relish the idea of climbing over the mountains to get to Foggia. While in the traffic pattern the engine was vibrating so badly that I though it would shake itself loose and tear off a wing. Smoke was pouring out of the engine. It looked like it was on fire. The crew was in the radio room prepared for a crash landing.

After a good landing the plane slowed down. At about 30 knots the prop just fell off the plane. This field was an A-36 (P-51 dive bomber) base. While on my final approach the tower called and told me to go around because the A-36s were starting to land. I replied to the tower that if any planes got in my way I would run over them. It was a sight. Planes buzzing all around me. We had to spend the night because the plane needed an engine change. A plane came in the next day to take us home.

Mission No. 49, Toulon Harbor, Feb. 4th:

It was pretty rough today. An hour late to the target because of 100 mph head winds. We reached our altitude of 24,500 feet and flew there for over an hour. Four planes in my squadron turned back. Our group must have had at least fifteen returnees.

We were on oxygen for four hours. It sure was cold, then we sweated gas. I don't think that we did well with our bombs. We had heavy flak. We lost a plane and the 2nd also lost one. We then headed for Corsica in order to refuel.

It was a chaotic rat race with thirty-five to forty planes trying to land at one time. There was no semblance of a traffic pattern as everyone was pretty low on fuel. Flying in this area we encountered some of the worst turbulence ever. The field was located in the midst of mountains. After we landed I couldn't stay in the plane because it was too cold. I stayed around a fire in a tent along with others and didn't sleep a wink.

I spent a good part of the next day waiting for the gas truck and finally took off at 1415 hours and I was plenty mad because I was one of the last to leave. It was a rough trip home. I had to stay above the clouds all the way. We hit the coast at 16,000 feet with very little oxygen left. We finally got broken overcast with much turbulence and eventually landed in a 40 knot wind.

Two planes are still missing. I saw them leave well before me. I hope that they landed somewhere else and are O.K. One more mission and I'll have it made.

*　　　　*　　　　*

Homeward Bound:

After he flew his fiftieth mission to marshaling yards at Verona, Italy on Feb. 14th, Horowitz had to wait around before going stateside. On March 26, 1944 he landed in Newport News, Va. He said he could have flown back, but since he'd never been on a ship before, he chose instead to return on the USS Gen. Mann. He characterized the trip as one of a leisurely tourist.

CHAPTER 15

Retired at Fifty

If one were to let their fingers walk through Joseph C. Kenney's war diary, one would have to favor that walk with superlatives. Awesome is perhaps one word I'd choose to describe a litany of aerial combat anecdotes revealed in the 346th squadron radio operator's diary. I'm adding my personal comments in italics where I find them appropriate.

Joseph Cady Kenney died April 29, 1993 at his home in Lander, Wyoming at the age of 69. He was a founding member, past president and chaplain of the 99th Bomb Group Historical Society. He sold real estate in the Casper area and was circulation manager for the Casper Morning Star. He was a retired real estate appraiser and retired as the owner/manager of the Fremont Title Company.

A radioman like Joe, just beginning, knew he faced 50 combat missions. Before the 50-mission quota was set, combat crews had to put in 25 raids before they could go home. Those were the early days of the vicious air war over Europe. They say that 15 missions was the average lifespan of a bomber crew. And those boys never flew mission number 13. It was always 12-A.

Joe wrote this about his diary before he died:

"I have attempted to get this down as nearly as I possibly could from my diary along with some recollections of things that I recalled when I was working this up. There may be a couple of discrepancies of occurrences attributed to missions that may have occurred on another mission, but it should be abundantly clear that what has been written here did happen. These being as I saw them from my own viewpoint. In no way can I express myself with a clarity that would mirror my own, actual feelings and emotions."

And when his tour ended, he wrote: "I had very mixed emotions. First, the great relief that some of those big problems were behind me. And along with this, elation and happiness that it was all over. Then next, quite strangely for me, was regret that I would not be flying combat any more and that, somehow, I was letting down first, the crews I flew with, and my friends who were still flying, and then our country in getting this rotten war over with."

I'm not about to relate every single mission this intrepid radio gunner participated in. but you should know he crewed the same ship--the lead plane of the 5th Wing with Col. Ford Lauer as pilot and Brig. Gen. Laurence, co-pilot as they embarked on the historic shuttle to Russia on June 2, 1944. Also, I'm hoping to focus on his forebodings, anxieties and apprehensions that certainly possessed him as a combat crew member who flew both the earlier "F" models and then the "G" when it became available.

To know Joe better is to know his job. On the day he is scheduled to fly and as a radio operator he must attend the mission briefing with the pilots, navigators and bombardiers. It's also where he picks up the escape kits and the first aid kit along with briefing information. He gets the "Code of the Day' sheet along with information about the recall code word. When he arrives at his plane, he distributes the escape kits and then briefs the gunners about the mission they will fly.   Joe would board the B-17 and ready the radio room for the mission. He'd assemble his machine gun and hook up ammo belts without charging the gun. He'd set up his radio log with the initial entries. He signed "On Watch" at the specific time of engine start and remained on watch from then until he was deep in enemy territory and always beyond the time where the recall code word might come through. When that happened he'd enter into his radio log, "Off watch to man the battle station."

The radio operator had a rather restricted view through the sights of his machine gun mounted above him. His field of fire was limited to shooting straight up. Otherwise the gun, when fired, might hit both wing tips, the dorsal fin or the radio antenna. With his bomber at the I.P. preparing for the bomb run, his job mandates that he dump chaff or window to foul German radar on their flak guns. Yes, the chaff chute was installed in the radio room. After dispensing the chaff, the radio operator hears the bombardier call "bomb bay doors opening." He then opens the bulkhead door into the bomb bay and watches the doors open, reporting them open when their cycle is complete. The bombardier finally calls "bombs away" and the radioman on intercom will report "bombs all gone." The bomb bay doors close and Joe would report them closed when that occurred.

Only one plane in the group sends back the "bombs away" message. If Joe were flying group lead, he was responsible for encoding the message and tapping it out to base. When it was received and a receipt acknowledged, he'd complete the entry into his log.

Joe was more than just a radio operator. The ship's flight engineer early in their practice missions would have shown Joe how to transfer fuel. At this time, then, the copilot would call him and have him transfer fuel from one tank to another. He had signed "On Watch" when he sent the "bombs away" message and he remained there, unless he had fighters to contend with, until they landed and the engines were shut down. This was the time to close your log; clear up the radio room, pick up the escape kits and the first aid kit and turn this material and information over to proper authorities. Radiomen on non-operational days went to school where they either drilled in code and radio operation or got lessons in first aid. They were invariable considered the medic of the aircraft.

Every mission is a window into his conduct under fire. What I hope to do as we pursue his missions in chronological order is to seize the moments of agony and fear along with the exhilaration of survival.

I want you to know his feelings of foreboding at a morning briefing when a diabolical target like Ploesti is disclosed to crews flying that morning. I want you to experience the same anxious moments he experienced when bombers one by one were crashing on takeoff--I want you to feel his desperation as his own crew began passing out for want of oxygen right before his eyes in the waist of the bomber. And finally, I want you to appreciate his helplessness and fear as a flock of friendly but disoriented B-24 bombers plowed through his formation on a bomb run.

Now to explore the explosive and stimulating excerpts provided in the war diary of Joe Kenney.

Mission No. 2, March 18, 1944, Target: Villaorba Airfield, northern Italy.

This raid points up the hazards of carrying a load of fragmentation bombs. Five hundred and one-thousand pound bombs were a more stable bomb load, but every time one of Joe's subsequent missions called for frag bombs to the target, he'd think back to this particular mission and its grave ramifications.

...We were attacked by 67 ME-210s which came in on us in waves of four, launching rockets from just out of range of our defending 50 caliber machine guns. They really hit us hard with both the ME-210 and Me-109s working us over. The B-17 group to our right took the heaviest of these attacks which resulted in their loss of three bombers.

On the bomb run the flak was intense and we were all of us taking battle damage. At "bombs away" our plane ran into problems. The two lower bomb stations on the left side of the bomb bay hung up. The bombs from the upper hangers came off normally as did the right side of the bomb bay. Since these were again frag bombs, they come in clusters and as soon as they are released the clusters break up. Those clusters came apart above those hung up stations and we wound up with the left side of the bomb bay being full of loose frags.

It was part of my duties to watch the bombs go. I reported our condition to the bombardier and he salvoed. The bombs fell helter skelter from the bomb bay. I checked to make sure the bomb bay was clear. It was. As I glanced out the bomb bay I saw a B-17 drifting to our left, very close, underneath us. About this time our ball turret operator reported a

B-17 drifting to the left with its dorsal fin blown off. The tailgunner had been blown from his position and believed not to be alive. We watched as the B-17 continued to the left and we counted nine chutes as the rest bailed out. It was reported (*probably in error*) that the plane made it home safely and that the fin had been blown off by a German rocket. We believe the tail was blown off by a frag bomb from our ship. We were under attack for some 48 minutes.

Mission No. 9 and 10, May 24, 1944, Target: Atzgersdorf Aircraft Factory, Austria.

Two missions in one day reflects the Air Force policy of the time in awarding two missions for an extremely difficult one. This raid explores the singularly isolated ways a man can be killed on a combat mission.

We flew B-17 No, 855, "Weary Willie." This was the first combat mission for this aircraft. We were again flying lead ship with Adams as our pilot. Flying squadron lead (*German flak gunners on a clear day pick off lead planes in squadron and group if the can*) the flight was pretty much routine until we got into the target area. The B-17 group ahead to the left and below our formations was attacked by fighters and two B-17s were lost. One appeared to go pretty much straight in and I have no idea as to how many or if any were able to leave this plane.

The second one was on fire and eight men had bailed out. The plane did a steep 180 degree turn flying directly back over these eight men where it exploded. It set four of the chutes on fire.

This incident has been with me and bothers me greatly. Those four men did not get a second chance. I must point out that I, personally, was not able to see this because of the nature of the radio room. all of this was related by others on the crew. I considered this to be a rough one since we had some mighty rough flak over the target.

Missions15 and 16, June 2,1944, Target: Debreczen, Hungary.
America's 1st Shuttle Mission to Poltava, Russia:

This was the most   important mission of the war to date,

according to General Twining who was present at the two hour briefing. He said that future operations in Russia depended largely upon the results of this mission. And who was in the lead plane but Joe C. Kenney whose pilot and C.O. of the 99th Bomb Group was Col. Ford Lauer and whose copilot was Big. Gen. Laurence. They led the wing in what was the first of an operation called F.R.A.N.T.I.C. The flight was comprised of 140 Flying Fortresses. Destination: Poltava, Russia.

Aerospace historian Russell Bradshaw, in his article reprinted in the 99th Bomb Group newsletter of May, 1992, disclosed the shuttle was a priority mission. It had been planned on a top secret basis involving his 2nd Bomb Group along with the 99th and 97th and a colonel from the 8th Air Force. The briefing was held in an underground wine-cellar. They were going to try something that had never been done before--a one way mission to Russia. Once set up at Russian bases, they would fly a series of missions in support of the Soviet army on the Eastern front. The plan had been conceived at the highest level. The need for secrecy was implicit as the element of surprise was paramount. It would be the first time in history that regular combat units of a foreign country would be operating from Russian territory.

It was raining as they approached the city of Poltava. They'd hit the Debreczen marshalling yards with excellent results. The 97th Bomb Group lost one plane. Poltava was pretty much in rubble, but the streets looked wonderfully clean, like they had been scrubbed and polished. Its people were not beggars. They were proud, even hesitated to accept candy or cigarettes without giving the Americans a souvenir in return.

Poltava was located in the heart of the Ukraine which was the bread basket of Russia. The visiting Americans could see the red clover growing there and plenty of potato patches--even in the streets of the town. The greenness of the country made a great impression on the flyers. Flowers bloomed and the grass was well kept. The Yanks were impressed with the cleanliness of the children too.

The landing field was large and up to date. It had been used by the Russians as a training field before the war. All the main buildings were destroyed and the airmen lived in tents that were waiting for them. The runway was of steel matting which had been laid for them mostly by women. The Russian woman did the same work as men and did it cheerfully. Girl soldiers marching around with long rifles with fixed bayonets was nothing to be laughed at. Russian men and women fought together and worked together. It was their destiny if they were to drive the Germans from their country.

An unhappy and deadly reversal of fortunes visited 8th Air Force B-17s who followed up with a second shuttle mission to Russia. They landed at Poltava, according to Samuel B. Hess, a 99th Bomb Group Communications officer, in his story reprinted in the 99th newsletter, March 1, 1985. They used the same base we used the week before, he reported.

After they landed , a German reconnaissance plane flew across the Russian base to take pictures. Anti aircraft batteries opened up but failed to hit the plane. It was a costly miss. That night, according to Hess, the Germans bombed the field, flying in from about 8,000 feet and succeeded in destroying sixty-four of the seventy-two planes parked there. There were only two casualties in the raid. No missions were flown from Poltava by the remaining eight 8th Air Force B-17s, but they did bomb Rumanian oil fields enroute to Italy.

Col. Ford Lauer, pilot; Brig. General Charles Laurence, copilot. We led the 5th Wing on this trip. Eventual destination Poltava, Russia after striking our assigned target. It was the first Shuttle Run into Russia. Our flight was composed of 140 B-17s of the 5th Wing of the 15th Air Force. We hit the Debreczen marshalling yards with excellent results. The initial force from our bombs was so great that the entire red tile roof of the depot was seen to rise to a significant height before it disintegrated.

As I remember it we did have a little flak but this was of not much consequence. However a B-17 from the 97th Bomb Group exploded just off target for unexplained reasons. We flew on to Poltava which is located approximately 65 miles southeast of Kiev, Russia. Our experience in Russia was an education in itself. We were appalled by the incredible amount of destruction done to Poltava and the plight of the citizens during the German occupation was horrible. We could not help but notice the single track the Russians were on. I saw women off-loading bales of steel mat runway from railroad flat cars and they were doing this impossible job by hand.

Mission No. 20 and 21, June 13, 1944. Target Oberpfoffenhofen airdrome at the southern edge of Munich.

Fear of flying is one thing even some few people in peacetime have difficulty with. Fear of dying afflicts us all and especially a combat airman. Every mission he flies is fraught with danger and the real possibility of being killed. This mission is a case in point. Being assigned to a ship that flies either group or squadron lead increases the chances of that crew's demise. German pilots and German flak batteries know if they can pick off those lead ships, they create confusion in the formations. True, there are deputy leads, but the adjustment under stress can be difficult if not fatal. Joe would fly squadron lead on this raid with all the attending premonitions.

I recall the awful forebodings I had on this one--the dread before takeoff. I briefed the balance of the crew along with a stray photographer who was to go along. We had his cameras in place but it was rough enough that this photographer cancelled because of sudden "illness". I think the rest of us were kind of ill as well. One thing that really bothered us was the fact that two B-24 groups had gone into this same area a week before and had lost half their airplanes.

The flak over the target was intense and accurate with most of us suffering battle damage. Even though we heard that fighters were around, none ever attacked our formation. We took a number of hits including one that went through the top turret without hitting Adam Zanoni, the engineer. Another put a hole in one of the oxygen tanks and the system began to exhaust itself. I was able to save four walk-around bottles and others in the crew did the same before pressure became too low. Adam came through and collected those bottles so the pilots could maintain their alertness. We went off oxygen at about 22,000 feet, as I recall, and flew across the Austrian Alps before we could get down to more dense air. I can remember the rotten headache I sustained from the lack of oxygen.

Missions 22 and 23, June 23, 1944, target: Ploesti.

Our group began flying missions to this dreaded target April 5th. This day marked the fifth time the 99th targeted Ploesti and Joe's first. We would go on to punish Ploesti seven more times with the end coming August 18th as Russian ground forces captured the oil rich area.

Capt. Chamberlain was our pilot and we flew squadron lead. Strong resistance from enemy fighters. Our P-38 escort did a magnificent job of keeping them out for the most part. However one of Hermann Goering's "yellow nosers," a part of Goering's Flying Circus, made a direct frontal attack on our airplane. As he neared with that tremendous closing speed, I heard the top turret fire several bursts and then saw tracers ripping down the length of our plane followed by that flickering shadow of the FW-190 as it came over the length of our plane as well. I saw that he was trailing smoke and it began a spiral to its left and that began to tighten up as it burst into flames. The pilot did not get out. T/Sgt Daly, the engineer, got him cold with superb use of his Sperry automatic computing sights. The flak was again unreal and we were in that intense and accurate stuff for about thirty-five minutes and that is one heck of a long time. We were a force of 139 B-17s and lost six of them.

Mission No. 33 and 34, July 21, 1944. Target: Brux, Czechoslovakia an industrial oil refinery.

It's enough to face enemy fighters and flak in combat. And further, just to stay alive and to cope with sufficient oxygen, heated suits that work and to keep one's concentration on the immediate job at hand. But not on this mission. Add to it a grievous human error happening to Joe. Always a threat and sometimes a reality in formation combat flying is the ugly chance of a mid-air collision with one's own.

Pilot is Capt. Karnes and we were flying squadron lead. We were briefed for intense and accurate flak with the possibility of 250 fighters in the area and these considered to be aggressive. Our trek into Brux was pretty uneventful. Our escort was effective in keeping enemy planes from our formation and we eventually turned on our I. P. for an unusually long bomb run.

Our bomb bays were open and our bombardier was calling for "level" when we were suddenly engrossed in violent evasive maneuvers to avoid a B-24 group in a tight left turn at our altitude. That B-24 group literally flew through our bombers with most of us salvoing bombs to help us get away. We were low squadron and did not drop our bombs and had suffered two aborts leaving us with only five planes in our squadron. We reformed and did not go over Brux. There were no losses sustained in this melee. It was an incredible event that no one was hurt or killed.

Captain Karnes was never one to bring bombs back home and since we still had our bombs our bombardier, Chris Christensen, began the process of selecting a suitable target. We pulled from formation, flying a bomb run on a fairly good size community with a large marshalling yard with a train in it. The drop was perfect and the loads from three planes would not have been overly significant but that train was an ammunition train and exploded like dominos and I guess literally obliterated that town.

This mission had more in store for us. We discovered we couldn't transfer fuel from one of the Tokyo tanks. We were very low on usable fuel when we returned and came out of formation for a straight-in approach. A British colonel cut us from the final approach and we were obliged to go around for a second run. It was mighty close call on fuel.

About those B-24s that sliced through our formation. I feel at this late date a note regarding a bombardier named Roy Buckmeier who lives right here in Lander, Wyoming. He was in one of the B-24s that flew through the 99th that fateful day. He mentions heavy losses in his group just moments later over Brux, including three B-24s out of his squadron alone.

Mission No. 37 and 38, July 25, 1944. Target: Linz, Hermann Goering Tank Works.

An easy mission is considered a milk run. When, as Joe writes, "the whole war seemed to engulf us," you can be sure this one wasn't just a milk run. In truth, it was a vivid display of air to air, ground to air combat that illuminates the vicious struggle American air crews had to contend with.

This was the roughest mission I have flown to date. However there have been other times when incidents occurred where we were individually closer to getting shot down, wounded or killed. We didn't receive any great amount of battle damage to our plane. However fighter attacks began early on with a B-24 group below and somewhat behind us taking attacks with devastating results. As more and more fighters showed up, more and more of us became involved and shortly we were involved in a full blown aerial battle. The whole war seemed to engulf us.

On the bomb run the flak became very intense and it was accurate. This, too, began to take its toll in battle damage and further loss of heavy bombers as we progressed on into the target. In one instance, the wing was blown off a B-17. There were no survivors. Several B-17s exploded. Any place you looked in the sky you could see a trail of smoke and/or a ball of flame. There were parachutes almost everywhere you looked. At "bombs away" we flew through the blast and wreckage of a B-17 that had exploded above and ahead of us. Capt.Karnes took suitable evasive action to avoid that wreckage and it was pretty much of a terrifying experience for us.

We sustained some battle damage, but not serious. We counted 34 heavy bombers going down or in trouble including the one that exploded in front of us. I have no idea of the actual number of bombers lost on this one since some of those in trouble made it back.

Mission No. 45, August 10, 1944. Target: Ploesti.

It's oxygen, or the lack of it, that's the focus of this mission. Certainly it was the latter that created havoc aboard "Bugs Bunny," the B-17 Joe flew on this mission. Lack of oxygen can cause a person to become irrational and then dead. Medical science calls it anoxia. Depending on the severity (length of time an individual is deprived of oxygen) a stricken flyer at an altitude of 28,500 feet can be dead in two minutes. This mission caused the temporary unconsciousness of not one of the crew, not two, but three crewman. The use of a walk-around bottle with its three minute supply of oxygen is available to all crew members in an emergency or otherwise. But they must unplug from the main system to venture forth. Flying group lead, let Joe describe this hectic raid.

At briefing, as always, that awesome foreboding feeling because this in the past has been a raunchy target. The flak, again, at briefing, very intense, very accurate. Those boys had certainly had enough practice. The flight from takeoff, assembly and positioning into the 15th Air Force bomber stream was entirely routine. Our altitude over the target was 28,500 feet.

It seemed difficult to believe,but the outside temperature at that altitude on August 10th was 60 degrees below zero. I suspect that our inside temperature did not differ very much from what we had outside. When we were finally into the bomb run our tailgunner discovered he had rings in both his parachute harness and the chute he was to snap into the harness. He reasoned that, under these circumstances, this would probably be the day we'd get shot down. He headed for the waist position to select a chute that would work, but did not have a walk-around supply of oxygen and passed out next to the tail wheel. The left waist gunner grabbed his emergency supply, went off oxygen and got the tailgunner plugged in. The left waist gunner passed out with the right waist gunner rescuing left wait gunner and he too, passed out with the left waist fixing him up.

After "bombs away" I reported the bomb bay clear, but when the bombardier tried to close the bomb bay doors, they remained open. The engineer was on a walk-around bottle when he squatted on the catwalk trying to crank those doors closed. He ran out of his (oxygen) supply and I went off oxygen, taking my walk-around bottle to him and he was conscious enough to take the bottle, plug it in and get back to his position, leaving the doors open. I returned to my position only to get somewhat hung up in the bulkhead door into the radio room where I was rescued by the radar navigator. All of this with that intense flak throughout the bomb run. I have to say that the catwalk through that bomb bay with the doors open seems mighty narrow and 28,500 feet appears to be a long way down. When we got down to lower and warmer altitude the doors closed.

We saw no enemy fighters on this mission, but out of 414 heavy bombers that went over the target, we still lost sixteen of them--again being subject to a heavy loss of men and bombers.

Mission No. 49, Aug. 15, 1944. Target: Beachhead No. 261, just south of St. Tropez, France.

This mission was in support of the invasion of southern France. Bombing altitude was only 13,000 feet--at least a 10,000-foot departure from the normal bombing altitude. As our Flying Fortresses flew on to their target, they overflew seven divisions of soldiers below them. There were three American and four Allied divisions participating with French and British forces about 1000 feet off shore. The bombers' objective was to destroy enemy land mines, enemy ground personnel and their communications.

Takeoff, especially in the pitch black of night as this mission was, is always a time for guarded optimism. Pilots are tense under the yolk as their bomb laden Forts lumber along the steel matted runway gaining the necessary ground speed to get into the air. Crashes on takeoff are the bane of their existence under combat conditions. And takeoff crashes are particularly unsettling to others in the formation.

John Plummer, 347th squadron, flying right wing of the second element lead in his squadron formation on the same dreadful morning, corroborates what Kenney has written. Plummer said, "the three explosions we observed after takeoff and destroyed my night vision, were reported to have been three B-24s that had exploded shortly after takeoff. The unofficial reason for the explosions was that it was the work of saboteurs who had placed explosives within the wing root area of the aircraft and was detonated by an aneroid (barometric) device. Thirty fine men died in those explosions."

Joe describes the terrible beginnings of this mission as he once again takes to the air in a familiar squadron lead position. If somebody were to tell him he'd be digging fox holes for the infantry, he would have laughed in their face. But truth sometimes is stranger than fiction.

Our "H" hour was midnight. Breakfast was cold dehydrated eggs (green in color), cold, slick flat pancakes with cold watery syrup, cold greasy stale sausage and that washed down with the vilest coffee you could ever dream of. Takeoff time was 0300 and the night was pitch black.

Shortly after takeoff we saw a plane explode as it crashed on takeoff. It think it was a B-24 from another field. Just seconds later a second plane crashed, also a B-24, and it exploded as well. A third B-24 was seen blazing away as it bounced along the ground and it also exploded. Two B-17s collided and exploded when they hit the ground. A third B-17 was on fire, salvoed his bombs and made a spectacular trail across the sky as he made for the airfield where he landed safely. (Imagine, all this a prelude to a mission that hadn't even formed yet. What must those aircrews been thinking). With all this going on, we couldn't help but wonder if we were not being subjected to some sabotage, frightening to say the least.

We flew to an area just north of Corsica where we entered a great circle with all these bombers from the 15th and 12th Air Forces there. Each group in this tremendous circle was formed to split off this circle to go into their assigned targets at specific times. A very spectacular sight. We had some low clouds below us and could not see much going on on the surface. Our radar navigator showed me on the scope what radar was picking up and we could see the action of the assault boats going in clearly beneath those clouds. Our altitude was 13,000 feet, which was the lowest mission I have flown and we did not need oxygen. As we went in on our bomb run the clouds thinned as we approached the shore. We had a camera installed in the camera well and I could see around it and view what was going on below. I saw a large number of invasion craft churning in toward the beachhead. Our bombs were 100-pounders and their only purpose was to create ready-made fox holes for the troops as they hit that beach. Quite a tremendous occurance and we hit just as the sun was beginning to rise.

Joe Kenney's fiftieth mission turned out to be a genuine milk run. He was not overjoyed with the frag bombs they had to carry in "Weary Willie" being piloted by Harold Rickerson. And true to form a problem did develop causing a scare until the bombardier could resolve it. Seems the armorers before takeoff forgot to safety wire their load. Joe tells of seeing some of the tiny arming propellers turn, but he alerted the bombardier who toggled them off in what he called perfect sequence--"all falling without a hitch."

CHAPTER 16

The Evader

He didn't know it on that infamous mission to Castelfranco, Italy on Dec. 29, 1944, but three fourths of the 99th Bomb Group's Flying Fortresses launched that morning were damaged, with half receiving major damage. And he was shot down, the only plane lost on the mission.

Because the events I'm about to relate occurred on a day I didn't fly (I'd flown the 26th and 28th of December) it is with some misgivings that I can only give a second hand account of everything that happened. But in war mistakes are made and this mission was a lulu. And I would be remiss if I didn't attempt to explain the whole embarrassing episode.

This is 346th Squadron Leader Homer (Mac) McClanahan's story. His plane was the lone casualty of the mission. It was a chaotic day in the skies over Italy and Austria and when it was played out to the fullest, recrimination against the colonel, deputy commanding officer of the 99th, flying group lead, permeated the group in the wake of the raid. So inept was the colonel's leadership performance that day that squadron pilots throughout the group swore they would refuse to fly if the colonel was to lead another sortie.

Ask Mac what he thought of the colonel as a group commander and he will tell you years later that he had only negative thoughts about the man. Never mind Mac wasn't the only loser, standard operating procedure could have saved the mission. Like everybody else, takeoff that Dec. 29th from Foggia was normal. The formation proceeded up the Adriatic Sea, but instead of taking a northerly course along the coastline, they turned left right smack into a bunch of flak guns. The 88s were known to be in that location. It was the colonel's first mistake. He subsequently would get sacked for his part in this crazy, mixed up raid.

Mac's navigator was screaming into the intercom that extreme danger was imminent, but Mac could only follow his group lead. Mac said it was his understanding that only one ship in his squadron made the target and it got pretty well shot up. All made it back except Mac.

The 99th's primary target was Castlefranco, as stated. But it turned into a melee with confused pilots searching for targets of opportunity, the most celebrated being Innsbruck, Austria. Their flight through the Brenner Pass was difficult, but it did set the stage for things to follow.

The 99th launched 28 planes and possibly one or two mickey (radar) ships. For fourteen aircraft to sustain major damage, half the group's committed number, command ineptness again proves our capacity for human error.

Enemy resistance on that Dec. 29th raid is described by 416th intelligence in their report as follows: At 1154 hours, four JU-88s made an attack on the 346th squadron, the one McClanahan was flying the lead ship. And theirs was second position at 23,000 feet in the Innsbruck area. The JU- 88s came in from 3 o'clock high to 9 o'clock low making one pass. In the Udine area, six enemy aircraft were observed at 1227 hours, but they did not attack. Two jet propelled aircraft were seen at 1145 hours, Innsbruck area, at 26,500 feet. They flew off to the side and made no effort to attack.

Flak, according to the official report, was as follows: At Innsbruck at 26,000 feet, flak was slight, inaccurate and heavy, however our group ran into considerable flak in the Brenner Pass area. It ranged from moderate to intense, very accurate and heavy, both barrage and tracking. One aircraft was lost. Twenty-one of our aircraft suffered damage. Fourteen ships received major damage and seven minor damage. Six crew members were wounded, four seriously.

The 346th squadron leader thinks the only reason they deviated from their chartered course was because the colonel left his seat to tell the navigator how to navigate. He was so intent on not missing the target that everything got screwed up. Once Mac's plane was hit and caught fire, the crew bailed out. Eight were captured by the Germans and he and his waist gunner were picked up by Italian partisans--ex-Alpine troops. They landed in different mountain ranges and were split up. Freedom for Mac didn't come until Allied tanks pressed into the Po Valley.

Only the 348th squadron hit the railroad and marshaling yards in Castelfranco and that was not on the first or second try, but the third try. Other squadrons hit Udine and Innsbruck. Mac's squadron took the initial shock of enemy resistance in the pass and the remaining three squadrons came under intense fire soon after. Planes scattered like a clay pigeon hit at a skeet shoot. Formation discipline evaporated.

That was the picture leading up to the loss of Mac's ship, his bailout and subsequent life on the run in the Alps with Italian partisans until the war ended.

Squadron Leader McClanahan Tells His Story

We were to bomb Innsbruck and our ship was flying lead for the 346 squadron. Our position was the left hand squadron of the 99th. All was going well as we approached the Italian coast at the northern end of the Adriatic where, according to our briefing, we were to continue in a north-westerly direction to Innsbruck. (Note: the official record lists Castelfranco as the day's target). Instead we made about a ninety degree turn to the left and proceeded inland until we made a right hand turn into the Brenner Pass. As we turned right into the pass, being the left squadron, we caught hell first. Jerry had a lot of JU-88s protecting his main supply line (the railroad and the highway). I was told later that only one plane from my squadron was able to continue to the target.

Our engineer, Jackson, reported No. 2 engine on fire. It was feathered and very soon a fire in the bomb bay was reported. We left the formation and salvoed the bombs. The fire appeared to be getting worse so a decision was made to abandon ship. After I thought the crew was gone, I went into the bomb bay to check aft. Waist gunner Orban was still there. I motioned for him to jump and he did. I noticed that the fire had burned through the bulkhead from the wing root and was being fed by gas from the wing. I returned to the cockpit and while recharging my walk-around bottle I looked out the window and saw the upper wing skin behind No. 2 engine bubble up and peel back revealing a wing full of fire. I then went down to the forward hatch, sat down with legs hanging out, ducked my head and rolled out.

From this point my story differs from the other crew members as I never saw any of them again until years after the war. After leaving the plane, I lost consciousness--from fright, I think. Since I didn't have a head injury, that would explain it. I came to in my chute. My oxygen bottle and mask were gone, but otherwise I was in one piece. It would appear that I was going to land in a fair size town, but by slipping the chute I landed in a small village on the other side of the river which ran between the two. Later I was told there had been a German detachment in the larger town but they had to go ten miles downstream to a bridge to cross over. I was gone before they arrived.

With the luck of the Irish I swung into a tree when I landed which knocked me out temporarily. When I recovered a bit I realized that there were several women and children standing around and a man in a priest's robe was helping me to stand up. I had landed in a graveyard beside a little Catholic church.

Before I was fully recovered, two men walked up. They were dressed in civilian clothes and each had a submachine gun slung over his shoulder. They motioned me to follow them and started walking off so I fell right in behind them. We proceeded up the mountainside which was all terraced vineyards. Each time we approached a farm house one of them would go ahead and meet us on the trail with a glass containing a clear liquid. I found out it wasn't water, but distilled wine which the natives used extensively. After I had a drink we would continue up the hillside. That was pretty strong stuff because I didn't remember getting to the farm house where we stopped. My next recollection was being awakened about 10 o'clock at night. I was laying on a straw mat with a couple of blankets. They had fetched a doctor up from down below to check me over. I guess

I passed muster as they let me go back to sleep.

I found out the next day that this farm house was the headquarters for an Italian partisan group. I was sleeping in a large loft on the second floor of the farm house. About twelve other men were also sleeping there. Several of them took me down to the kitchen for breakfast. There was the farmer, his wife and young daughter, plus another woman who I found out had been brought up from below to help out. The three women prepared and served the food. So far no one spoke English so I had a terrible time making the farmer's wife understand that I wanted my egg cooked. Turned out they tapped a hole in the end of the egg and sucked the inside out raw.

Late that afternoon the first English speaking men showed up. They were two English soldiers who had been captured by the Italians in North Africa early in the war. They had been in an Italian prison camp when Mussolini fell from power. The guards walked off so these guys took off for the mountains and joined the partisans. They gave me a run down on the organization which was composed mostly of former Italian Alpine troops who had deserted and gone into the mountains under Mussolini's rule.

These partisans had a semi military organization with their men scattered around at different spots in the mountains. They used buildings which were used by Italians in the summer when they took their cattle to higher elevations to graze. The group had a radio which was used mostly to arrange parachute drops of supplies from our air force. They notified their contact in Rome that I was there. They brought me back a message which suggested that if I could find a suitable location to land a small plane, they might pick me up. I consulted my British friends since they had been running around these mountains for a couple of years.. They assured me that such a place did not exist. A message so stating was sent back to Rome.

A few days later I was moved to another of their posts, located a little higher up with no women to cook. Over a period of several days I was joined by several other men who had also been shot down and were in the custody of the partisans. A P-51 pilot, a B-25 pilot and a couple of his crew were involved. They had gathered us up into one location with the idea of helping us get to Yugoslavia. In addition to the supplies which the air force dropped by parachute, they were also supplied with money and were able to buy anything that was for sale. It was decided that the B-25 pilot and I would attempt the trip first. Then, if we made it, the guide would return for the next two and so on. We were furnished skis and since neither of us had been on skis before, we spent about a week practicing. My buddy, the B-25 pilot, was fitted with shoes with ice cleats on the soles. They weren't able to get any in my size so I had to do with what I had.

The guide picked us up and we started out with skis over the shoulder and a bed roll. On the second day I slipped on ice on the trail and went sliding down about a thirty degree slope covered with snow and ice. The last thing I remember was being tangled up with those damned skis. I came to about a week later. I was at another one of the partisan posts. My buddy said that I had ended up about 1,500 feet down the mountain from the trail. They had obtained help from the men at this post and had transported me to their post. I had received a rather large cut on the head. They taped it up the best they could with their first aid kit. They did a pretty good job. I have no ill effects today.

The guide had gone back and picked up two more men and before I was able to travel we received word that they had been machine-gunned crossing a bridge. That ended our Yugoslavian bid for freedom.

By the time I was able to travel, someone had decided to gather up all of us shot-down folks and escapees in one place. That place was over in another range of mountains and required a dangerous crossing of the valley. I was to be picked up by a group which was making the trip.

After I joined the group I found that it consisted of the high command of the partisans. Some of them wore red kerchiefs around their neck which indicated they were communists. The valley we had to cross had a major highway and railroad. We came to a mountain village in late afternoon from which you could look down and see the highway and railroad tracks. The village put on a big feed that evening (I was in the with big shots) and afterward they had a dance. Then, after midnight, we started down the trail to cross the valley.

In preparation for our crossing, they sent down an advance party to set up machine gun posts on each side of the valley. They had received word back that they were in position before we left the village. We crossed the railroad tracks adjacent to where they entered a tunnel. We hesitated there while several men laid plastic explosive charges on the rails well up into the tunnel and connected them by a fuse wire and a trip switch. We then continued on up the trail on the other side. We stopped about halfway up and waited for a train coming up the valley. After it entered the tunnel it really blew, big time!

When I got to my destination a couple of days later I found I had lots of company. As I remember there were eventually around thirty including mostly American, but several British, one Frenchman, one Indian (from India) and two majors from "A" force. They had parachuted in along with radio gear and a radio operator. Their mission was to arrange to get us back to our own forces.

The first plan was to bring a Catalina flying boat, have it land on a lake and pick us up. I never did know where the lake was and if I heard the name, I don't remember it now. Two days before we were to start our march to the lake Jerry moved in antiaircraft guns around the lake which, of course, killed that plan.

The next plan was to build a landing strip. There was a mountain valley down the hill from where we were staying. It was photographed by our air force to check the approaches, length, etc. We were told it was okay and when and if we got a suitable strip built they would send an aircraft to pick us up. There was considerable leveling and grading to do, but the big item was a large pond which had been dammed up to collect water for the cattle which grazed there in the summers.

This work, of course, would have been impossible for us. But as I've said, the partisans were supplied by parachute and it included money. As a result, laborers were hired. They came up the mountainside every morning and went back down every evening (at least they disappeared from our area). They brought with them several teams of horses, lots of wheelbarrows and shovels. Because we were anxious to catch a plane out, we joined the labor force where we could. As I remember, there were about seventy-five people working on the project.

The valley was surrounded by forest, so trees were cut down and branches trimmed. The trees were dragged by the horses to the stock pond. They were placed in the pond perpendicular to the (to be) runway. The brush was tamped between the logs. We then carted tons of dirt to cover the whole thing. That was the main use for all those wheelbarrows. I don't remember how long it took, but shortly it was completed and it was a pretty fair landing strip. In fact, I felt I could safely get in and out with a B-17 with about fifty percent of capacity load. Headquarters in Rome was notified and we waited impatiently for a plane to come and pick us up.

In the meantime two British men arrived and said their orders were to fly out with us. Turned out they were British agents who had been operating in Venice which was south of our location. They were carrying intelligence information for the coming drive across the Po Valley. These agents said that the rumor down in Venice was that we had a squadron of fighters up here. Needless to say we were on the radio every day to ask when that plane was coming and we were told that they couldn't spare the fighters to protect a plane. That answer didn't set well with us but all we could do was sit around and cuss the air force headquarters. We did have a diversion during this time. A British Spitfire fighter made a forced landing on our strip. Wheels were up and the pilot was not injured.

After about a week, the British must have decided that they couldn't depend on the air force to bring their agents out and they sent a plane at night to pick them up. By prearrangement via radio we gathered wood and prepared to light fires to mark the runway. The first were lit on an agreed upon time and the plane landed without incident.

The plane taxied back, turned into takeoff position and sat with the engine idling waiting for the two agents and their baggage to be loaded. The plane was open cockpit (two in front and pilot in back) so I went up to the plane and introduced myself to the pilot and asked him what he though of our strip. He said it was wonderful and he surely didn't expect anything this good. Very briefly I told him our problem and asked if he would go to air force headquarters when he got back and give them my name and tell them that I said they had shit in their necks. He laughed and said "I'll do it Yank and you can bank on it." I believe he did because the next day we got word that they would be coming the next day.

Again the luck of the Irish, the weather socked in. It had been beautiful for weeks, but on that morning the peaks were all in the clouds. We didn't expect anybody to make it under those conditions. However we did hear them circling above the clouds which did improve our attitude. The weather stayed that way for what seemed like weeks. Anyway the bad weather persisted until the big offensive drive across the Po Valley was begun. On getting word of this we moved to another location where it would be convenient to go down and greet our army when they arrived. When the tanks rolled up the valley we went down the mountainside and gave ourselves up to friendly forces.

I was loaded in a truck along with the others and transported to a delousing station (which I needed badly). After delousing, squadron 346 sent a B-17 to pick me up. I didn't find many people still with the squadron who I remembered. But there were a number who remembered me and the circumstances concerning my being shot down. That's when I found out what really happened concerning the leadership of our ill-fated mission. I've been mad as hell ever since.

To top it off, I was sent home on a banana boat (United Fruit Co.) and every time we went over a large swell the prop would come out of the water. The resulting vibrations reminded me of the day I had a runaway prop over Vienna.

CHAPTER 17

My Guys

Neely's crew, or what was left of it, began to come together February 23, 1996 when I received a call from Vic Fabiniak from his home in Vermilion, Ohio about "finding" John "Red" Patterson, my tailgunner.

I first met Vic at a 99th Bomb Group reunion in Rapid City, South Dakota, the first week of September, 1992. He was tailgunner on Len Smith's 346 squadron crew I saw get shot down over Augsburg and became interned in Switzerland for the duration. I was to serve with Len on the host committee for the 99th's reunion in Tucson, Arizona in May of 1999. Vic became connected with the Swiss Internees Search Committee and in the ensuing years was responsible for locating a number of "missing" internees. He became an expert tracer of lost persons and offered to do what he could to locate any of my crew. I provided him with army serial numbers of the enlisted men, but couldn't do the same for our officers. Locating Red was the culmination of many months of searching by Vic.

In any case the phone rang on a sunny, moderately warm February Friday morning in my Fountain of the Sun retirement community home in the southwest desert city of Mesa, Arizona and it was Vic on the other end with the exciting news that he had located Red. I was ecstatic. He also gave me Red's phone number in Santa Barbara, California. As soon as Vic and I had finished I got on the horn to Red. An astonished one time tailgunner answered and for the next half hour we lost ourselves in conversation. He was unaware of the 99th Bomb Group Historical Society and its newsletter until I told him about it.

Fifty-one years is a long bridge in time, but it helps bring into focus what we all experienced together as a combat crew. Red was born Nov. 2, 1925 in Butler, Pennsylvania. He enlisted in the aviation cadets before he turned eighteen and entered active duty on Dec. 1, 1943. He took his basic training at Miami Beach and gunnery school at Kingman, Arizona. He flew most if not all our 30 missions with me and the rest of our crew.

Red took advanced ROTC while attending Michigan State University and became a commissioned officer in June, 1950--just as the Korean War was beginning. he saw active duty from 1951 to 1952 as Administrative Officer at Pope AFB and Clark AFB in the Philippines. He concedes "I had a lot more fun in WWII as an enlisted man and a member of a close knit bomber crew."

His civilian career began as a high school history teacher and subsequently counselor and administrator in Berkeley, California. He is married to Donna Thomas and has one son, John, Jr., and one daughter, Stephanie, from his first marriage. He has four grandchildren--one named John III.

The best way I know to really introduce Red is to let him tell his end-of-the-war story which he calls the *Last Flight of the Old Lady*. We'd flown three mission in her--two to Vienna on Nov. 18, 1944 and March 21, 1945. The third mission was April 24, 1945 to a bridge in Obr Drauburg. In all we flew in a dozen different B-17Gs during our combat tour of duty. Let's hear what Red has to say about The Old Lady in his own words:

On July 4, 1945 Don Power and I were standing in the 301st Bomb Group's noontime chow line out on the San Severo road. Suddenly our names were called out over the "bitch box" to report to the orderly room where we were informed to grab our gear and get over to base operations as we were heading for the Gioia del Colle and home.

Good news at last! We were delighted to learn that the plane that was to take us home was *The Old Lady* from our own 348th squadron.

Then, 1945

John "Red" Patterson

Tailgunner
Neely's crew
Red, 18 years old, was from
Bulter, Pennsylvania

Youngest member of Neely's crew, this photo of Red taken in 1995. "Found" after 51 years by Vic Fabiniak, 346th Squadron in time for '96 San Diego reunion. He now lives in Santa Barbara, California.

We'd flown three missions in the old girl and we thought of her as a reliable and trustworthy friend. Don was the right waist and I was the tailgunner on Neely's crew and why they broke us up at war's end for flying home purposes with strangers I will never quite understand. Don and I had been together through training and combat since gunnery school in Kingman. We were both from western Pennsylvania and were excited to be heading home together.

The Old Lady was just that, an old aircraft that had flown missions dating back to the early months of the war in North Africa. She'd taken many hits, some of them major, had engines knocked out but always brought her crew home. It was easy to see where flak holes and major damage had been, as indicated by patches on wings, tail surfaces and fuselage.

We were weathered-in that morning and it was not expected to clear before noon, so everyone took off for the mess hall or for further sack time. We were left the lone crew at base ops milling around and bitching about state-side ground pounding officers and wondering how the hell we were going to remove that paint. And then, as they say, out of the blue came a voice, obviously not the major's, informing us that the weather was clearing over the Gulf of St. Lawrence and that we were cleared to leave. I think we set a record that day for how fast a crew could get a B-17 into the air. We were cleared for immediate takeoff. There were no other aircraft around and we never stopped rolling as we rounded the end of the runway.

An hour or so later our radio operator became very ill with a serious attack of appendicitis. We received permission to land at the nearest field inside the USA--the civilian airport at Bangor, Maine, where an ambulance would be waiting to get him to a hospital as soon as possible.

The Old Lady was a mild sensation there while we waited to be cleared by customs officials. Many civilians came out of their offices and places of work to see and touch this old war weary bird and hear her story and talk to the boys who flew her. It was awkward to be held in such awe. It was a strange feeling to be back in the states. Did we really belong

Don Power

Waist Gunner
Neely's Crew
Don, 24 years old, from
Cochranton, Pennsylvania.

One of three known survivors of Neely's crew, "found" by Red Patterson after 52 years and reunited for first time at Baltimore reunion in September, 1997

here? It was like we had come from another place in time.

At Marrakech, French Morocco, our engineer gunner assisted by our ball turret gunner procured a can of bright red paint and painted cartoon-like explosions on *The Old Lady's* exterior wherever combat damage had occurred. When they were finished she was indeed a sight to behold.

Our bombardier was not feeling well and spent most of the trip rolled up in a blanket and asleep in the waist. I was happy to occupy his bombardier's chair and play with the Norden bombsight as we crossed North Africa and the many miles of ocean to America. We were flying just high enough to keep nice and cool and I will always remember what fun it was to pick up ocean-going ships through the bombsight and the beautiful icebergs covered with sea birds on the leg from the Azores to Newfoundland. Oh, how I would like to make that trip again.

At Gander, Newfoundland, the line officer, a major, chewed all ten of us out for defacing government property entrusted to our care and said that he would not clear our aircraft to go on to the states unless we cleaned off all the red paint. We countered with the argument that we had actually lost planes "entrusted" to us, here and there, over southern Europe and that there were several at the bottom of the Adriatic Sea--and this aircraft was, in otherwise good flying condition. But to him we were only smart ass insubordinates.

So we were late getting to our original destination at Bradley Field in Connecticut. We were still at work unloading our gear from the bomb bays when a gas truck pulled up along with a basic flight crew who informed us that *The Old Lady* was going somewhere to sell war bonds. Wherever she went, I know she made a grand appearance. We last saw her heading out to the runway through the gathering dusk.

*   *   *

An abiding feeling of terror was a constant in flying. Close as we were, it came down to great concern for our own well being. Recalling our fifth mission over Regensburg, Red told me he saw everything I saw

The Enemy at Home

Our neighbors' Tent burns down
Cause: unknown

The plains of Foggia, campsite of ten thousand tented homes, was Italy's answer to interlopers from abroad. it was not enough we boiled under tents in summer and froze in tents in winter. Immune we weren't from nature's wrath and man's frailties.

T/Sgt John Trapuzzano stands in the debris of his wind-blown tent to attest to the savagery of what he termed a "whirlwind that swept through camp". The 348th squadron operations building can be seen in the background.

But nature's wrath doesn't compare to man's carelessness. The tent consumed by fire next to the abode of Neely's crew speaks to not so uncommon occurrence in not only our squadron area, but in all other areas of billeted troops as well.

We were vulnerable to our creative heating systems in winter. High octane aviation fuel, gravity fed into half 55-gallon drums widely used as makeshift furnaces, when not carefully maintained, were the cause of many fire destroyed tents over time. An undiscovered leak in the line, a careless match and the tent was history.

So were the comforts of home away from combat. Always a fragile interlude between missions that provided additional incentive to finish your missions and rotate back to the states.

only from a different angle. Looking up at all those open bomb bay doors as our own bombers passed over and around us affected Red just as it affected me. We were consumed with helplessness as the bombs fell around us and frozen in frightful moments of fear. He remembered that after the mission and back on the ground that we were very quiet and just sort of stood around looking at each other, thankful to be alive.

Red's position in the tail was unenviable to be sure. The holes we sustained in the rudder on our sixth mission, close to Red's compartment, were caused by flak bursts as the tail surged up and down and back and forth causing him to hit his head hard on the roof. He told me he never used that little seat belt provided the gunner in the tail because it was just one more impediment to leaving the ship in a hurry should Neely order a sudden bail out.

Not enough that flak should cause problems, but Red pointed to our seventh mission when the temperature had dipped to 60 degrees below zero. This was one of those missions, he said, when he was so cold that he thought that he would surely suffer frostbite. He sang and chewed gum and hit himself in the face (mask), chest, arms and moved around as much as he could in a vain attempt to keep warm. But this experience led to better days.

"I bitched so loud at Bob Neely and some ground pounder that I got an electric heated muff to help keep my hands warm. It worked and I guarded it with my life. There were times over the Alps when I thought it probably would be better to bail out to get warmed up as it couldn't possibly be that cold on the ground even in all that snow," Red said.

Commenting again on that seventh mission, Red told Don he recalled how Don had so much trouble getting Aunt Henrietta, Hank our ball gunner, under control. He had become unhinged when our ship lost an engine to flak and he thought the worst. Red said there were a couple of missions like this when he had his chute on ready to go--otherwise he kept it back by the escape hatch. How many times he thought to himself his dream of sliding back there, popping that door off--and heading out with or without a parachute.

Alex (Radio Operator) surveys
muddy front yard

Mess Call:Elmer Nelson, 21 (left)
with yours truly, Waist Gunner
from Albany, California

Memorial Services for F.D.R. (gathering of the clan)

Speaking of escape hatch, how about escape kits. Red surprised me with his recollections of the Intelligence briefings we got--special briefings, he said, not the morning ones before a mission. I was unaware of the contents of these kits so many years later, but Red insisted they contained 48 one dollar bills. They were replaced, he added, by a little folder in our photo I.D. that said, "This airman will write out an obligation to reward you for the help you have given him...etc." And he was quick to remind me that the escape kits were always checked out so "you couldn't bankroll your evening poker games," meaning me, of course, knowing of my weakness for poker.

Red further commented on those briefings. "This is what I remember," he wrote. "We were told to avoid German soldiers and citizenry and if we came down near towns or cities to try to get into the country. Turn yourself in after dark at a farm house," Chances of escape with the aid of friendly civilians was greater, we were told. And Red was quick to point out that it was a fact that there were more returned airmen in the 15th Air Force than any other Air Force operating during WWII. We were more likely to elude capture because the countries we flew over lacked the big industrial cities common to 8th Air Force targets.

"It must have been sheer hell living in the heavily populated cities in '44 and '45. I would not have wanted to have been an American airman arriving by parachute during or just after an air raid. It could only have been worse if you were in the R.A.F.," Red surmised. After months of being pounded around the clock, German civilians were dangerous people for a downed airman to have to confront.

Take it from a former POW. The German treatment of POWs in accordance with the Geneva Convention, was for the most part good fiction. George Guderley, a former POW who flew with the 463rd Bomb Group, said this was particularly true of the Air Force POWs who were considered "Terror Fliegers" or Luft Gangsters". Early in 1945, Guderley pointed out, Hitler directed the Luftwaffe Chief of Staff, General Koller, that in the future when the capture of Allied airmen was accomplished, that members of the German military would not prevent their lynching or

Elmer & me.

Capri: Donkey transport

No! I didn't shoot it down.

Henry "Hank Soriano," (left) in a chance meeting in Tiajuana, Mexico with Somers in November of 1945, a month after the author was discharged at Drew Field in Florida. It's the last time anyone has seen or heard from Soriano.

*Elmer Nelson
Albany, California*

murder by irate civilian mobs. Any German military member who protected the Allied POWs from the mob would be shot. This testimony was included in the War Crimes testimonials of what transpired at Hitler's bunker in Berlin. A copy of the original document reposes in the USAF Academy library at Colorado Springs, Colorado, according to Guderley, whose gripping story of participating in a German death march of Allied airmen is told in Chapter VII.

Don was to tell us of a gentleman living near him--and this was in letters written to me and Red in April of 1996--who was a German anti-aircraft gunner living in Vienna during the war. This German, who became a Russian prisoner of war, told Don that their flak guns were not too accurate and the best they could do against us was to put up barrages. Asked if our chaff affected their aim adversely, the German gunner said just the opposite. He told Don they could pick up the aluminum as the sun would shine on it and from the ground they could easily see it.

Red told Don in a letter over fifty years later, "It is hard to believe your new friend's 'very few radar guns' story. Perhaps it was true where he physically was, but think of all that chaff you threw out and once we even saw it work when there was a huge barrage of flak off in an area where there weren't any bombers." It was Red's contention that there had to be a lot of radar operated gun batteries down below or the intensity of our chaff dispersal in the bomb run wouldn't have been justified.

It was at the 99th Bomb Group's San Diego reunion in May of 1996 that I met Red for the first time in 51 years. I first spotted him coming through the door of our large hospitality suite in the Hanalei Hotel. Marilyn and I had just returned from viewing a recruit graduation at the Marine Corps Recruit Depot in San Diego. Would I recognize him after all these years? You bet. Despite the fact that his red hair had turned gray, its tousled look was a dead giveaway, kind of like when I remembered him in Italy. He hesitated at the entrance to the room, looking. It was him! There was mutual recognition as he spotted me waving my arms above my head in greeting. We bear hugged. Our reunion was underway. Among the many introductions, Vic was paramount. He just had to meet the guy who was responsible for bringing us together. Another gentleman needing an introduction was the "colonel." Rank is never used during these reunion socials, but the case of Col. Ray Schwanbeck, our group commander from January until the war ended in May, we made an exception. The colonel was going blind and his wife, at his side much of the time, enabled him to get around pretty good.

A little bit about our C.O. since the occasion has arisen. Commissioned a 2nd lieutenant in February, 1936, his first assignment was with the 2nd Bomb Group at Langley Field, Va. He later served with the 19th Bomb Group at March Air Force Base, California and moved with them to the Philippines in October, 1941--two months before the Japanese launched their sneak attack on U.S. forces in the South Pacific.

Col. Schwanbeck's decorations include the Silver Star, the Distinguished Flying Cross with one cluster, the Air Medal with two oak leaf clusters and the Distinguished Unit Citation with one OLC. His campaign medals include the Asiatic-Pacific campaign medal, EAME campaign medal, certificate of meritorious service, PH, Philippine Defense ribbon, Army occupation, Korean service medal and Occupation medal (Japan).

The colonel and Red were engrossed in conversation in the hospitality room. Red said he was fascinated by Col. Schwanbeck's experiences at Clark Field in the Philippines on Dec. 6, 1941 when the Japs destroyed the B-17s parked on the field around him. To this day Red had been miffed about the way they busted up crews and sent them back to the United States after the war ended. He confronted the colonel with his pet peeve, but said he got no satisfactory answer.

Fifty-one years of darkness--and then there was light. Seeing Red brought back a flood of memories. One of the missions Red referred to was the only one we ever aborted. I'd neglected to note it in my diary when and to what target we never reached.

"It's that aborted mission we were in the greatest danger," Red recalled. "We were jumped by 109s and saved by P-38s," I recall the incident, but I find it difficult to place in our chronology of events.

52 Years Later...

Last year it was in San Diego Red patterson and I met for the first time in 51 years. The next year, in September of 1997, it was at the Baltimore reunion that the three of us on Bob Neely's crew in the 348th squadron met for the first time in 52 years. Don Power, our waist gunner now living in Florida, joined to make it a threesome. Red lives in Santa Barbara, California and I live in Mesa, Arizona.

We flew 30 combat missions together over target in the underbelly of Europe in World War II and lived today to tell about it. L.R.: Bill Somers, engineer/gunner Red Patterson, tailgunners and Don Power, waist gunner as we look in 1997.

The 348th Bomb squadron of the 99th Bomb Group presents itself as they are in 1997 at the Baltimore reunion in September. Survivors all!

The Old Lady

Of twelve different B-17Gs we flew in combat, The Old Lady, No. 164, put up with us for three missions--our first, twenty-second and twenty-ninth and would bring Red and Don home after the war.

NEELY'S CREW, front row, L.R. : Elmer Nelson, waist; Hank Soriano, lower ball turret; Bob Neely, pilot; back row, L.R.: Bill Somers, flight engineer; Red Patterson, tailgunner and Don Power, waist. Absent: Thomas, Kaptain, Wyatt and Leitman.

It was only a few weeks after "finding" Red that Don was "found." And it was Red who found him. He'd remembered Don had a brother in Pennsylvania in an area he was familiar with. He managed to track him down with some difficulty and learned that Don was living in Florida.

On January 24, 1944 Don was sent by train to the induction base at New Cumberland, Pennsylvania. His records were not at the induction center and he was told he would have to go into the infantry until he gave them his Air Corps enlistment information that cleared the way for the Army Air Corps. He was sent to Miami Beach for basic training and was disappointed when he failed to become a cadet. After basic he was shipped to Kingman for gunnery school. Upon completion and a furlough, he ended up in Tampa as Neely's crew was being formed.

After disembarking on the side of a sunken ship in Naples harbor, our enlisted crew were taken to a tent city at Caserta a few miles north of Naples. Neely's crew were given an army truck and directed to the Arno River to get a load of sand to soak up some of the mud that surrounded them. Don's recollection of that duty continues: "We arrived at the river where the bridge had been blown up by retreating Germans. The Italians had placed a rope across the river to hold onto while crossing in small boats.

"While shoveling sand onto the truck an Italian with a bottle of wine came across the river. I do not recall how we dealt for the wine, but it was our first experience with real Italian wine. I personally do not recall our return to tent city with the sand or the unloading of it," he said, his smile betraying his amusement.

A few days after tent city, Neely's crew were off on a narrow gauge railway, riding on the floor of box cars, over the mountains in about a 90 mile trip to our destination--Foggia. The next day we were given a tent which would accommodate all six enlisted men and told where to erect it in the 348th squadron area. We spotted the location of a pile of bricks and after dark the six of us carried the bricks to floor the tent with.

Don describes what it was like to hear from the both of us the same day so many years later. He proceeds to fill in the blanks of his life as he tells his story:

"Last Sunday night the two telephone calls I received were like a bomb dropped from 28,000 feet from a B-17. Those phone calls hit dead center and I have thought about them all week," Don wrote us on March 15, 1996, a few days after receiving our calls. He wanted to fill in those five decades we'd been out of touch.

He told us that in 1948 he and his wife Fern had visited Bob Neely and had dinner with him and his wife. But since then he hadn't heard a word from Bob or any of our other three officers.

Don writes: "Red and I were both home when the war ended in the Pacific. We returned to Indiantown Gap and we both shipped out to Sioux Falls, South Dakota. That's where Red and I got separated. Fern and I bought and operated a Denver restaurant but after three years we decided it was not our cup of tea so I applied to Farm Bureau Insurance Co., now Nationwide, for a position in the claims department. I was hired and after six weeks of training I was assigned to Erie, Pennsylvania. After more than ten years with the company, I was promoted to claims manager. The last two years before I retired at the end of 1983 I negotiated law suits in New York and New Jersey," he concluded.

Don has two sons. Greg lives near them in Florida and is a professional musician. Their second son, Jeff, is adopted and resides in Connecticut. He is single and Greg is divorced. There are no grandchildren. Don was ready for retirement after having spent almost thirty-five years in the insurance business. Five years before he retired they bought a home in a mobile home park in Jensen Beach, Florida where they still live today.

In the ensuing correspondence Don often would refer to specific missions. At one point he began, "you may both remember on our last mission a large piece of flak came through just to the right of me and cutting off all the control cables on the right side of the fuselage. The flak continued between the left waist gunner and me and went out on the left side just above the floor. Both holes were at least six inches in diameter. There was not much space between my right side and the right side of the left waist gunner. I think Elmer was flying nose at the time," he said.

My turn. When the war ended I went to college like thousands of other under the G.I.Bill. In my four years at Syracuse University I majored in English and minored in Journalism. My first job in 1949 after graduation was in Pleasantville, New York, the village I graduated from high school in 1942. Its small town weekly newspaper was the beginning of my journalistic career and I was hired on as a reporter/advertising salesman/circulation manager all rolled into one. Ours was a small but affluent community in one of the wealthiest counties--Westchester--in the United States at the time. In fact in 1999 the next village bordering Pleasantville, Chappaqua, saw Hillery Clinton, the president's wife, purchase a million dollar mansion to establish residence in the state in order to undertake a senatorial race.In any case, I subsequently became editor of The Townsman but it was short lived. Here's what John T. McAllister, my publisher, said of me in an editorial at my departure from the newspaper:

"All over this country, for the third time in our generation and for the second time in a decade, young men are being forced to interrupt their educations and normal occupations to take up arms. Like many businesses, large and small, The Townsman this week is adjusting itself to the loss of a key member of the organization. Our editor and business manager has left to go on active duty with his unit of the Air National Guard."

His editorial continues: "Bill had had only five short months to serve as general factotum at this newspaper before his call came. He was doing a great job, as columns of advertising, sharp circulation gains and evident public approval all bore witness."

The editorial concluded with this paragraph: "Many in the community will join us in wishing Bill the best of luck and happy landings as he goes back into service again. We hope that within our lifetimes the world will become a place where men like Bill can pursue their chosen careers without the senseless interruption of war."

When my Air National Guard unit, a fighter outfit in White Plains, New York was mobilized in 1950 it was destined to be in Korea eight days after it was alerted. I traded my machine gun expertise and sergeant's stripes for lieutenant's bars this second time around and my new MOS dictated an assignment to March Air Force Base in California as Assistant Public Information officer. I served in that capacity throughout the Korean War. It was there that I supervised the publication of the base newspaper, The Beacon.

After the war ended I went to work as farm editor for The Evening Tribune in Hornell, New York. I quit that daily after a couple of years and started a weekly shopping guide in the same town. I married and had one son, Michael. My shopper flourished. I sold out eighteen years later and moved to Arizona with my second wife, Marilyn, having divorced my first. And it's in this southwest desert location I now call home.

CHAPTER 18
Rest and Deliverance

It wasn't until we'd flown our seventeenth mission--that to Augsburg--in the first week of March of 1945, that we were told to get ready for R and R. Call it rest and relaxation. Call it rest and recuperation, but my choice is rest and deliverance to a higher power. And it's not because we were delivered to the Isle of Capri rather than Naples, rather than Rome. It's because on that celebrated island I found myself, away from the sting of battle, a distraught and confused young man, seeking direction.

The Phoenicians were Capri's earliest settlers followed by the Greeks in the fourth century B.C. That's where I got to go in the middle of a war pretty much involving the whole world at the time. This isle was a safe haven for us now. It was for Tiberius too, this rugged island in the Bay of Naples. It is about four miles long and two miles wide and maybe a thousand feet tall in some places. It's steeped in ancient history, so ancient it predated the Roman Empire.

For us the war was not over. We knew we'd be going back and the thought had a nagging affect that diminished for me at least the real reason for being there. It was like an omnipresent cloud of negatives, imperceptible, but needing some kind of a positive response before we went back to flying. Mortality never occurred to me at the time. I truly was a gung ho kid. I earnestly, felt I owed a debt to my country. I wanted to pay that debt. Something happened.

I wasn't a very religious person then. Growing up the oldest with a brother and two sisters behind me, I was dutifully ushered off to church in the suburbs of Mount Vernon, New York on Sundays and entrusted with a nickel or a dime, sometimes more, for the collection plate. In the middle of the Great Depression this was a lot of money. My dad was a professional man, an optometrist working for a chain of optical stores. He managed, probably better than some, to provide the essentials for our family.

My folks never went to church, but made sure we did. Us kids had to pass a corner candy store on the way to and from church and the more money dad gave me, the easier it was to skim off the top. Bribing the others made it easy for me to garner a penny baseball card or two packed with a slice of reddish delicious bubble gum. Sought after cards picturing baseball players of that era were the likes of Babe Ruth and Lou Gehrig. I can still see, as I sat in my seat off first base with my dad in Yankee Stadium, the No. 4 on the back of Gehrig's shirt as he covered first base. The names of Charlie Gehringer, Al Simmons and Jimmie Foxx were not unfamiliar to me.

I was born in Manhattan. In those very early years of my life and from our 6th floor walkup apartment I still recall the spitting, angry chatter of jackhammers as they pounded the concrete that would establish Riverside Drive along the Hudson River. I became a dyed in the wool Yankee fan at a young age.

But like I said, religion was not a real part of my life before and right after my Capri experience. As I grew older and no matter where we lived my folks insisted we attend a church. It could have been a Methodist or a Presbyterian or whatever church, but church-going had to be a part of our young lives.

And that's why I found myself foundering in a dilemma on the way to Capri. We'd just come through some trying raids and on one I had the audacity to ask God to help us knowing full well my track record in that department lacked credibility. Yet God did answer my plea, hardly a prayer, and we survived to fly again. But why me? That's what got me to thinking and why I decided the trip to Capri was more of a deliverance than R & R in the contemporary sense of the word.

One of the outstanding points of interest on Capri was the ruins of Villa Jovis, A Tiberius pleasure palace and one of the most notorious of his twelve stately villas on Capri. It is said he dispatched his enemies and others in disfavor off the high cliff abutting his palace. Not only was the island a wartime haven for us, so it was for Tiberius too. He was the stepson and successor to Augustus Caesar and he disliked and feared Rome with a passion. He spent the last decade of his life on Capri, ruling his empire from afar.

During our visit, we stood at the site of the castle ruins which commands a breathtaking view of the Bay of Naples from its lofty perch. Capri, also known as the Island of the Goats, provided me gratifying escape, however brief, from the mental stress of flying. A memento I keep to this day is an oil painting of a B-17 flying over snow capped Alps and nestled in a carved wooden frame displaying the 15th Air Force emblem, gunners' wings and my squadron and group numbers.

I was on that island to collect myself. My sense of a Supreme Being was terribly lacking in my mindset. When I needed God, except for that one time, I shied away from asking Him. I didn't deserve any special favors from Him; I hadn't earned any. That's the way I looked at it. But on Capri I had plenty of time to think it out. I felt the way to God and salvation was with a religious sect that could provide structure and discipline. This was to prove out once I got married, but not while I remained in service.

For one thing I wasn't prepared for scary situations. I never had a prayer in my head when I needed it. All I could say was "God help me." How did I change. I really didn't until after the war, but the Capri experience planted the seed. I would go back to Foggia feeling better, knowing there was a Somebody to look after me if only I would look to Him. I didn't worry after that about saying the right thing when things got tough. I realized then He was always with me. And my conscious soul was at ease for the first time since we began our combat tour back in November.

A highlight of our Capri experience was the Blue Grotto off the island's rugged northwest corner. The grotto's exquisite azure color results from light refraction off the walls and water through the cave entrance. To get from town and the expansive hotel we were billeted in to the Blue Grotto you took the funicular to the Grand Marina. Then a guide would row you to the entrance, a distance of maybe two kilometers. That's what Alex, Red, Hank, Don and I availed ourselves of. Elmer, our armorer, didn't make the trip with us because of classes he had to attend. Tony, our guide, rowed us to the entrance. Another way of reaching the cavern was on foot below Villa St. Michelle on the Anacapri side of the island which we chose not to do.

Tourists today pay a pretty penny to visit this sanctuary of the rich and famous. But to us G.I.s we felt privileged. I guess you could say it didn't come cheap for us either.

ISLE OF CAPRI

(Bay of Naples)

Town square 1945

The hotel where we lived during R&R

THE ISLE OF CAPRI

My 17th mission, a rough one to Augsburg on Feb. 27th, was history when we were given, to use the navy's more apt description, liberty. We got the first week in march to use for rest and recuperation.

We went to a rugged, tiny island in the Bay of Naples. it was about four miles long and two miles wide and maybe a thousand feet tall in some places. it was steeped in ancient history, so ancient it predated the Roman Empire.

Below is a photo of the ruins of Villa Jovis, a Tiberius pleasure palace, one of the most notorious of his 12 stately villas on Capri. It is said he dispatched his enemies and others in disfavor off the high cliff at right.

An hour's walk up the hill from town is the ruins of Tiberius, castle.

Bath house on Capri looking out into Bay of Naples.

Date in __28 Feb.__ , 1945

Expires __6 Mar.__ , 1945   № 43243

Issued to __William F. Powers__
name

S/Sgt   12219726
rank   ASN

This is your PASS-BOOK for all activities in connection with your Rest Camp leave.

U S AIR FORCES REST CAMPS

OPERATED BY ARMY AIR FORCES SERVICE COMMAND
MEDITERRANEAN THEATER OPERATIONS

Cover of my R & R pass booklet issued to me for use on the island. For rules governing our stay, see next page.

RULES TO PLAY BY
ON THE ISLAND OF CAPRI

NOTICE
TO ALL ENLISTED MEN VISITING U. S. AIR FORCE REST CAMPS

1. We have arranged for you the finest possible program for entertainment, relaxation, rest and fun : and during the week of your stay your food, service and facilities will be the same as those provided for the officers, exept that your housing and messing are in separate buildings to comply with Army Regulations.

2. The Officers will be charged, and will pay $ 1 per day for their accommodations (by authority of NATOUSA Circular 63, 27th April, 1944).

3. There exists no authority to charge Enlisted Men anything for their accomodations. therefore we request that each enlisted man contribute voluntarily in advance the sum of $ 1 per night for each night of his intended stay to help us meet our payrolls. Refunds will be cheerfully made to any man who is not entirely-satisfied that he has received the greatest dollar value anywhere obtainable.

1

Lieutenant General IRA C. EAKER, Commanding General of all U S Air Forces in this theater, has ordered that all combat crews within the combat units of his command be afforded a rest, as the situation permits.

It is expected that you will conduct yourselves as gentlemen at all times, being especially careful of property. Please remember that thousands of others will follow you and they have the same right to enjoy fully the facilities which have been provided for your rest and relaxation.

Property such as sheets, blankets, glassware, etc. cannot be easily replaced in this theater.

We want you to enjoy yourselves fully while you are with us, and we shall expect your cooperation as gentlemen.

BY COMMAND OF BRIGADIER GENERAL WHITTEN
EUGENE C. FLEMING
COL. A. C.
SPECIAL SERVICE OFFICER

2

SIGHT-SEEING THE ISLAND

The Phoenicians were Capri's earliest settlers followed by the Greeks in the 4th century B.C. . The Americans sought refuge there in the mid 20th century during a war involving me and pretty much the whole world.

To get from the town down to the Blue Grotto you took the funicular, right, to the Grand Marina. Then a guide would row you to the entrance, a distance of two km. or one could access the dazzling cavern on foot below Villa St. Michelle on the Anacapri side of the island.

Of the many colorful grottos, the Blue is the most famous, but it is said not the most beautiful. There is also the green Grotto, the Yellow Grotto and others. We saw the Grotto azzura. it was lovely.

The Isle of Capri in wartime was a safe haven for us. It was for Tiberius too. He was stepson and successor to Augustus Caesar. Tiberius disliked and feared Rome. He spent the last decade

Funicular between Grand Marina and the town of Capri.

of his life on Capri, ruling his empire from afar.

His castle ruins, Villa Jovis, commands a breathtaking view of the Bay of Naples from it's lofty perch.

The Isle of Capri, known as the Island of the Goats, provided me gratifying escape from combat flying. A memento I keep to this day is an oil painting of a B-17 done by a native of the island.

Rowboat guides attend grotto entrance.

THE BLUE GROTTO

Against the rugged shoreline of the northwest corner of Italy's famous island resort, Capri, exists the popular Blue Grotto. So it was for American soldiers on R & R during World War II and so it remains today. In the photo below is Alex, myself and our guide, Tony. Red "sleeps" in the jeep.

The rowboat we're sitting on will take us the two kilometers to the grotto. The grotto's exquisite azure color results from light refraction off the walls and water through the cave entrance.

Tourists today pay a great deal of money to see the Isle of Capri. To the G.I.'s who were privileged, it didn't come cheap either.

What I wouldn't give for that leather jacket today!

L. to R., Hank, Don, Alex. I'm in a straw hat.

A picture postcard reproduction of Blue Grotto

CHAPTER

Epilogue

Still reeling from a punishing Depression that beset our nation, its people, an awakened sleeping giant following the surprise and "dastardly" attack on Pearl Harbor, responded en masse to the colors, to the factories and to the business of war in general after Dec. 7, 1941.

A determined and courageous nation of people performed their class act cloaked in patriotism and love of country as never before in its collective history. Men and women left the classrooms, the farms and small town America in appalling numbers to right the wrong of Pearl Harbor.

Resourceful Americans, leaving their cares and woes behind them along with the unsettling decade of economic turbulence and material devastation, turned to a common goal in their war efforts. Hitler's madness, Tojo's treachery were to be confronted head on by a generation of Americans never before threatened by such an unsavory scenario.

As part of this generation I felt the pride and anger that swept the country. This shocking development, however, provided us the opportunity to pay a debt I felt we all owed to our country. Maybe we'd pay with our blood and our tears, but we would pay just to say "thank you" for the privilege of having enjoyed the luxury of freedom we'd taken for granted all these years.

Neely's crew, a microcosm of the millions of uniformed patriots who served our country in need, joined together in battle from all over the United States of America. They came from Arkansas, Georgia, New York, Connecticut, Alabama, Pennsylvania and California. From all walks of life they combined to form a knowledgeable and efficient combat team and pay their just debt to a glorious society that nurtured them in its womb of independence.

The United States became the envy of the world in turmoil. And those of us who chose the air to engage the enemy did so with a dedication equal to those sailors, marines, paratroopers, infantry and armored personnel who were also engaged.

That we might be free to fight without moral or material encumbrance, a willing ally in our civilian population provided food and fiber to sustain us. Farmers in our nation's bread basket stayed the course and proved their mettle in sustaining the war effort to final victory. Women poured into our nation's capitol and secured the sometimes impossible battle of red tape. They displaced men in factories or joined the military themselves all in a devotion to a country they loved and wished to preserve. Factories, converted from civilian use, provided the guns, ships, tanks and planes to do the job. By 1944 we had 12 million men in uniform. The conversion of a peaceful giant into a formidable adversary against the prevailing forces of evil was all but complete.

And those of us involved in fighting our country's battles around the world did so with an unrequited zest to preserve what other would deny. In the case of Neely's crew, we sustained no personal loss. We did our job and did it well and then went home to pick up the threads of our lives. We were survivors who had paid our common debt to a nation that never owed us a living, only a sweet legacy.